Praise for the Previous Edition of *Getting Started in Bonds*

This book not only does an outstanding job of introducing basic bond concepts, but also introduces the reader to more sophisticated investing strategies. Sharon Wright does a fantastic job demystifying a subject many people find intimidating—this book is not only understandable, but also entertaining and fun.

> **—Brian M. Storms,**
> President, Prudential Investments

Ms. Wright has produced an excellent, easy-to-read guide for the novice bond investor. The book is well organized and allows its readers to identify and focus in on the security types most suitable for them. Even experienced investors will find this book a refresher course in bond fundamentals.

> **—Richard Lehmann,**
> Publisher, *Income Securities Advisor Newsletter*

Getting Started in Bonds is a thorough, straightforward, and accessible introduction to the world of fixed income securities. Wright does an excellent job of covering basic concepts as well as explaining the broader factors that affect bond prices. This book is a valuable and essential tool for the novice investor.

> **—Gail C. Scully,**
> Partner and Portfolio Manager, Gofen and Glossberg

The recent volatility of world equity markets is sure to increase interest in fixed income investing. *Getting Started in Bonds* successfully introduces investors to the dynamic world of buying and selling money. Furthermore, it does so in an easy-to-read, entertaining format.

> **—Jefferson DeAngelis,**
> Managing Director, Northwestern Investment
> Management Company

Getting Started in
Bonds

Second Edition

Sharon Saltzgiver Wright

John Wiley & Sons, Inc.

Published by John Wiley & Sons, Inc., Hoboken, New Jersey.
Published simultaneously in Canada.

For general information on our other products and services, or technical support, please contact our Customer Care Department within the United States at 800-762-2974, outside the United States at 317-572-3993 or fax 317-572-4002.

Wiley also publishes its books in a variety of electronic formats. Some content that appears in print may not be available in electronic books.

For more information about Wiley products, visit our web site at www.wiley.com.

Library of Congress Cataloging-in-Publication Data:

Wright, Sharon Saltzgiver, 1961–
    Getting started in bonds / Sharon Saltzgiver Wright.—2nd ed.
      p.   cm.—(The getting started in series)
    Includes index.
    ISBN 0-471-27123-3 (pbk. : alk. paper)
    1. Bonds. I. Title. II. Getting started in.
  HG4651 .W75 2003
  332.63'23—dc21   2002032435

This book is dedicated to my partner,
my computer artist, my proofreader, my best friend,
my great enabler, and the love of my life,
who auspiciously all walk around in the same body
(my husband's), Doug.

Preface

Have you ever noticed how people's eyes glaze over when you mention "bond investing"? They belong to the legions of uninformed whose ignorance is relegating them to the boat of missed opportunity. The fact that you are reading this indicates you're already more savvy than the average investor. You've identified the fact that it is absolutely essential to understand and invest in fixed income.

Welcome to the Wonderful World of Bonds. Read on, and you'll discover bonds are not narcoleptic; they are stimulating, dynamic investment vehicles. Once you devour this book, you'll be able to dazzle folks at your next soiree with tantalizing tales of fixed income prowess.

"Aren't you totally jazzed the Fed lowered rates? I had extended out the curve and am long a bunch of zeros."

"Did you see the T-bill's dead cat bounce?"

"I just thought of a cool way to balance my mortgage-backeds' negative convexity."

The possibilities are limitless. Yes, Virginia, bonds do have sex appeal. Although bonds have been known to intimidate and obfuscate, don't be discouraged by your lack of fixed income acumen. A number of folks working in the finance industry don't properly understand bonds. All the more reason you need to understand these seemingly elusive creatures yourself.

I believe the best way to learn a subject is to have fun while doing so. It's not productive if you fall asleep reading the first chapter. In this book, there will be a number of chances to "get" a concept. There will be analogies, real-life examples, and different approaches to help you through the material. One of the reasons bonds have remained enshrouded in confusion is the jargon used when talking about them. To simplify your learning process, investment terms will be set in bold and defined in the margin where they first appear in the book and then collected at the back of the book in a reference glossary.

The book is divided into four sections. Part One covers the types of bonds you have to choose from. Part Two explains how you can identify a good bond and covers some simple bond math. Part Three reveals factors that can affect a bond's value and will help you forecast future interest rates. Part Four shares a number of valuable bond investing and portfolio strategies.

So, put on your seatbelts. Prepare to be surprised and to have a ball demystifying the bond market. The sky's the limit.

SHARON SALTZGIVER WRIGHT
November 2002

Acknowledgments

I can't give the people who helped me polish and buff this book riches or 15 minutes of fame, but I do extend my heartfelt gratitude as I now name some of them.

First, thanks to my teachers in the bond biz who now know that some of what they imparted actually sank in! This is a group of very bright and patient individuals who also happen to be really nice people: Jeff DeAngelis, Jackie Conrad, Keith Cich, Zonder Grant, Shari Cedarbaum, and Chris Ray. Thanks also to the folks who hired me to the great jobs that taught me so much: Mike Emmerman and Herb Wein, Bill Landes, Tim McKenna and Sherif Nada.

Those of you who have bought this book will want to join me in thanking the next group of stalwart laborers who braved rough drafts of the manuscript and contributed their enlightening suggestions. First, Doug Wright and Pere Saltzgiver gave me the layperson's perspective (only relatives who love me dearly would have persevered through the versions these two saw). Then, Chris Ray, who is one of the smartest and most honorable people in finance, proved that he is also a steadfast friend when he invested hours reading the book and counseling the author. Thanks, too, for the other financial folks who read sections that corresponded with the areas of their expertise: Rodney Brown, Stan Carnes, Jeff DeAngelis, Ron Loukas, Charlie Poole, and Mitchell Sherman.

Appreciation is also lavished on those who helped with information: Amanda Buvis, Sue Fulshaw, Noel Johnson, Ed McCarthy, Steven Rudnyai, Susan MacNeil Varney, Anne Vosikas, Roger Young, and the librarians at the Kirsten Business Library. Thank you also to Jonathan Pond for his kind support and advice.

I also have to thank those that helped me on my inaugural foray into the publishing world. Deborah Moules from dance class who introduced to me Didi Davis the delectable cookbook author who put me in touch with her agent Doe Coover who encouragingly gave me Super Agent Denise Marcil's name who signed me to her team and got me hooked up with the publisher John Wiley & Sons where I was chosen and advised by editor Mina Samuels.

In addition, for their help with the book's second edition, I would like to thank Susan Ricker, Thomas Lapointe, and Bob Pickett for reviewing sections, and Wiley editor Debbie Englander.

My greatest debt and gratitude go to the two people who throughout my entire life have guided me with their vast wisdom, noble example, and infinite love, my parents, Pere and Cyndi Saltzgiver.

S. S. W.

Contents

"Soon that tuppence, safely
invested in the bank
Will compound

And you'll achieve that sense
of conquest
As your affluence expands
In the hands of the directors
Who invest as propriety demands

You see, Michael, you'll be part of
Railways through Africa
Dams across the Nile
Fleets of ocean greyhounds
Majestic, self-amortizing canals
Plantations of ripening tea

All from tuppence, prudently
fruitfully, frugally invested
In the, to be specific . . ."*

BONDS

*Excerpt from "Fidelity Fiduciary Bank," from Walt Disney's *Mary Poppins*. Words and music by Richard M. Sherman and Robert B. Sherman. © 1963 Wonderland Music Company.

Bond Building Blocks

"THE NAME'S BOND"

All you have to do is mention the word **bond** and people start to nod off. Perhaps that's why the world's largest investment sector is also the most misunderstood. It's about time someone let you in on one of life's best-kept secrets: Bonds are incredibly exciting and dynamic. Believe it or not, bonds have sex appeal!

Around the globe bonds have built bridges, airports, and cities. They have transformed basement start-ups into international conglomerates. Bonds are the primary instrument that has financed our nation's innovation, growth, and global influence.

Don't worry if bonds baffle you; you're not alone. Even though they are the most common financial investment in the world (see Figure I.1), even some of the folks who work in finance don't fully understand **fixed income investments**.

By taking a couple of hours to read through this book, you'll have a leg up on the majority of the investing public; and, in the market, knowing more than the next person is more than half the game.

 bond
debt security.
Investors loan
the issuer money
who pledges to
pay back the
money plus
interest.

1

WHO CARES?

 fixed income investments also known as bonds. Bond issuers are obligated to pay the income stipulated in the contract until the security matures. At that time the issuer pays back the principal borrowed from the investors. Most bonds have level income payments. A few pay variable income streams that change according to a set formula. Bonds with their promised income are different from stocks, which pay income only when it is earned.

Let's go over some of the unique characteristics that make bonds so popular with investors. The two major features that distinguish bonds from other investment alternatives are:

✔ Steady income.

✔ **Maturity** date when the bond's **face value** is paid (usually the amount loaned).

This predictability has led many people to assume that bonds are either boring or mediocre contributors. However, the fact is that bonds' unique traits can significantly impact a **portfolio**'s performance. All types of investors, from staunch conservatives to wild speculators, can benefit from fixed income. Here's how savvy investors use fixed income investments to fulfill their diverse requirements.

Bonds can:

✔ Pay expenses or be reinvested in stock or bond markets.

✔ Enable you to meet future expenses with confidence.

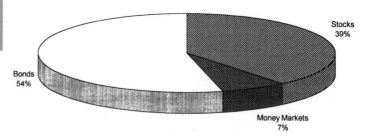

FIGURE I.1 Where we invest.
Sources: U.S. Department of the Treasury; Federal Reserve; Freddie Mac; *Emerging Markets Fact Book, 1997.*

✔ Balance a stock portfolio (through **diversification**).

✔ Provide steady performance so more risk can be taken with the rest of the portfolio.

✔ Customize your portfolio to fit your needs.

✔ Provide significant growth that results from **compounding** the higher income stream.

maturity
the length of time until the loan ends. When the bond matures the borrower pays the investors back the borrowed principal and any remaining interest owed. This ends the contract between the investors and the borrower.

Bonds' predictable income means investors can budget to meet monthly expenses. Bonds are usually the primary investment choice for investors who are living off their investments' income because the amount paid out is constant and can be confidently counted on. In fact, given that most bonds pay interest twice a year, you can buy six bonds that have different payment dates and structure a portfolio that pays monthly income. If you don't need the income to live on, the predictable income can be used to **dollar-cost average** into the stock market or back into bonds.

When investors expect to have a big bill to pay in the future (e.g., house, car, college), they can rest easy knowing the money will be there when the bond matures. Many investors choose bonds with maturities that will coincide with their future needs. Bonds are especially useful when the expense looms in the near future. For example, your child is 16, planning on college, and you become nervous about a stock market correction. Since you probably would not have enough time to recoup substantial stock losses you decide to reallocate the college savings fund into fixed income **securities**. This way you can rest assured you'll receive the face value in a lump sum when the bond matures and be able to meet those expenses.

face value
amount the borrower must pay the investor at maturity. This amount is used to calculate the interest payments.

There are a number of reasons fixed income securities can effectively diversify a stock portfolio. The first reason is that bonds tend to experience less price volatility in the secondary market than stocks do. This tends to pull the portfolio's performance back from the extremes. In addition, bonds' higher income stream is a constant contributor to the portfolio's **total return**. This cash supplement not only adds to your return but can also help further

portfolio
a collection of investments made by one entity.

diversification
spreading out your risk by splitting up your investable assets among several different types of securities. The hope is that they will react differently to stimuli, like interest rates or unemployment figures, so your investment returns won't all go down at the same time.

compounding
interest is earned on both the principal and all the interest that was earned before and reinvested.

buy the market's impact on your portfolio's value. The last reason bonds can balance stock performance is that their prices tend to react differently to economic indicators. Therefore, bonds often will not compound your stock holdings' price moves.

When managing your money, you should target an amount of **risk** that you are comfortable with. Each investment doesn't need to exhibit this degree of risk, but the sum total of your overall portfolio should. For example, if some investments are more conservative than the target, the others can be more risky. Since with a bond its interest and maturity value are known quantities, you may feel comfortable taking more risk with your other investable assets when some money is invested in bonds.

Most people snort that fixed income securities are too pedestrian; what they don't know is that some bonds can give you as a wild ride as stocks. This variety gives you a lot of flexibility in designing your portfolio, and also explains fixed income's wide appeal to an incredibly diverse range of investors. It's like a furniture maker: The more varied the tools in his/her shop, the easier it is to tailor pieces for many different tastes. Bonds offer the discerning investor a broad range of tools, so you can customize your portfolio for your specific requirements.

EITHER A BORROWER OR A LENDER BE

Okay, so what is a bond?

It's a loan. When a company or governmental entity needs to raise capital, it can borrow the money from us, the investors. To do this, it issues a bond. Investors buy the bond and in so doing loan the issuer/borrower money.

A bond is a contract detailing the terms of the loan. It says when the issuer will pay us back our investment as well as how much **interest** it has to pay us for our loaning it the money. This contracted interest is called the **coupon**.

Most bonds pay interest six months after they are issued and every six months (i.e., **semiannually**) thereafter (see Figure I.2). The last interest payment is made on the bond's maturity date when our **principal** is paid back.

THE TOPIC OF INTEREST

The reason most investors buy fixed income securities is for their namesake: fixed income. Stock dividends can

dollar-cost average
to invest equal dollar amounts in an investment at equal time intervals. This technique has been found commonly to result in a lower average cost than trying to time the market.

securities
financial instruments that you can invest your money in; bonds or stocks.

FIGURE I.2 Interest is paid twice a year.
Drawing by Ken Wright.

total return

a comprehensive measure of your investment's performance. It includes change in price, plus income, plus or minus any change in currency valuation if it's denominated in a currency other than U.S. dollars.

Δ price + income ± Δ in currency value = total return

 risk

chance the investment could go down more or up less. As investors, we are usually more worried about the going down part.

vary and are paid only when they are earned, but bond issuers must pay the promised amount of interest regardless of how their business is doing. It's this steady stream of income that is attractive to so many investors.

Rule 1: The Longer the Maturity, the Higher the Interest Rate

Investors demand that issuers pay them interest because they are giving up the use of their money for a period of time. Generally, the longer they have to do without this money the higher the interest rate they will want. Note that this is not always the case; there have been times when longer rates have yielded less than shorter rates, but those times have been fairly brief.

Rule 2: The More Risk, the Higher the Interest Rate

Investors also need to be compensated for the amount of risk they are taking. The riskier the investment, the more interest they will have to be paid.

Rule 3: The Higher Expected Inflation, the Higher the Interest Rates

Investors want to earn a targeted real rate of return. An investment's real rate of return is what you are left with after inflation takes its bite. To prevent inflation from eroding away their profits, investors include an inflation premium in the interest rate they demand. For example, if investors want to earn 3% and inflation is expected to be 3%, they will want the issuer to pay them 6%.

The first two rules governing fixed income interest are illustrated by the Figure I.3. You can see how yields increase as creditworthiness declines and as maturities get longer. The lower the rating, the less creditworthy the issuer is and the higher the yield their bonds will have to offer.

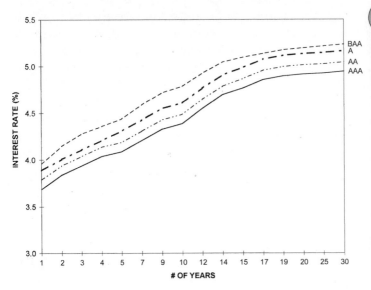

FIGURE I.3 Credit spreads: general obligation (GO) municipal bonds.

interest
money that a borrower owes the lender in addition to the amount borrowed. It is the cost of borrowing. Lenders demand this additional money for the inconvenience of being unable to use the money they have lent to the borrower.

coupon
stipulates how much money the lender/investor will earn. A 10% coupon means the investor will receive 10% of the amount she or he lent for as long as the contract states. For example, $1,000 lent will earn $100 a year until maturity, when the $1,000 is paid back.

CREDIT QUALITY

You need to be a smart consumer. The dictum "Let the buyer beware" certainly holds true in the fixed income market. Unfortunately, people think more about whether their brother will be able to pay them back $20 than they do about whether the company that issued the $20,000 bond they just bought will be able to pay them back.

When you buy a home, your bank is the lender and the mortgage is your debt. When you buy a bond, you are a lender and the bond is the issuer's debt.

Lender	*$*	*Debt*	*$*	*Borrower*
Mortgage banker	→	Mortgage	→	Homeowner
Bond investor (you)	→	Bond	→	Bond issuer (corporation, government)

semiannually
every six months
(i.e., half year).

principal
amount of money
the borrower
must pay back to
the lender/
investor at
maturity. It is
usually the
amount borrowed
from the investor.
Also known as
the **face value**.

So, when you're buying a bond, you need to adopt the mind-set of a loan officer at the bank. What's the borrower's credit history? Is the issuer fiscally responsible? What's the chance you're going to see your money again in the future? Are you being fairly compensated for the risk you're taking?

A loan officer for a credit card company or mortgage bank looks at your credit record to determine how much money he/she is willing to loan you. Similarly, you can look at an issuer's **credit rating** to determine whether you are comfortable lending it money. The two best-known credit rating services are Moody's Investors Service and Standard & Poor's. The ratings are summarized in Table I.1 from the most to the least creditworthy.

THE RISKS OF BOND INVESTING

Not only do rating agencies consider the issuer's cash flow and operations, but they also consider the likelihood of potential business risks. When you are evaluating a bond, you should consider the following risks.

TABLE I.1 Bond Credit Ratings		Moody's	Standard & Poor's
Investment Grade Bonds	Highest quality	Aaa	AAA
	High quality	Aa	AA
	Good quality	A	A
	Medium quality	Baa	BBB
High Yield Bonds	Speculative elements	Ba	BB
	Speculative	B	B
	More speculative	Caa	CCC
	Highly speculative	Ca	CC
	In default	—	D
	Not rated	N	N

Credit Risk

Credit risk, aka default risk, measures how likely it is that the issuer could get into financial difficulty and not make its interest and principal payments. Of course, if the issuer is not paying investors their interest, or if the principal payment is in danger, investors will flee from the bonds; and the price of the bonds in the secondary market will plummet.

Researching the issuer's credit history, familiarizing yourself with the corporate management's competency, and investigating the issuer's product/service's competitive market position will help you to avoid investing in bad credit situations and also minimize your exposure to this type of risk.

Credit risk can also be positive. When an issuer's financial picture improves, the yields it must offer in order to borrow money will decline, and the prices of its **outstanding** bonds should rise. Of course, people aren't trying to protect themselves from this type of credit risk.

Reinvestment Risk

Reinvestment risk is related to the fact that we don't have a clue about where future interest rates will be. Not a single one of the best-informed or highest-paid financial pundits can tell you with absolute certainty where rates are going to be even five minutes from now. Any projection is just their best guess.

With reinvestment risk, you face the possibility that when your bond matures, interest rates could have fallen well below where they were when you originally bought the bond. If rates are lower when you reinvest the principal you received back at maturity, the new bond you invest in will provide less income unless you take on more risk (see Figure I.4). This is especially dire for people living on this income.

For example, if you had bought a 20-year **municipal bond** in 1981, its yield was around 11.37%. If you'd bought $25,000 face value, you would have been earning each year about $2,842.50 tax-free. If you reinvested in

credit rating outside evaluation of a borrower's credit standing and ability to pay financial obligations. In the case of a bond rating, it evaluates the issuer's ability to pay bond investors the money owed them.

outstanding has been issued and has not yet matured or been called.

municipal bond debt obligation issued by a state or local governmental entity.

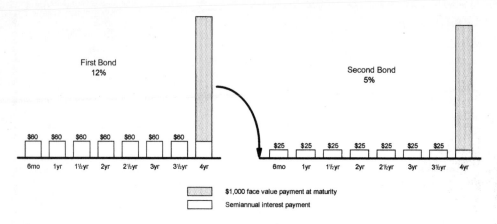

FIGURE I.4   Reinvestment risk.

2002 when 20-year minicipal rates were 5.11%, thus providing $1,277.50 in tax-free income a year, your annual income would take a $1,565.00 hit.

Inflation Risk

Inflation risk is the risk that inflation will erode away the money you make. If you earn 7%, but inflation is 7%, you actually haven't made anything. You have 7% more dollars, but everything you want to buy with the money costs 7% more. So, the purchasing power of your money hasn't changed; therefore, neither has your wealth. This is why investors are concerned about their real return.

Money earned – Inflation = Real rate of return

Call Risk

Call risk applies only to **callable** bonds. It is the chance that the issuer may **retire** your bond prior to the maturity date. Issuers tend to call bonds when interest rates fall, which, unfortunately, is when reinvestment options are less attractive. In effect, the issuer returns your principal and causes you to reinvest in a new bond that will have a lower coupon. In order to receive the same level of income, you may have to take on greater risk than before. As the investing public has become more savvy, the number of callable bonds being issued has dropped dramatically.

Event Risk

Event risk is the result of an unpredictable catastrophe. For example, a hurricane levels all manufacturing facilities, the government investigates the entire management team, swarms of radioactive rodents take over the grocery chain's warehouse. . . . Such dire events could affect the bond's value and may curtail the issuer's ability to pay interest or principal. Some corporate bonds have catastrophe calls allowing the issuer to retire the bonds early in the face of such tragic circumstances. There is also positive event risk: For example, a strong company merges with the company you have lent money to. Your bond could be upgraded (improving the credit rating), or it could be retired earlier than its maturity, which is usually done at a premium (above the price it was issued at).

The next three fixed income hazards do not apply to investors who hold their bonds until maturity. They only affect investors who will need to sell their bonds before they mature. Since these investors sell their bonds at whatever the current market price is, their return is affected by the bonds' price fluctuations in the secondary market.

Interest Rate Risk

Interest rate risk (aka market risk) is the effect that interest rate changes have on your bond's value. Since a bond's coupon doesn't change, your bond's value in the

callable
a callable bond can be retired by the issuer before the maturity date. It is called at a premium, above the price it was issued at, after stipulated dates. For example, a bond could become callable five years after it's issued at a price of 103. It remains callable at that price until two years later when it becomes callable at a price of 101. If it is not called, it will mature at 100.

retire
the issuer pays off the loan/bond in full, so the issue is no longer outstanding.

secondary market falls as current interest rates rise because its relatively lower interest rate makes it less appealing to investors. Its price will fall until its yield is the same as new yield levels for similar bonds.

Interest rates $\downarrow$: ☞ your bond's price $\uparrow$

Interest rates $\uparrow$: ☞ your bond's price $\downarrow$

Having your bond's price fall is a definite drag if you need to sell.

A dramatic example of how interest rates can affect bond prices in the secondary market occurred in 1987. In January of that year, long-term Treasury bonds (T-bonds) were yielding 7.28%. By October 15, long rates had risen to 10.22%, and prices had dropped more than 27%. If you had sold then and lost almost one-third of your investment, you'd have been crying in your soup because the next week (following the stock market crash), the bond market staged the biggest one-week rally in its history to date. In fact, by December 24, 1987, rates were back down to 8.75%, and you'd have made back most of your money. Who says the bond market isn't exciting?

Of course, if you're holding the bond to maturity you just blissfully ride out these market moves unconcerned knowing that you'll receive your principal back at maturity.

 tanks
traders' slang for plummets precipitously with astounding momentum. Other expressions conveying the same meaning: bites the dust, falls out of bed.

Sector Risk

Sector risk is the risk that investors suddenly hate all bonds of a certain type regardless of the merits of an individual issuer. Just as the tide affects all the boats tied up at the pier, even bonds issued by a company with strong performance can be negatively impacted by dour industry forecasts.

An example of sector risk is when unemployment rises and all consumer goods companies' bonds trade off. Another example would be when oil prices skyrocket, and the entire airline sector **tanks**.

Liquidity Risk

Liquidity risk affects thinly traded bonds. If there is not sufficient interest in the bonds you are selling, you may have to really discount the price in order to entice buyers out of the woodwork.

WHAT'S YOUR FLAVOR

During the 1980s, fixed income investments transformed themselves from being pedestrian, safe-deposit box keepsakes to being the dynamic, radical alternatives we see today. Wall Street whiz kids invented new fixed income marvels faster than you can say, "Yield, please." Many of these manufactured confections were so esoteric they defied description. Even their creators often couldn't predict their behavior.

The rules of thumb are:

If you don't understand it—don't buy it.

If something about it makes you uncomfortable—don't buy it.

If it sounds too good to be true—it probably is.

There are a few basic bond types (see Figure I.5). They are differentiated by:

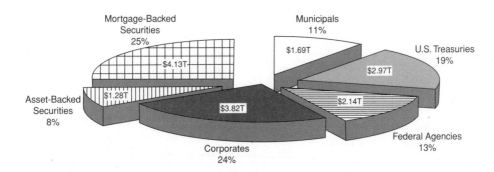

FIGURE I.5 The U.S. bond market in 2001.
Data source: The Bond Market Association.

Who Issued Them	*How the Interest Is Paid*
✔ U.S. Treasury bonds.	✔ Coupon bonds.
✔ Municipal bonds.	✔ Zero coupon bonds.
✔ Corporate bonds.	✔ Adjustable rate bonds.
✔ Mortgage-backed bonds.	✔ Convertible bonds.
✔ Foreign government bonds.	✔ Inflation-adjusted bonds.
✔ Foreign corporate bonds.	

Combining characteristics from each group (i.e., U.S. Treasury zero coupon bond), it's clear there's myriad combinations you can choose from. This variety enables you to tailor your investment portfolio to best meet your financial needs and risk tolerance. Let's look at each bond alternative, so you'll be able to judge what's right for you.

Congratulations! You've already digested the basic bond tenets and fixed income investment commandments, and you're ready to move on to the next course. We'll now cover the diverse delights you can choose from on our tasty bond buffet.

PART ONE

TYPES OF BONDS

Chapter

1

When Uncle Sam Needs a Dime: U.S. Government Bonds

L ike any business, governments need to raise money to pay for the services we ask them to provide. They have three sources of income:

1. User fees (e.g., tolls).
2. Taxes.
3. Bond issues.

Our national government has borrowed so much money from investors that 16 cents of each dollar you pay in taxes is currently used to pay investors the money owed them. You get no actual utility from that portion of your taxes; it's money the government spent long ago. (This is actually a big improvement. In 1997, it was 33 cents of every dollar collected.) Our government has borrowed $5,989,198,647,537.[1] In 2001 alone, the federal government paid roughly $360 billion in interest on that debt! So, what is the government selling us to raise that kind of dough? Bonds, baby.

[1]As of May 13, 2002, as reported in "The Debt to the Penny and Who Holds It" at www.publicdebt.treas.gov.

mutual reciprocity
the agreement between the federal and state governments that they will not tax the interest from each other's bonds. It applies only to interest. If the bonds are sold before maturity any capital gains would be subject to the applicable tax rate.

institutional investors
large investors such as pension funds and insurance companies.

retail investors
individual investors who invest smaller quantities than institutions. You and me.

One of the government's best-kept secrets is that you don't have to pay state income taxes on U.S. government bond interest. This is because back when our country was being formed and the federal and state governments were at loggerheads to see which would become the dominate power, they agreed not to tax the interest earned from each other's bonds. This agreement between the state and the federal governments provides a guideline known as **mutual reciprocity**. If there'd been no such agreement, one could tax the other's bonds so much it would be impossible for them to raise money, and they would be out of business.

The U.S. Treasury sells four types of fixed income securities to individual investors:

1. U.S. Savings bonds.
2. U.S. Treasury bills.
3. U.S. Treasury notes.
4. U.S. Treasury bonds.

There is another type that is sold mainly to **institutional investors** because the minimum trade is in the millions. They are a very short-term instrument known as cash management bills. But, let's look at each of the four types that we mere mortals, the **retail investors**, can afford, one at a time.

U.S. SAVINGS BONDS

Savings bonds are the Mennonites of the bond world: steady, hardworking, and faithful to their own rules. With years of experience trading bonds, I was unfamiliar with U.S. savings bonds because they aren't traded. When you say Treasuries in the financial world, you do not mean savings bonds, so I found it ironic that when much of the public thinks of bonds, this is what they think of.

We buy savings bonds when a baby is born, for weddings, and for graduations. We buy them for ourselves. In fact, more than 55 million Americans own savings bonds, making them one of the most popular savings tools in the country. One of the attributes that makes savings bonds attractive to so many people is that all Treasury securities (including savings bonds) are backed by the full faith and credit of the U.S. government, which pledges to pay back the principal you invested, as well as the interest your money earns. In this section we are going to look at what makes the savings bonds that are currently being issued so interesting and so unique.

 savings bonds type of bond issued by U.S. government. There is no secondary market, and there is a penalty for early redemption.

Savings bonds are the only type of bond still issuing paper certificates (see Figure 1.1). They look a lot like a check and are mailed to the owner after purchase. Don't worry if you're as disorganized as I am; the Treasury replaces lost certificates free of charge.

Principal and interest are payable only to the registered owner whose name is printed on the certificate. This means savings bonds are not transferable to anyone. When you purchase a new savings bond, there are three ways they can be registered:

1. Single ownership.
2. Co-ownership.
3. Owner with beneficiary.

Minors can own savings bonds, unlike other securities. Corporations, associations, as well as individuals

FIGURE 1.1 Savings bond.

may also own them—the key is having a Social Security or tax identification number.

Savings bonds pay interest for up to 30 years. They are unique in that if you buy the bond the last day of the month you are entitled to interest for that whole month even though you didn't own the bond during most of the month! With all other bonds, you get only the interest for the exact number of days you own the bond. Savings bonds pay you the whole month's interest because the interest accrues monthly, not daily, and is posted the first day of the next month. So beware—don't redeem your savings bond January 31 because you will not get the interest you earned in January; wait until February 1.

Another beautiful thing about savings bonds is you never pay a commission or fee when you buy or redeem them. As always, you can buy savings bonds at 40,000 banks, credit unions, and savings and loans across the country, and now they are also available for purchase through payroll deductions and over the Internet at the Treasury's web site (www.publicdebt.treas.gov) with a credit or debit card ($5,000 limit per transaction). This comprehensive web site is an easy-to-understand information resource about all Treasury securities: what they are, how to buy them, tax treatment, historical data, current rates, etcetera. The site's EasySaver Plan allows you to buy savings bonds at regular recurring intervals by debiting your personal checking or savings account. You can also manage your savings bond inventory on your computer using the web site's Savings Bond Wizard, which can calculate your redemption value and earned interest.

Savings bonds are different from other U.S. government bonds, in fact from all other bonds, in that they are *not* a **liquid** investment; the Treasury refers them as nonmarketable securities. This is of crucial importance because it means that there is no secondary market for savings bonds. You cannot sell them to someone else at a market price that is determined by supply and demand. However, after six months you may redeem savings bonds for cash at the Treasury for a price mathematically determined by the terms set at issuance. Many savings bond investors like not being at the mercy of unpredictable

 liquid
there is a significant amount of interest in the issue, so buyers can be found if you want to sell. The bond can be easily traded in the secondary market.

market forces. It's important to note that there may be a penalty—forfeiting a set amount of interest—if you redeem you savings bonds before a certain date.

The result of savings bonds being nonmarketable is that you do not buy these securities hoping to make **capital gains**. When interest rates drop, the prices of these securities do not rise like prices of most bonds; therefore, there is no way to make any capital gains (happily, there are also no losses when interest rates rise). This means that savings bonds have no market risk; it is also correct to say that there is no market for them, that is, that they are not marketable. You buy savings bonds for the interest and for the interest alone.

As with all U.S. Treasury securities, you do not pay state and local taxes on savings bond interest. However, unlike other Treasuries, savings bonds offer an unusual benefit called the Education Tax Exclusion. Qualified taxpayers can exclude the interest earned on Series EE or I bonds from their gross income for federal tax purposes if the money is used to pay college tuition and required fees. There are a few requirements. The bond must have been issued after 1989 to a taxpayer at least 24 years old who is also the person responsible for the college expenses. *Note*: The bonds cannot be in the name of the dependent, even as co-owner (beneficiary is fine). If the taxpayer is married, a joint tax return must be filed in order to qualify for this exclusion. The eligible expenses, which do not include room and board or books, must be incurred during the same tax year when the bonds are redeemed. There are income limits to qualify for the education exclusion. In 2002, the limits for the full exclusion are $86,400 for married couples filing joint returns and $57,600 for single filers. Above these levels the benefits phase out.

Three comments before we look at the different types of savings bonds in detail. If you see savings bonds being auctioned over the Internet, these are not interest-bearing securities since savings bonds are nontransferable; you would be buying only a piece of paper, not an investment. Secondly, buying savings bonds as part a chain letter or other pyramid scheme is prohibited. Lastly, savings bonds cannot be posted as **collateral** for a loan.

 capital gains aka cap gains. When you sell an investment for a higher price than you paid for it.

 collateral hard assets, things that are pledged when someone borrows money. If the borrower does not have money to pay off the loan, the items pledged must be given over. Your house is collateral for your mortgage—if you don't pay your mortgage, the bank gets your house.

accrual bond
the bond's interest is added to the principal amount and isn't paid out until maturity.

The Treasury is currently issuing Series EE/Patriot, Series I, and Series HH savings bonds. (See Table 1.1.) Series EE/Patriot and Series I bonds are **accrual bonds**, meaning they accrue interest monthly, which is compounded semiannually. The interest is added to your investment every month, but you don't get the cash until you redeem the bond. Series EE bonds are sold at a discount and mature at the face value or higher; the difference in value is the variable interest rate you have earned. You buy Series I at the face value and have a fixed interest rate that is adjusted for inflation and added to the face value. In contrast, Series HH savings bonds are current income securities. The interest is paid directly into your checking or savings account every six months. The Treasury no longer issues Series E (stopped in 1980) and Series H (stopped in 1979) savings bonds; however, you may still own some. For information on them visit www.publicdebt.treas.gov or call 304-480-6112.

TABLE 1.1   U.S. Savings Bonds

Series EE	Series I	Series HH
Buy at a 50% discount	Buy at full face value	Buy at full face value
Buy for cash	Buy for cash	Exchange into with proceeds from Series EE
Accrual bond	Accrual bond	Current income bond
Interest not taxed until redemption	Interest not taxed until redemption	Interest taxed in year paid
Annual purchase limit $15,000 (i.e., $30,000 face)	Annual purchase limit $30,000	No purchase limit
Variable interest rate set semiannually	Fixed interest rate, with an adjustment for inflation	Fixed interest rate reset after 10 years
Interest earned monthly paid at redemption	Interest earned monthly paid at redemption	Interest paid out semiannually
Interest automatically compounds semiannually	Interest automatically compounds semiannually	Interest paid out; no compounding
Pays interest for 30 years	Pays interest for 30 years	Pays interest for 20 years

Series EE Savings Bonds

Series EE savings bonds are popular with retail investors because you only have to invest a fraction of the face value now. They are what is known as **discount bonds** or **zero coupon bonds**. For example, if I spend $500 today, in about 17 years little Benjamin could redeem the bond for $1,000.

The purchase price for Series EE bonds is one-half the face amount, and you can buy Series EE savings bonds for as little as $25. It's a great way to make people think you're spending tons of money on their kids because they see the face value and don't know what you really spent. Series EE bonds are sold in different face values: $50, $75, $100, $200, $500, $1,000, $5,000, and $10,000. As you hold these bonds, interest is added to the amount you originally paid. So, when you cash in Series EE savings bonds, you receive the amount you invested as well as the compounded interest the bonds have earned.

Only $15,000 in Series EE bonds ($30,000 face amount) may be bought in any one calendar year by/for any person. Series I has an annual limit of $30,000 invested; however, it is computed separately from Series EE bond purchases. After six months you may redeem the Series EE bond for its current accumulated value; however, if you have not held the bond for five years you must pay an early redemption penalty equal to the last three months' interest.

The Series EE bonds earn interest for 30 years and are accrual securities. This means you do not receive the interest you have earned until you redeem the bond. Each month the interest is added onto the previous month's redemption value.

A keen benefit of an accrual bond is that the interest is reinvested internally, automatically compounding. Furthermore, both the Series EE and the Series I savings bonds earn more of a return than stated relative to other bonds because you are compounding your earnings tax-free since you do not pay taxes on the interest until redemption, so more money goes back to work for you.

The Series EE's variable interest rate is set for all Se-

> **discount bond** or **zero coupon bond** bond sold at a price way below its face value. No interest is paid until the bond matures. At maturity, the principal, interest, and interest-on-interest is paid to the investor. The interest-on-interest calculation assumes semiannual reinvestment of "phantom" interest at the bond's interest rate.

ries EE savings bonds in May and November at 90% of the five-year Treasury note's average yield over the previous six months. Each bond will reset to this new rate on the next six-month anniversary of its issuance. The bond's redemption value on that date is also the one used to compute the interest for six months.

For example, if you buy a savings bond in July, it will earn the rate set the previous May for six months (from July until January); notice that the rate does not change in November when the new rate is set; it will be reset to November's rate in January. It will reset every six months thereafter.

While Series EE bonds pay interest for 30 years (final maturity), they are guaranteed to have reached full face value by 17 years (original maturity). So, this is a bond with two maturities—go figure.

Since a Series EE savings bond's interest rate changes, it is unknown how long it will take to reach the face value (double your money). For example, a bond earning an average of 5% would reach face value in $14\frac{1}{2}$ years, while a bond earning an average of 6% would reach its face value in 12 years. If the market-based rates are not sufficient for a bond to reach face value by the original maturity in 17 years, the Treasury will make a one-time adjustment to increase the redemption value to the full face value at that time.[2]

The final maturity is 30 years after issuance. This is when the bond stops earning interest. You are responsible for turning in the bond at that time to receive the amount you originally invested and all the compounded interest you have earned. If you have been postponing paying taxes on the interest now, this is when you do so, unless you roll it into a Series HH bond (more on that later).

Patriot Savings Bonds

Patriot savings bonds are Series EE savings bonds. The only difference is that these Series EE certificates are in-

---

[2]*U.S. Saving Bonds: Investor Information*, May 1995, Department of the Treasury, Bureau of the Public Debt, Washington, DC 20239-0001; also at the Bureau of the Public Debt web site, www.publicdebt.treas.gov.

scribed with the words "Patriot Savings Bond." The Treasury issued them in response to investors who wanted to express their support for the rebuilding and war efforts following the September 11, 2001, terrorist attacks in the United States.

Series I Savings Bonds

Series I savings bonds (I bonds) offer a guaranteed fixed interest rate, but what really makes them appealing is that the interest is adjusted to keep pace with inflation, so your earnings' purchasing power is protected! Therefore, it is actually more accurate to say I bonds pay a fixed *real* interest rate.

Series I, like Series EE, is an accrual bond—the interest is added to the bond value monthly and not paid out until the bond is cashed. However, Series I is different from Series EE in that you purchase it at its face value, not at a discount—you pay $50 for a $50 I bond. The value then increases every month by the amount of interest paid.

The value also increases with inflation or decreases with deflation. So while the interest rate is fixed, the amount of money you have earning that interest changes with inflation. It also grows with reinvestment and compounding. Therefore the number of current dollars your bond earns changes every six months.

The semiannual inflation rate used in this calculation is announced in November and May, and it is based on what inflation was the previous six months. Even though it is the principal that is inflation adjusted, the Treasury releases a composite rate to help you know what your money is earning; this is the fixed interest rate adjusted for inflation. *Note:* Your actual total return will be higher because the composite rate does not reflect the compounding effect or the fact that your earnings are growing tax-free.

Because of the attractiveness of earning a guaranteed return over and above the inflation rate, one would expect the I bond to offer a lower interest rate than other bonds whose earnings are not protected from inflation. For example, Series EE bonds issued from May until November 2002 earned 3.96%, while I bonds issued during the same period were assigned a fixed rate of 2.00% with a 2.57% composite rate. However, this is not always the case because the Treasury uses different formulas for computing rates for the different types of savings bonds and may sporadically change these formulas, so at times the I bond can yield more. Also, if deflation is expected, which means I bond earnings would be declining, the fixed rate for new I bonds could be higher than that for new EE bonds because at that time the I bonds would be judged to be more risky—the risk being a declining redemption value and interest payout. However, if there is a period of deflation, the Treasury will not decrease a bond's value below the most recent redemption value. Very cool.

With Series I bonds as with Series EE, all of the interest earned since inception is compounded every six months from when you bought the bond. This is done automatically without you having to reinvest the interest—another advantage of accrual bonds. And as mentioned before, since you can postpone paying taxes on the interest until redemption, your return gets an extra boost because you are compounding tax-free.

I bonds are sold in $50, $75, $100, $200, $500, $1,000, $5,000, and $10,000 denominations. I bonds have the same purchasing limit of $30,000 face amount per calendar year as Series EE; however, since the limit is computed separately from the limit on Series EE bond purchases, you could invest $15,000 in Series EE ($30,000 face value) and $30,000 in I bonds per Social Security number per year. As with Series EE, I bonds can be sent directly to a person receiving them as a gift, if you wish. You cannot redeem I bonds for six months after purchase, and bonds sold before five years are subject to a three-month earnings penalty. I bonds are also available for the Education Tax Exclusion if you qualify.

Series HH Savings Bonds

Series HH Savings Bonds, unlike other savings bonds, are not accrual bonds; they are coupon bonds that pay out semiannual interest. Therefore, they provide investors with current income. The interest rate is set when you buy them and then reset 10 years later. Well actually, you cannot buy Series HH savings bonds; you can only exchange Series EE bonds for them. People do this because they want their interest paid out semiannually or because they want to postpone paying taxes on the Series EE interest. Series HH are not issued at a discount; you get them at the full face value that they will mature at. Because Series HH are coupon bonds that pay out their interest, the face value does not increase. In 2002, new issue Series HH were still paying the 4% interest rate set March 1, 1993.

They are sold in $500, $1,000, $5,000, and $10,000 denominations. A minimum of $500 redemption value in Series EE bonds is required to make the exchange. If you are exchanging Series EE savings bonds valued at $900, you may add $100 in cash to buy a $1,000 Series HH savings bond or you may buy a $500 Series HH bond and receive the remaining $400 in cash. There is no limit to the amount of Series HH bonds you exchange into in a calendar year, and Series HH are not included in the Education Tax Exclusion program.

U.S. TREASURY BONDS, NOTES, AND BILLS

These are the creatures that Wall Street thinks of when you say Treasuries. Unlike savings bonds, these securities are actively traded in the secondary market. In fact they are *very* actively traded. Their judged safety makes them an investment of choice the world over. Also unlike savings bonds, since 1986 they have all been issued in book entry form, meaning they are stored only within computers' memory. This is true of all traded securities because shipping paper around would be too cumbersome, time-consuming, and open to loss or theft.

The Treasury issues two types of securities: fixed-principal and inflation-indexed. Fixed principal means you know how many dollars in principal you will be getting at maturity. With inflation-indexed securities, you

Treasury bill (T-bill) short-term (maturities up to a year) discount security issued by the U.S. government.

Treasury note (T-note) intermediate debt obligation (maturities 2 to 10 years) issued by the U.S. government.

Treasury bond (T-bond) long-term debt obligation (maturities greater than 10 years) issued by the U.S. government.

simple interest interest is paid once, so there is no compounding during the year; the interest rate used for discount securities.

know your principal will have the same purchasing power when it matures; however, the number of dollars is not known since the amount of future inflation/deflation is not known.

These two types are divided into three classifications: **Treasury bills (T-bills)**, **Treasury notes (T-notes)**, and **Treasury bonds (T-bonds)**. Whether a security is a Treasury bond, bill, or note is determined by how many years will pass between its conception and its maturity. (See Figure 1.2.) Treasury bills are issued with 3-month, 6-month, and 1-year maturities. Treasury notes are issued with 2-year, 5-year, and 10-year maturities. At the time of this writing the Treasury was not issuing any long bonds (maturing beyond 10 years). In the past, the U.S. Treasury auctions have included 3-year, 4-year, 7-year, 20-year, and 30-year securities.

You may look in the newspaper and see some securities called T-notes that will mature in less than a year. That is because when a 10-year Treasury note has been around for nine years and has one year left until maturity, it will still be called a note. Even though the T-note has kept the same name through out its life, with one year left to maturity it will now act almost exactly as if it were a 1-year Treasury bill. In other words, it will have the same volatility and be priced to yield the same as a current 1-year T-bill.

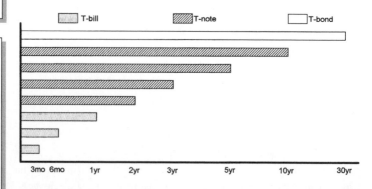

FIGURE 1.2 U.S. Treasury maturities.

Treasury Bills

Treasury bills or T-bills are sold at a discount from their face value. The difference between the purchase price and the face value at maturity is the interest you earn on your money. Therefore, unlike coupon bonds, T-bills pay all their interest at maturity. A T-bill is also different from other Treasuries in that it is traded using its yield not its price. (See Table 1.2.) The T-bill's yield as calculated by the U.S. Treasury is the discount rate. This is an annualized rate of return based on the par value when the T-bill is issued. Even though the 1-year T-bill is outstanding for 52 weeks—364 days—the Treasury calculates all T-bills' discount rates on a 360-day basis (12 months with 30 days each).

Simple interest is the rate you earn if you buy the T-bill at some time other than at issue. It is the difference between what you pay and the face value

You should not use the T-bill discount rate or simple interest when comparing its rate of return with other instruments. Since most other bonds that are outstanding for more than a year pay coupons that you can reinvest to compound your earnings, you need to convert the T-bill's simple interest rate to a **bond equivalent yield (BEY)**—also known as the investment rate or equivalent coupon yield—in order to make a fair comparison. If you don't use the BEY, you'll be comparing apples and oranges. The simple or discount yield would appear inaccurately higher

bond equivalent yield (BEY) a cash equivalent or short-term discount instrument's simple yield will look higher than a coupon bond because the coupon bond pays interest and can be compounded every six months. To compare the two, you must translate the discount's simple yield into a bond equivalent yield. BEY = 365 x Discount rate/ 360 – (Discount rate × Days to maturity) To calculate the BEY for money market instruments that use a 360-day year, such as CDs, substitute 360 for 365 in the numerator.

TABLE 1.2 Treasury Bills					
Maturity	Days to Maturity	Bid	Ask	Change	Ask Yield
Jun 20 '02	6	1.65	1.64	−0.04	1.66
Jul 11 '02	27	1.69	1.68	−0.02	1.71
Sep 12 '02	90	1.69	1.68	−0.02	1.71
Dec 12 '02	181	1.78	1.77	−0.03	1.81

June 2001

than it should because you have not included the longer maturity's compounding effect.

Treasury Notes and Bonds

U.S. Treasury notes and bonds are coupon bonds that pay interest semiannually.

For example, if the bond's coupon rate is 10%, a $1,000 investment will pay the investor $50 two times a year (i.e., 5% each coupon payment). The $100 that the investor gets each year is a 10% annual return on the investment. (See Table 1.3 and Figure 1.3.)

U.S. treasury notes are federal securities issued with maturities ranging from 2 to 10 years. Currently, T-notes are issued with 2-year, 5-year, and 10-year maturities.

govies
trader slang for government securities.

U.S. Treasury bonds are "**govies**" issued with maturities beyond 10 years. In October 2001, the Treasury decided to suspend its auctions of the 30-year T-bond in its effort to trim borrowing and the nation's debt burden. The last Treasury issued with a 30-year maturity was the $5^3/_8$% coupon maturity in February 2031, which was auctioned in February 2001 and reopened in August 2001. Then a 30-year 6-month TIPS (inflation-indexed Treasury) was issued in October 2001 with a $3^3/_8$% coupon maturing in April 2032. The most recent Treasury issued with a 20-year maturity was the $9^3/_8$% maturity in February 2006,

TABLE 1.3 Government Bonds and Notes					
Rate (%)	Maturity Month/Year	Bid	Ask	Change	Yield
$6^3/_8$	Aug 02n	100-25	100-26	. . .	1.51
$12^3/_8$	May 04	117-15	117-16	4	2.93
$3^1/_4$	May 04n	100-15	100-16	3	2.98
$6^1/_8$	Aug 07n	108-18	108-19	9	4.25
$7^7/_8$	Nov 02–07	102-17	102-18	. . .	1.66
$5^1/_4$	Feb 29	94-10	94-11	13	5.66

June 2002

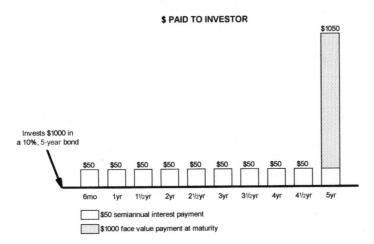

$ PAID TO INVESTOR

FIGURE 1.3 $ Paid to investor.

issued January 1986 at 100; in June 2002 just before it could be called, it was trading at 118³/4.

Treasuries that are currently being issued are noncallable. However, there are still some callable Treasury bonds outstanding, like the 20-year just mentioned, that were issued when the government was issuing callable bonds. Notice in Table 1.3, the bond 7⁷/8% November 2002-07. This means the Treasury was first callable in 2002; its final maturity was 2007. You can tell the bond was called by looking at its yield, which was trading to its call date instead of its maturity (1.66%), a yield more like six-month securities than like noncallable 2007 bonds that were yielding around 4³/4% at the time. We will discuss callable bonds when we talk about municipal bonds.

Here are two more U.S. government debt securities: U.S. Treasury zero coupon bonds and TIPS.

ZERO COUPONS

The Treasury itself does not issue any zero coupon bonds; however, there are two types of zero coupon Treasury securities that differ only in how they are created. From an investment perspective, the investor perceives no difference between them. In all cases, the zeros are created by taking a large quantity of a Treasury issue, taking it apart, separating the interest payments from each other and from the principal payment and selling each separately. So, a 2-year T-note could be separated into zeros maturing in 6 months, 1 year, 1$\frac{1}{2}$ years, and 2 years.

Zeros that are created by investment firms in concert with the U.S. Treasury are known as **STRIPS**, an acronym for Separate Trading of Registered Interest and Principal of Securities. While STRIPS are not issued or sold by the Treasury, they are considered an obligation of the Treasury and backed by the full faith and credit of the United States. The other type of Treasury zero is created by investment firms that buy Treasury coupon bonds and then separate the coupon and principal payments themselves. The firms then sell each payment separately as individual zero coupon bonds. These securities have been bestowed with many imaginative acronyms, including CATS and TIGRS (pronounced "tigers").

SOME T.I.P.S.

TIPS stands for Treasury Inflation Protection Securities. They are the Treasury's marketable (tradable) inflation-indexed securities and are designed to protect your returns from being eroded away by inflation. For example, if inflation rises 2% a year, the bond's face value rises 2%. Therefore, the interest will also increase because there is more face value earning interest.

How this works is that while a TIPS coupon interest rate is fixed at issuance, the principal is adjusted semiannually for inflation. Then in order to arrive at the interest payment earned the last six months, the inflation-adjusted principal is multiplied by half the fixed interest rate. For example, you own $10,000 face value with a 5% coupon, so you earn $500 a year. If inflation rises by 3% the next year, the face value rises to $10,300, the coupon is still fixed at 5%, so you'll earn $515 a year ($10,300 × .05), paid in two semiannual payments of $257.50.

STRIPS stands for separate trading of registered interest and principal of securities. They are Treasury-issued zero coupon bonds. They are issued at a deep discount from the maturing face value. The difference is the interest and interest-on-interest.

TIPS stands for Treasury inflation protection securities. They are inflation-indexed Treasuries.

The IRS has decided that you not only have to pay taxes on the interest paid every year but also on any inflation adjustment to your principal. Paying taxes on the inflation adjustment to the principal each year doesn't really make sense since it is a capital gain only on paper that won't be **realized** until you sell or the bond matures, but that's the way the IRS ball bounces. At least in terms of tax treatment, you can take the downward adjustment of principal as a loss against the interest paid out that year, and carry forward any loss balance to be applied against future income.

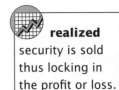

realized
security is sold thus locking in the profit or loss.

So what happens if there is deflation—something we haven't experienced since the Great Depression, but which is still a possibility? Well, the face value will adjust downward by the amount of the deflation. However, remember that in a deflationary environment the prices of the things you are spending money on have declined, so you have not lost any purchasing power. And the great part is, if deflation causes the principal to decline below the face value (the amount of money you loaned the government when the bond was issued) at maturity, the government will still pay you back the original face value. The government has guaranteed that you won't lose money with these bonds. Pretty neat: upside with no downside. You gotta love that.

This adjustable feature also helps to protect the bond's market value from falling as interest rates rise. This is because interest rates tend to rise when there is inflation in an attempt to keep inflation from getting out of control. Most bonds' principal and interest are fixed; so when interest rates rise, their prices fall (this is explained in full Technicolor detail in Chapter 10). However, while a TIPS coupon is fixed, the amount of interest paid and the principal value will rise as inflation increases. So if interest rates are rising because of rising inflation, TIPS tend to not fall in value as much as other bonds.

These advantages mean TIPS do not have to offer as much yield as other bonds. In the summer of 2002, a 10-year inflation-indexed bond yielded about $3\frac{1}{2}\%$, while traditional 10-year Treasuries yielded roughly $4\frac{7}{8}\%$. So, if inflation averaged more than $1^3/8\%$ a year over the next 10 years, the inflation-indexed bonds would outperform their traditional counterparts.

Even with price downside and inflation protection, current investor interest has been lackluster (a relative term since by June 2002 $147 billion had been issued since January 1997). One would expect a much bigger difference (yield spread) between TIPS and fixed principal securties than currently exists; in other words, you would think TIPS yields would be much lower than they are. The reason that is not the case could be because in recent history inflation had not been a problem. In times of deflation, one could imagine TIPS actually yielding less than fixed-principal bonds (although probably not a lot less since you know TIPS will pay full face value at maturity regardless). However, should inflation again become a problem these securities will become very popular since many other inflation hedges, such as gold, do not pay interest. In this case, holders of inflation-indexed bonds would be sitting pretty as other bond investors see the purchasing power of their fixed interest and fixed principal decline—a decline probably magnified by higher interest rates decreasing the value of their holdings in the secondary market.

THE TREASURY AUCTION

Okay, now that we know all about what kinds of Treasuries there are, how do you buy the things? You can buy them either from the government (Treasury) when they first come out (the **primary market**) or from a previous owner after they've been issued (the **secondary market**).

When the government wants to borrow money from investors, it offers bonds in the primary market through regularly scheduled auctions. A tentative schedule is published on the Treasury web site months ahead. About a week before the auction the Treasury announces the size and other details of the offering in a press release. (See Table 1.4.) If the normal auction day is a holiday, the auction generally is held the next business day.

primary market
when bonds are first sold to investors by the issuer. This is not a physical place; it is more a point in time and a transaction.

secondary market
when bonds are traded by investors after the bonds have been issued and are outstanding (i.e., between the issue date and the maturity date). The trade involves two parties other than the issuer, who is no longer involved. This is not a physical place; it is more a point in time and a transaction.

TABLE 1.4 U.S. Treasury Auctions			
Term	Minimum	Multiple	Auction
13-week bill (3-month)	$1,000	$1,000	Weekly
26-week bill (6-month)	$1,000	$1,000	Weekly
52-week bill (1-year)	$1,000	$1,000	Every 4 weeks
2-year note	$1,000	$1,000	Monthly
5-year note	$1,000	$1,000	February, May, August, November
10-year note	$1,000	$1,000	February, May, August, November
Inflation-indexed security (TIPS)			January, July, October

You can submit an electronic bid through your investment adviser, through one of the 12 **Federal Reserve Bank** branches (Figure 1.4) by standing in line or by mail, or through the Treasury's web site (www.publicdebt.treas.gov). Most investment firms do not charge a commission on bonds bought at Treasury auctions, but they may charge a nominal fee to cover the expense of processing the transaction. Many investors choose this route for its convenience. Of course, if you go directly through **the Fed** or Treasury there are no fees or commissions. In this case, the Treasuries can be held in a TreasuryDirect account or transferred to your **broker** or account with your investment adviser.

If you decide to deal directly with the Treasury through a Federal Reserve Bank, or through the Treasury's web site or automated phone system (800-722-2678), and have a TreasuryDirect account, interest and principal can be paid directly into your bank account. If you choose, you can set up your account so that the principal will be automatically reinvested when the security matures. TreasuryDirect doesn't cost you anything unless the par value in the account exceeds $100,000, when there is a maintenance fee. If you are holding Treasuries in your Treasury-

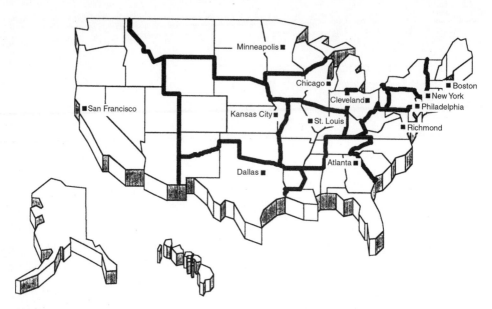

FIGURE 1.4   Locations of Federal Reserve Banks.

Direct account and want to sell them, you can sell them through the Treasury's Sell Direct program, which will go to a number of different brokers for their bids and sell your bonds for the highest price offered for a modest fee; or the Treasuries can be transferred to your account at a broker or investment adviser to be sold with the broker or adviser's markup taken out.

Most individual investors enter a noncompetitive bid in Treasury auctions. This is a nonspecified bid meaning we don't say what yield we want to receive. We say how many bonds we would like and agree to accept the yield that's determined by the competitive bids that are accepted by the Treasury. Competitive bids are entered with one of the Federal Reserve Banks by large investment firms and **size** bond buyers. These bids are submitted stating how many bonds they'd like and what specific yield they are willing to buy them at. Noncompetitive bids (individual investors) cannot be for more than $1 million in T-bill auctions or more than $5 million in T-note and T-bond auctions—I don't know about you, but I don't think that's going to cramp my style.

Until late 1998, most Treasuries were sold via multiple-price auctions. Competitive bids (*big* buyers) were entered, and the Treasury awarded bonds at the different yields bidders had entered from lowest to highest until all the securities were sold. Noncompetitive orders (you and me) were awarded the average of these various accepted competitive bids.

In November 1998, the Treasury adopted single-price auctions, which had previously been used only for 2- and 5-year maturities and TIPS. In single-price auctions, competitive and noncompetitive bidders all receive the same rate—the highest accepted rate. The Treasury starts at the lowest yield a competitive bidder submitted and keeps moving higher until it has sold all the bonds it has to sell (the size of the auction). It is this highest yield that everyone (comp and noncomp) receives. (See Table 1.5.)

The reason single-price auctions were adopted is that the Treasury found this method awards bonds to a greater number of bidders. Also, participants tend to bid more aggressively. They are more willing to bid with lower yields since everyone is awarded the same yield—the highest one accepted. Previously, bidders didn't want to go in with a low yield because that was the yield they got while others could get higher yields. Today's more aggressive bidding lowers the Treasury's—and therefore our (the taxpayers')—borrowing costs.

The auction's awarded yield determines the issue's coupon. If the coupon is lower than the awarded yield, you will pay slightly less than the face value to raise what you earn to its proper yield level. If the coupon is higher than the yield awarded, you will pay slightly more than the face value, but this rarely happens.

If awarded yield > coupon, then you pay < par (i.e., less than 100).

If awarded yield = coupon, then you pay = par (i.e., 100).

 Federal Reserve Bank the United States' central bank, charged with maintaining the health of the country's banking system. There are 12 Federal Reserve branches owned by the member banks in their region. These branches monitor the member banks to make sure they comply with the Federal Reserve Board regulations. They also provide member banks with emergency funds when needed at below market rates through their discount window. The Federal Reserve is also charged with monitoring and maintaining the country's economic health. They do this by affecting monetary flows.

TABLE 1.5   Single-Price Auction

$100,000,000 auction

–   5,000,000 noncompetitive bids

$ 95,000,000 competitive bids

	Bid	Face Amount	Competitive Bidder
	5.14%	$ 8,000,000	Ocean Funds
Awarded yield →	5.13	15,000,000	Apple County Pension
		(5,000,000)	
	5.11	**4,000,000**	University Trust
	5.10	**25,000,000**	Hilltop Asset Management
	5.10	**2,000,000**	Mr. & Ms. I. M. Rich
	5.09	**11,000,000**	Merrill Lynch
	5.08	**6,000,000**	GE Corp.
	5.08	**35,000,000**	Chinese Treasury
	5.07	**7,000,000**	XYZ Investments

Accepted bids are bolded and total $95,000,000. Everyone, including the $5,000,000 noncompetitive bids, receives 5.13%, the highest accepted bid.

the Fed
short for the Federal Reserve Bank, the United States governing bank authority.

If awarded yield < coupon, then you pay > par (i.e., more than 100).

Sometimes the coupon of an existing issue is so close to the new issue's yield that the Treasury will reopen an outstanding coupon. This means it will add to the size of the old issue and issue new bonds with the same description except for the issue date. In recent years the Treasury has done this regularly with the 10-year note. For example, on November 15, 2001, the Treasury reissued the 5% coupon maturing August 15, 2001. So investors were actually buying a security with a 9-year, 9-month maturity. Investors paid a premium 106.17, which will be explained in detail in Chapter 10, but it doesn't mean they over-paid—only that rates had dropped to around $4\frac{1}{4}\%$ in November and they were buying a bond with a 5% coupon. It's also true that when a coupon is reopened you pay for the interest (in this example three-months' interest) that you will receive at the next coupon payment, but which you don't deserve because you didn't own the bonds for those three months. If this is totally confusing, don't sweat it; as I said, we'll be covering this later.

GETTING BACK WHAT'S OWED YOU

When it issues Treasury securities, the U.S. government has pledged its reputation and taxing authority that it will pay you your borrowed principal back with interest. This is why U.S. government bonds are considered the safest investment you can make.

If you hold Treasuries in a TreasuryDirect account, when a bond matures you will receive notification 45 days before asking whether you want to automatically reinvest the principal. If you don't respond by 11 days prior to maturity, the Treasury will send you a check when your bond matures. Your other choice is to roll all or part of the proceeds into a new issue. For 3- and 6-month T-bills you can schedule automatic reinvestment to continue for up to two years. If you hold your Treasuries at your financial adviser's, the proceeds at maturity will be paid into that account.

Whether savings bonds or Treasuries, U.S. government securities are popular the world over. They are backed by the full faith and credit of the United States government. International respect for this country's ability to meet its obligations has meant our securities are considered a safe haven. In times of uncertainty, investors flood to the perceived safety of U.S. securities, helping to buoy Treasury prices. This abundance of ready buyers also means that marketable Treasuries are one of the most liquid investments available. Go U.S.A.!

broker
a third party that serves as an agent, trading securities on your behalf. With bonds, brokers will mark up the price when you're buying and mark down the price when you're selling. Therefore, their cut is included in the price, so you can't see how much they're making. There is no commission like with stocks. Don't panic. With bonds, comparing yields is more important and relevant than price in determining value. If the broker took "too much", the yield would become unattractive.

size
large quantity.

The "I Hate Taxes" Bonds: Municipal Bonds

A ll right, you've mastered one type of bond. Let's move on to another delectable morsel. As the name suggests, municipal bonds—also referred to as municipals or munis (pronounced *mew-knees*)—are issued by a municipality when funds are needed either to run the local government or to build and maintain specific projects such as highways, bridges, or sewage treatment plants.

As we mentioned before, the federal and state governments don't tax each other's bond interest, so you don't have to pay federal taxes on the interest you earn on municipal bonds. (Yea!) In many states, the income is also exempt from state taxes. (*Yea!!!*) (See Figure 2.1.) This is to encourage investment in projects that are felt to be for the greater good.

As long as there are taxes, people will be clamoring for an investment that is tax-exempt. This constant demand means prices tend to remain steadier; municipal bonds tend to have more subdued highs and lows than other fixed income securities. This does not mean municipals cannot experience dramatic changes in their value in reaction to surprising economic news, or big swings in the new supply of or demand for muni bonds.

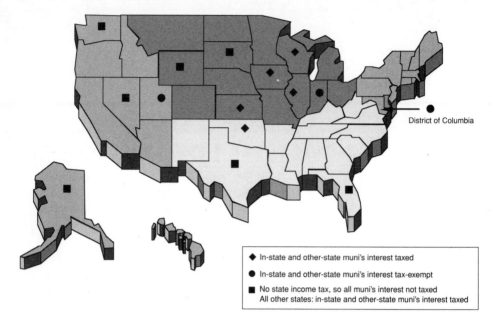

District of Columbia

◆ In-state and other-state muni's interest taxed
● In-state and other-state muni's interest tax-exempt
■ No state income tax, so all muni's interest not taxed
   All other states: in-state and other-state muni's interest taxed

FIGURE 2.1 Municipal bonds taxation by states.
Source: The Bond Market Association at www.investinginbonds.com.

Because municipal bonds are tax-exempt, a trait that makes taxpayers' blood pound with excitement, local governments can issue bonds with lower yields and still attract interested investors.

So, how does one decide whether to buy a higher yielding taxable bond or a lower yielding but tax-free bond? Comparing these bonds is like comparing those old apples and oranges again. It's next to impossible to fairly judge which is the better deal unless you know how to break the code.

SECRET DECODER: TAXABLE EQUIVALENT YIELD

This is the most important information to remember when you're buying municipal bonds, so if you've started dozing, go splash cold water on your face, and come on back.

In order to take your tax-exempt bond and decode

its yield so that it resembles a taxable bond, you will need to calculate the muni's **taxable equivalent yield (TEY)**.

For example, Table 2.1 shows the TEY for AAA-rated municipals. It's the yields in the TEY column that you would compare with a taxable bond's yield to see which offers the better opportunity.

Here's how you calculate the TEY for municipal bonds. Let's assume a federal tax rate of 25% and a tax-exempt yield of 5.45%.

First find the **reciprocal** of your tax rate:

1 – Your tax rate

1 – 25% = 1 – .25 = .75 or 75%

Then divide this into the tax-free yield to calculate the TEY:

TEY = Tax-free yield ÷ (1 – Your tax rate)

= 5.45% ÷ (1 – 25%)

(convert percentages into decimal form and do the math)

= .0545 ÷ (1 – .25)

> **taxable equivalent yield (TEY)** converting the yield of a tax-free bond into the equivalent yield it would have if it were a taxable bond in order to land the same number of after-tax dollars in your pocket.

> **reciprocal** as used in calculating a municipal bonds' TEY; the reciprocal of a number is found by subtracting the number from the number one.

TABLE 2.1 Taxable Equivalent Yield		
Years until Maturity	Muni GO-AAA Yield-to-Maturity	TEY at 30 Percent Combined Tax Rate
2	2.14%	3.06%
5	3.25	4.64
7	3.76	5.37
10	4.25	6.07
15	4.82	6.89
20	5.11	7.30
30	5.15	7.36

June 2002, Bloomberg.com.

$$= .0545 \div .75$$
$$= .07266$$
$$= 7.27\%$$

This means you wouldn't care whether you owned a taxable bond yielding 7.27% or a tax-free alternative yielding 5.45%, because your after-tax return would be the same. So, if the taxable bond you are considering yields less than 7.27%, you would want to buy the municipal bond. However, if the taxable bond yields more than 7.27%, it becomes the better alternative—except in the unlikely event that the income you earn on the bond pushes you into a higher tax bracket, in which case the call is your accountant's.

What we've just gone over is the generally accepted method of calculating your TEY, and it's the simplest. If you want a more accurate method you need to adjust for the fact that state taxes are deducted from your federal tax bill. To calculate your federal tax rate adjusted for the state tax deduction, first multiply your federal and state tax rates together; then, subtract this amount from the federal rate. However, the easiest and most accurate method is just to look at last year's federal tax form.

Let's adjust the federal tax rate in our previous example:

Federal tax rate: 25%
State tax rate: 5%

You need to calculate what percentage your state tax rate is of your federal tax rate (Step 1). This is the amount you deduct from your federal rate (Step 2), so I call it the adjustment factor.

Step 1

Federal tax rate × State tax rate = Adjustment factor
$$.25 \times .05 = .0125$$

Step 2

Federal tax rate – Adjustment factor
$$= \text{Adjusted federal tax rate}$$
$$.25 - .0125 = .2375$$
$$= 23.75\%$$

Our adjusted federal tax rate is 23.75%. However, this formula is good only if municipal interest is taxed in your state. If you live in a state where municipal bonds are free from *both* federal and state taxes, **double tax-free**, the math's a little different—one more easy calculation: Simply add your adjusted federal tax rate to your state tax rate to get your combined tax rate.

$$23.75\% + 5\% = 28.75\%$$

 double tax-free you don't have to pay state or federal taxes on the interest you earn from the bond.

Now that you've computed your combined tax rate, follow the same procedure as before, *just substitute the combined tax rate for the federal tax rate* we used in the original TEY equation to get the break-even yield (i.e., the taxable equivalent yield).

Combo tax rate:	28.75%
Bond's tax-exempt yield:	5.45%

$$\text{TEY} = .0545 \div (1 - .2875)$$
$$= .0545 \div .7125$$
$$= .07649$$
$$= 7.65\%$$

All done! Sounds worse than it is.

Notice the original TEY we calculated was 7.27%, when we took into consideration the state tax deduction, but when we recognized that munis are double tax-exempt in our state the TEY became 7.65%. If we had not redone the calculation, we might have bought taxable bonds with yields of 7.27% to 7.65% when munis would actually have been the better buy.

When you are comparing a municipal with a U.S. Treasury alternative, you need to calculate the TEY for the Treasury also, since Treasuries are exempt from state taxation. To do so, subtract your state's tax rate from the number 1. Then divide this into the Treasury yield-to-maturity (YTM).

$$\text{U.S. Treasury's TEY} = \text{YTM} \div (1 - \text{State tax rate})$$

To summarize, U.S. Treasuries are free from state taxation. Municipals are free from federal taxation and in most states free from state taxation (their own issues). So you need to calculate the appropriate TEY for each in order to equitably compare them. Corporate bonds are fully taxable, so there is no need to calculate a TEY.

Moral of the story: Do the math; it will make you money.

But if you're still stymied and realize how important it is, many online investment sites provide TEY calculators.

GENERAL OBLIGATIONS (GOs)

backed the interest payments are pledged to be paid by (e.g., the bond could be backed by a bank, equipment, escrow account, etc.).

General obligation (GO—not pronounced go; it's *gee-oh*) municipal bonds are **backed** by the taxing authority of the issuer. In other words, the local government is pledging to pay back your principal and interest with money it receives either from taxpayers or from future bond issues. No specific project is pegged to raise funds to pay GO investors. For example, the issuer has not said investors will be paid back with money earned from the state's water project. The issues are paid off with money from the general coffers of the government.

GO ratings reflect how fiscally responsible the issuing governmental agency is. As with any bond, the better the government's credit standing the better its rating is and the lower the interest rate it can borrow at. If it is less of a risk, it can offer lower rates and still attract investors.

For example, Weston, Massachusetts, a wealthy Boston suburb, is AAA-rated and rarely issues bonds because it doesn't need the money. If Weston had issued a 10-year bond in the summer of 2002 it would have had about 3.80% **yield-to-maturity (YTM)**. At the same time an Aa/AA muni would have yielded approximately 3.90% YTM.

Some investors prefer GOs over other types of munis because they feel a government is less likely to go out of business than a project such as a tunnel. However, wary investors do not allow themselves to be lulled into complacency by such assumptions. Incidents such as Bridgeport, Connecticut, threatening to go bankrupt in 1993 and Orange County, California, declaring **Chapter 11** in 1994 shook the muni market to attention.

This doesn't mean GOs are bad investments; in fact, they are very safe. Just pay attention to the bond's rating, read research reports, and consult with investment professionals. And unlike most things in life, the most important element here is the easiest. Just use your common sense. (Remind me to mention this again in the investing section, because this goes for any kind of investment.)

yield-to-maturity (YTM) the yield you would receive if you reinvested the coupon you earn at a rate equal to the yield-to-maturity. It is a more accurate yield than current yield because it includes the positive effect a larger coupon has on your investment return.

REVENUE BONDS

This is the other class of municipal bonds. Revs, as these munis are affectionately referred to, are backed by the revenues generated by a specific project's user fees. The proceeds from the bond sale are used to build or maintain the project.

For example, the revenue bond description:

Denver Colorado City & County Airport Rev.,
Baa1/BBB+, 7³/₄% 11/15/2013

The issue is "secured by a pledge of the Net Revenues of the Airport System," meaning the issue will be paid off with money made by the airport. Other revenue bonds

 **Chapter 11**

when an entity is unable to pay its debts and has declared protection under the bankruptcy laws. This 1978 law keeps the company in possession of and in control of its business. It allows the creditor(s) and debtor a lot of freedom to reorganize the business and hopefully be able to pay off the debts and become a viable business again.

are backed by fees from toll roads, bridges, tunnels, civic/convention centers, and airports' landing fees.

The bond's rating reflects the financial prospects for the project: how much it will be used, how much consumers can be charged, whether constructing the project is likely to stay within budget, how much it will cost to maintain, and so on. Ratings can change when the prospects for the project improve or erode. For example, the Denver Airports mentioned in the preceding paragraph were rerated in 2000 from Baa1/BBB+ to A/A+.

Revenue bonds are commonly felt to have a little more risk than GO bonds since it is believed that there is more that could go wrong on a project and that you can't raise user fees as much as you can raise taxes. Whether this assumption is valid or not, it is the reason a revenue bond often yields a little more than a GO with a similar rating.

Another explanation for this difference is that revenues also have the risk of catastrophe, albeit slight to improbable: A tornado destroys the airport, exhaust fumes ignite and blow up the tunnel, fire levels the civic center. . . . While the media would lead you to believe this stuff happens a lot, it is actually a rare occurrence. We'll also be talking about how municipal bond insurance helps to mitigate what risk does exist.

GOs and revs are the two main muni issuers. They issue a number of different types of munis that include anticipation notes, alternative minimum tax (AMT) bonds, insured bonds, callable and prerefunded bonds. Let's look at each of these in turn. Then we'll look at whether buying munis makes sense for you, and, if so, how to decide which ones to buy.

ANTICIPATION NOTES: TANs, RANs, & BANs

Since we're muni bonds,
We have lots of fans.
But our time is short;
We're TANs, RANs, and BANs.

This little poem introduces three members of the short-term municipal family. It's as if the municipality is sitting in the middle of a desert, and there's rain on the horizon. Anticipation notes are the sprinkler that will sustain it until the rain gets there. Just as cash management bills and four-week T-bills are used in the Treasury market, anticipation notes are issued when municipalities need some stopgap cash to cover expenses until future revenue is received; but, unlike cash management bills, they are affordable for regular investors.

In the muni market, the securities called anticipation notes usually mature in less than a year. Like cash management bills and U.S. Treasury bills, their short maturity necessitates that they be discount securities. This means they are sold at a discount to their maturing face value, which includes both principal and interest.

One such security is the TAN; this stands for tax anticipation note. The government expects to receive tax revenue, but before the taxpayers mail in their checks, the government has bills to pay, so it issues TANs to raise cash to cover these interim expenses. When the expected tax receipts are received, the money will be used to retire this short-term issue when it matures.

There are a number of different anticipation notes:

BAN	Bond anticipation note
RAN	Revenue anticipation note
TAN	Tax anticipation note
TRAN	Tax and revenue anticipation note
GAN	Grant anticipation note
SAAN	State aid anticipation note

As you can see from the names, what distinguishes these issues is where the government is anticipating the money is going to come from to pay off these securities at maturity. BANs will be paid off with the money raised by a future bond issue. RANs are paid off from money earned from projects such as toll roads, civic centers, and airports. TANs bridge the gap until the government receives our tax checks and cashes them. TRANs are paid with a combination of revenue and tax funds received. GANs are paid with money from a federal grant that the municipality will be receiving. SAANs are paid with state aid the municipality is expecting to get in the future.

Some anticipation notes have an additional entity backing the issue's payments. They are **letters of credit** (LOC), which say that the named entity—usually a bank or large investment firm—will make the issue's payments should the issuer become unable to. LOCs can be used to enhance any bond's creditworthiness; however, in the current environment, insurance has become so inexpensive that insurance is usually used instead. We'll talk about insured bonds in a bit.

> **letter of credit (LOC)**
> a bank or large investment firm stands ready to make the issue's payments should the issuer become unable to make them itself.

AMT BONDS

AMT stands for **alternative minimum tax**. This lovely, immensely confusing concept assaulted our consciousness with the Tax Reform Act of 1986, when it was aggressively revamped from its 1978 origins. The alternative minimum tax was instituted so that regardless of their accountants' zealous efforts wealthy individuals and corporations would have to pay at least some tax. However, this is a tax that has outgrown its intentions since it was not indexed to inflation. In 1990, 132,000 taxpayers were subject to AMT. In 2000, the number had risen to 1.3 million. It is estimated that by 2010, 17 million taxpayers could be subject to the AMT tax.[1]

Don't panic yet; in 2000 only 1% of the population qualified for this still pretty elite form of taxation.[2] Accountants and the tax software programs available at of-

[1] *The Alternative Minimum Tax for Individuals: A Growing Burden*, Jim Saxton, Chairman, Joint Economic Committee, United States Congress, May 2001. On www.house.gov.
[2] *Alternative Minimum Tax: Overview of Its Rationale and Impact on Individual Taxpayers*, James R. White, United States General Accounting Office, testimony before the Committee of Finance, United States Senate, March 8, 2001. On www.gao.gov.

fice supply stores can tell you whether you are subject to this insidious tax.

So, why are we talking about ancillary taxes (ugh) in a book about bonds? Well, because there is such a thing as AMT municipal bonds, and because for 99% of us, these bonds offer an opportunity for higher tax-exempt yields— a very tasty investment choice!

AMT bonds are issued by entities that barely qualify for tax-exempt status. They are private-purpose bonds that are interpreted as serving the public interest, such as hospitals or higher education institutions. Investors subject to AMT do not qualify for AMT bonds' municipal tax exemption and have to pay tax on their interest. Therefore, they avoid AMT bonds and buy other types of municipals or higher-yielding taxable bonds instead.

Furthermore, people subject to AMT tend to be excruciatingly wealthy and usually buy huge amounts of municipal bonds, so their disinterest in AMT bonds dramatically lowers demand for AMT bonds and drives their yields higher. Historically, AMT bonds have yielded about 20–25 basis points more than straight municipal bonds (basis points are explained on page 148).

AMT yields also get an extra bump because a lot of people who could benefit from buying them stay away just because they don't understand what AMT is. So if we aren't subject to AMT, we now know to check to see whether AMT bond yields are higher than yields of other munis; and we'll be all over AMT bonds as long as the issue is sound, it meets our other parameters, and we aren't in danger of becoming subject to the tax. Hopefully, Congress will get its collective act together in regards to this issue so that the nonsuper rich don't become subject to AMT. Well, at least they are talking about it.

alternative minimum tax (AMT)
this tax applies to 1% of the population. Its intent is for the wealthy to pay taxes on private-purpose municipals. AMT adds together passive losses (such as those from tax shelters and deductions for charitable contributions) and income from private-purpose tax-exempt bonds, then subtracts a certain amount and taxes a percentage of this income that is above a minimum level.

CALLABLE AND PREREFUNDED BONDS

Municipal bonds come in both the callable and noncallable varieties. This is a description of a callable bond:

Mass Port 5¼% 7/1/18 call 7/1/08 @ 101, 09 @ 100

This means these are bonds issued by the Massachusetts Port Authority to mature in July 2018. However, they may be called (i.e., retired) by the issuer in July 2008 and after at a price of 101 and in July 2009 and after at a price of 100.

Both GOs and revs can be callable. A bond's callability can affect how it is priced and thus the yield it offers. So, pay attention. You should be paid more yield on a callable bond than on a similar noncallable bond because issuers tend to call bonds when interest rates fall. Just as homeowners refinance their mortgages when interest rates fall, bond issuers want to refinance when interest rates drop so they can pay a lower interest rate on their debt. From the investor's point of view this is a negative because you now have to reinvest your returned principal at lower rates. So, when issuers bring a callable bond to market they have to pay investors more interest due to the greater potential for reinvestment risk.

prerefunded bond (pre-re) outstanding higher-coupon bond whose interest is no longer paid by the issuer but is paid by a Treasury security.

Only callable bonds can be prerefunded. A **prerefunded bond** is known as a **pre-re** (pronounced with a long "e" at the end). If a bond you own is prerefunded, you, in effect, now own a tax-exempt U.S. government bond. The municipal issuer is no longer making the bond's interest and principal payment; instead, a U.S. Treasury bond makes the payments. Many people like to own prerefunded bonds for this added safety.

If the muni bond was rated below AAA before it was prerefunded, its price should appreciate to a level roughly equivalent to AAA muni bonds (sometimes even a little higher since it's basically a tax-exempt U.S. Treasury).

refunding bond new bond issued to raise money to prerefund an outstanding higher-coupon municipal bond.

Prerefunding is a way for issuers to lower their interest costs when rates have fallen. They can get the higher cost debt off their books before the bond's call date by prerefunding the issue. The issuer issues a bond, known as a **refunding bond**, which has a lower coupon than the old bond. The money raised in the new offering is used to buy a U.S. Treasury **slug** (SLGS— State & Local Government Series) which pays the interest on the outstanding muni until its first call date. On the bond's call date, money from the U.S. Treasury security retires the bond.

When issuers want to refund noncallable bonds, they are simply **escrowed to maturity**. As with pre-re's, there is a refunding bond that buys a U.S. Treasury slug (SLGS), which pays the muni's interest and principal instead of the issuer. This doesn't save the issuer interest since the bond isn't retired early; it just means it no longer has to keep a reserve fund, so that cash is freed up to be used for other things.

slug
U.S. Treasury bond that is created to exactly match the cash flows of a pre-refunded municipal bond (from SLGS— State & Local Government Series).

INSURED BONDS

Some investors like the added peace of mind that comes with buying insured municipal bonds. They are willing to forgo some yield to have an insurance company guarantee that the bond's interest or principal payments will continue even if the issuer becomes insolvent and cannot pay.

As with any type of insurance, you should know the financial health of the insurance company that is insuring the bond you are buying. You can study the company's annual report. In addition, many insurance companies have been evaluated by the rating agencies. The most well known and accepted insurance companies enjoy an AAA rating. These private companies insure most of the bonds in the insured municipal market. These industry leaders include:

escrowed to maturity
money has been put aside and held in a separate account to pay all of the bond's future interest and principal payments. The payments are assured and do not come from the issuer any longer.

MBIA	Municipal Bond Insurance Association
FGIC	Financial Guaranty Insurance Company
AMBAC	AMBAC Indemnity Corporation (formerly American Municipal Bond Assurance Corporation)
FSA	Financial Security Assurance Holdings Ltd.

Bonds can be insured a number of different ways. The bond can be issued as an insured bond, or insurance can be bought after the bond is in the secondary market. Insurance is available only for extremely large bond quantities. So, unless your last name is Gates or Vanderbilt, you probably won't own enough bonds to insure them yourself.

The cost of security insurance fell dramatically in the 1990s. For example, a bond that cost $20 to insure in the 1980s could be insured for about $2 a decade later. Since insurance became so cheap—largely due to strong economic times and competition among the insurers—roughly half of municipal bonds issued in the 1990s were insured.

CABs

capital appreciation bonds (CABs) municipal zero coupon bonds that are sold at a deep discount from the maturing face value.

There are also municipal zero coupon bonds available. They are usually known as **capital appreciation bonds** (CABs). The difference between the original discounted price and the maturing face value is considered tax-free interest. *Note:* You are also getting the internally reinvested income compounded tax free, which has a huge impact on your total return.

TO BUY OR NOT TO BUY

Whether you're buying munis in the primary or the secondary market, an excellent resource is the *Bond Buyer*. It is a daily newspaper detailing new issues, credit updates, and municipal market trends. It's pretty pricey, so you may not opt for a subscription; but it's available at many large libraries and online. Don't buy munis from someone who doesn't have access to a copy or whose muni research department doesn't subscribe.

The relationship between taxables and tax-exempts is a very important element in determining value. (See Figure 2.2.) If the difference between the yields is very unlike what it has usually been in the past, it can be a sig-

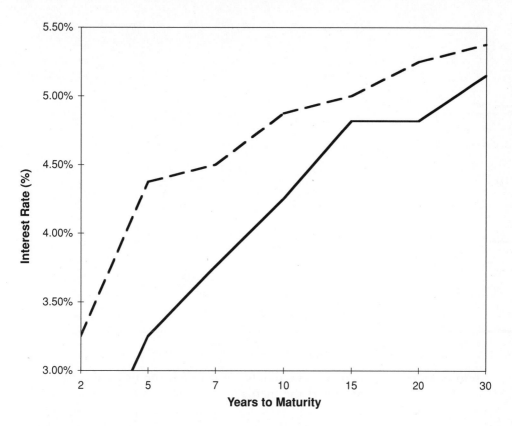

FIGURE 2.2   Taxable versus tax-exempt yield spread.

nal that munis are either cheap or expensive. This is because the pendulum tends to swing back to the norm.

Traders often look at what percentage of Treasuries'
yields munis are trading at. Historically, 30-year municipal bond yields tend to be around 86% of Treasuries. If
muni yields are greater than 86% of Treasury yields, munis might present a good buy relative to Treasuries. Less
than 86% could mean munis have gotten expensive versus
Treasuries. (See Table 2.2.)

The few rare instances in the past when tax-exempts
did not yield less than taxables were due to either extreme
uncertainty and confusion in the tax-exempt market or an
imbalance of supply and demand.

TABLE 2.2 Munis as Percent of Treasuries			
Years until Maturity	Muni GO-AAA YTM	Treasury YTM	Percent of Treasury (Muni/Treasury)
2	2.14%	3.25%	65.85%
5	3.25	4.375	74.29
7	3.76	4.50	83.56
10	4.25	4.875	87.18
15	4.82	5.00	96.40
20	4.82	5.25	91.81
30	5.15	5.375	95.81

June 2002

BUYING OUT-OF-STATE MUNIS

As we've mentioned, supply and demand dynamics can dramatically affect bond prices. High demand causes prices to rise (Figure 2.3). If demand declines and there are more sellers than buyers, bond prices go down and yields rise.

Prices can also decline when there's a large offering spilling a glut of bonds into the marketplace since there may not be enough demand to soak up the supply deluge. Bond yields may move higher in an attempt to get investors interested in buying.

There are often discrepancies between states' municipal supply. One state may have a lot of new issues coming to market and another may not have any. If excess supply is the only reason prices dip and yields rise, the effect is generally temporary and can present a buying opportunity for the alert investor. Eventually, the excess will be bought and prices and yields should drift back to their usual levels.

If a state has not had many new issues, supply is said to be tight; and the bonds become **rich** when compared to other states' municipals.

Part of the reason the municipal market is so vulner-

rich
expensive, pricey, costing more money, so the yield is lower relative to other bonds that have similar characteristics.

FIGURE 2.3 High demand.
Drawing by Steven Saltzgiver.

able to the vagaries of supply and demand is that people tend to buy only in-state issues, so any change in supply can have a big impact.

This tendency makes sense, since in most states only bonds from your own state are double tax-exempt. Also, it's usually wise to buy what you know; and since most of us know more about what's going on in our own state than elsewhere, it's often smartest to buy local issues. However, a little bit of research and some straightforward math can uncover some tasty out-of-state municipals.

Let's say you live in New Jersey, where there is lot of demand for municipals, but lately there's been very little supply. This means it may make sense to buy out-of-state bonds because New Jersey issues have gotten expensive.

Margaret's trying to decide whether to buy New Jersey's AAA-rated GO maturing in 20 years yielding 6.34% while similar bonds elsewhere are yielding 6.40%.

To figure which is the better buy, get out your TEY secret decoder ring (remember your combined tax bracket calculation on page 45). Margaret's is:

Federal tax rate: 25%

Margaret's state tax rate: 3%

Step 1

Federal tax rate × State tax rate = Adjustment factor
.25 × .03 = .0075

Step 2

Federal tax rate − Adjustment factor = Adjusted
federal tax rate
.25 − .0075 = .2425 = 24.25%

Step 3

Adjusted federal tax rate + State tax rate = Combined
tax rate
24.25% + 3% = 27.25%

So, Margaret's effective tax rate is 27.25%. Since out-of-state bonds are not state tax–exempt, we also need the TEY using just her adjusted federal tax rate: 24.25% (Step 2).

Now, she can compare apples to apples.

New Jersey GO

TEY = 6.34% ÷ (1 − .2725)
    = .0634 ÷ .7275 = 8.7%

Out-of-State GO

TEY = 6.40% ÷ (1 − .2425)
    = .0640 ÷ .7575 = 8.4%

Many states have graduated tax structures, so there is no one tax rate. The tax rate for interest income may be different from the earned income tax rate. A few states don't have any state income tax. To make sure you're using the correct rate to calculate the TEY, call your accountant and ask what rate your interest income is taxed at. If you don't have an accountant, look at past returns, or call your statehouse for information. Your state may also post the information on the Internet.

In this case, it still makes sense to buy the New Jersey GO because its TEY is higher than the out-of-state municipal.

Then during the next week, four different Arizona issuers bring insured bonds to market. New Jersey is still yielding 6.34%, but the flood of new bonds in Arizona pops yields there up to 6.78%. Let's run the numbers again:

New Jersey GO

TEY = 6.34% ÷ (1 − .2725) = 8.7%

Arizona GO

TEY = 6.78% ÷ (1 − .2425) = 8.9%

Now it makes sense to buy the Arizona bonds.

Here's another valuable trading tidbit related to supply levels. When there's a deluge of new bond supply, bonds in the secondary market often offer slightly higher yields than the new issue bonds. The main reason for this is that new issues benefit from investment firms focusing on them and promoting them to their clients. So, when there's a lot of new supply, be sure to check the yields on older, overlooked issues from that state being sold in the secondary market to see if they're cheaper.

Chapter 3

Investing in America: Corporate Bonds

A
s we leave the tax-exempt haven provided by munis, we venture into our country's business bayous. We are going to examine the bonds that have helped build our economic empire and provided us with products, services, and jobs.

America is a busy marketplace. Every day $15 billion in corporates are traded. During 2000, over $620 billion worth of corporate bonds were issued, bringing the total outstanding to $3.4 trillion!

As the name indicates, corporate bonds are issued by corporations. It follows that much of the research done when investing in corporate bonds is similar to that done for stock investing: evaluating balance sheets, products, management, competitive pressures, and so on.

In fact, corporate bond values often track the health of the company that issued them even more than they are affected by movements in interest rates. When interest rates are rising, a corporate bond's price could go down less than prices of other types of bonds because of the company's strong stock performance or improving credit profile. The lower a bond's rating, the more the company's health, measured by its cash position and ability to generate cash in the future, matters to its cost of capital. Poor health can cost the issuer 0.20% to 0.80% in additional interest cost.

Investors often look to identify and invest in lower-rated bonds they feel are on the path to future upgrades. The investors choose the bond instead of the stock because they are paid a substantial yield while they are waiting for the company to perform. In the finance industry this is known as "being paid to wait." Today hedge funds take a different view: they may **short** the security in anticipation of the troubled company's demise. Recently, this practice has contributed to—in fact, largely caused—dramatic downward pressure in the corporate market.

Hedge funds can also take large long positions hoping to make large gains. However, those positions can also result in large losses. In the end of June 2002, WorldCom was found to have misstated its financial position. Its bonds traded down to 40 cents on the dollar, and many hedge funds specializing in distressed issues bought them up (went **long**) thinking they would go up in value; however, the bonds continued to plummet to 15 cents on the dollar (a bond worth $10,000 when issued and $4,000 when the hedge fund bought it would then be worth $1,500).

There are different corporate market sectors:

✔ *Industrials.* Manufacturing, energy, mining, retail and, service industries are affected by consumer demand and economic cycles. These industries are also referred to as **cyclicals**. This is the largest segment of the corporate market.

✔ *Public Utilities.* Telecommunication, water, electric, and gas pipeline systems are affected by weather conditions, consumer demand, changes in government regulations, and technology.

short
when the trader has sold the bond before owning it (i.e., without being long the bond).

long
owning a bond or other security.

cyclicals
bonds issued by companies whose successes tend to follow business cycles: When the economy and consumer demand are strong, the company does well; when they falter, the company also struggles.

✔ *Banking/Finance.* Banks, savings and loans, brokerages, and insurance, mortgage, and finance companies are affected by interest rate changes and economic conditions.

The following classifications are all U.S. dollar–denominated issues and are also known as noncorporates. They comprise about 10% of the corporate market. We will discuss the implications of owning bonds from issuers beyond our borders in Chapter 5.

✔ *Sovereign.* Also known as Yankee bonds; bonds issued by foreign entities but denominated in U.S. dollars and traded on U.S. exchanges.

✔ *Supranational.* Multinational entities, such as World Bank.

Maturities fall into four categories:

1. Short-term—up to 4 years.
2. Intermediate-term—5–12 years.
3. Long-term—13–40 years.
4. "Absurd-term"—41–100 years.

The coupon structure also comes in different flavors:

✔ Fixed rate.
✔ Floating rate.
✔ Zero coupons.

As mentioned in the first chapter, bonds also differ in their creditworthiness. An issuer's credit rating measures how safe or how sketchy an issuer is.

INVESTMENT-GRADE AND HIGH-YIELD BONDS

Corporate bonds fall into two broad credit classifications: investment-grade and high-yield bonds. (See Table I.1 on page 8.)

The reason for the distinction between investment-grade and high-yield bonds is because at one time banks were allowed to invest only in bonds ranked in the top four rating categories. Thus, these bonds became known as investment-grade.

High-yield bonds were made famous in the 1980s by the marketing prowess of the now-infamous Michael Milken of the now-defunct firm Drexel Burnham Lambert. Although illegal trading practices would later land him in jail and leave the firm he worked for insolvent, Milken's efforts created alternative avenues for young companies to raise much-needed cash when more traditional methods of borrowing were closed to them. This sector of the fixed income market offers investors the greatest opportunity for growth if the start-up takes off. It also offers the best chance for the greatest loss if the start-up fails. (See Figure 3.1.)

Some traders make the distinction between top-tier high-yield bonds and low-grade high-yield bonds. In the

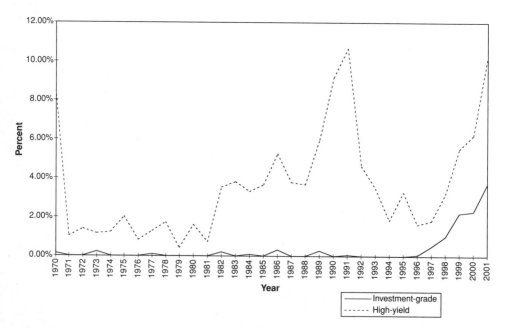

FIGURE 3.1 Historical default rate.
Data source: Moody's Investors Service, "Default and Recovery Rates of Corporate Bond Issues," February 2002 at www.riskcalc.moodyrms.com.

high-yield's heyday, folks in the business would say top-tier bonds were junk spelled "junque."

When a company gets into such serious financial trouble that it defaults on the issue and stops paying interest on its bonds, the bonds are said to be trading **flat** (without interest). These bonds trade at fractions of their face value. The hope is that they will do one or all of the following:

flat
the issuer is no longer paying interest on the bond.

✔ Begin to pay interest again.

✔ Pay the past interest in **arrears**.

✔ Pay the principal at maturity.

If they do, their value should move higher again.

Due to the collapse of Enron Corp. in 2001, rating agencies are rethinking how they evaluate credit. There seems to be more of an emphasis on company liquidity, as well as investor perception.

arrears
what was not paid and is owed to someone; back pay.

You will find corporate bonds listed on the New York Stock Exchange (NYSE). However, the vast majority of corporate bonds aren't traded on the **floor** but are traded between dealers **over-the-counter** (OTC)—which in this day and age would be more appropriate to call OTP for over-the-phone or OL for online.

floor
slang referring to a physical location where traders meet face-to-face to trade the securities that are listed with them. An example is the cavernous room where the New York Stock Exchange (NYSE) conducts its trading.

over-the-counter (OTC)
when stocks and bonds aren't traded on the floor of a formal exchange there is no physical place where the traders meet face-to-face to trade the securities; they are traded over the phone, fax, and computer line.

Corporate bonds are assumed to have a $1,000 face value unless otherwise stipulated. A 9% bond with a $1,000 face value would pay $90 a year, so each semiannual interest payment is $45.

The bond's **indenture** specifies all important facets of the bond issue including coupon, maturity date, and seniority—that is, where this debt (bond) ranks in the debt hierarchy on the company's balance sheet. This is important because you want to know where you stand in the line of creditors looking for their piece of the company's

> **indenture**
> formal agreement between bond holders and the issuer covering such issues as: type, size of issue, terms, what backs the issue, any provisions that further protect the investor (such as a sinking fund), call privileges, and appointment of trustee on behalf of bond holders.

> **debenture**
> bond whose interest and principal payments are not secured by hard assets that could be sold if the company goes under. The bond is sold on the basis of the company's past performance and good name.

assets if the company ends up filing Chapter 11 (Figure 3.2). Senior debt holders are second in line, with only banks standing in front of them in the creditor queue, whereas subordinated debt holders are further back in the line. If a bond is subordinated it will say so in the bond's description, usually abbreviated "sub."

The bond's indenture also tells you what, if anything, is backing the bond. Bonds that are not backed by any collateral and rely solely on the issuer's name or goodwill to attract investors are called **debenture** bonds. They are unsecured bonds and rely on the issuer's ability to make money to pay investors. If the issuer fails there is nothing to **secure** the bonds.

Many companies cannot issue debenture bonds due to their sketchy credit histories, so they have to post some kind of collateral in order to attract investors.

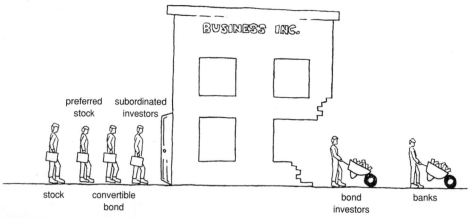

FIGURE 3.2 The lien line.
Drawing by Steven Saltzgiver.

secure
a hard asset backs the bond's interest and principal payments in case the issuer becomes unable to make the payment.

Equipment trust bonds are secured by . . . yes, equipment. For example, a construction company may need to borrow money to buy one of those huge cranes. If the company were to go bankrupt, the crane would be sold and the proceeds be distributed to the equipment trust bondholders. Equipment trust bonds are often **serial bonds**; this way the issuer's debt burden declines as the equipment is depreciated over time. As the value of the equipment erodes, the company owes less money because it has fewer bonds outstanding and so owes less interest than it originally did.

serial bond
portions of a serial bond issue mature at different times— the issue has a number of maturity dates. For instance, different bonds in the issue may come due each year for the next 10 years. The other type of issue is a term bond.

If a company has no hard assets to put up as collateral, and the trustees demand that the bonds be secured, they can specify bonds, stocks, notes, and so on to back the issue. These bonds are known as collateral trust bonds.

If real estate is pledged, they are **mortgage bonds**. The same real estate can be used to back many different loans and bond issues, so you need to check on what else it is pledged to and where your issue stands in the claims line.

Guaranteed bonds are backed by some other corporation—for example, the issuer's parent company.

mortgage bond
a bond backed by a property mortgage.

guaranteed bond
bonds backed by some other corporation; for example the issuer's parent company.

credit derivative
contract between two parties that bets on the future value of another security.

Credit derivatives are a noncash way to hedge or bet on a firm's ability to remain solvent.

Index bonds are bonds that have a sampling of corporate bond issues that is supposed to act similarly to a sector of the bond market. Investors get a broad exposure to that sector in one trade. However, at the time of this writing, it is such a new product that even the Wall Street pros are learning through experience how this creation will behave in different market conditions.

index bond
a sampling of corporate bonds that is supposed to act similarly to a sector of the bond market as measured by an index.

A company can also put aside money on a regular basis in an escrow account that is earmarked to retire portions of the bond on specific dates. These are **sinking fund bonds**. Which portion of the issue will be retired via the sinking fund is decided by lottery just before each designated date.

sinking fund bond
that is money put aside and held in a separate account to retire portions of a bond issue at different times.

put bond
investor has the option to put the bonds back to the issuer at set intervals.

Put bonds mean the investor has the option to put the bonds back to the issuer at set intervals. You would be paid a lower yield on these bonds because this is an advantage.

Whatever type of corporate you buy, you are helping to finance America's business. Just make sure the company is worthy of your loan.

Chapter 4

Bonds Including the Kitchen Sink: Mortgage-Backed Bonds

Now we're going to move a little closer to home. A mortgage-backed security (MBS) is a group of real estate mortgages like the one you may have on your home.

These groups of mortgages, known as pools (Figure 4.1), are then sold to investors who receive the mortgage payments as the MBS's income payments. Like the underlying mortgage, the MBS payments are made up of both interest and principal. Since homeowners make mortgage payments every month, MBSs pay interest monthly instead of semiannually like other fixed income securities.

MBSs are known as pass-throughs (Figure 4.2) because the interest and principal paid by the homeowner passes through to the bondholder. The issue's trustee or servicer administers all payments associated with the mortgage.

There are other types of pass-through securities that pool together other types of loans: auto loans, boat loans, credit card debt, student loans, equipment leases, and RV loans. These are known as asset-backed securities (ABS). The type of loan that can be packaged together and sold is

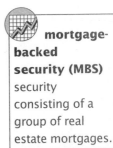

mortgage-backed security (MBS)
security consisting of a group of real estate mortgages.

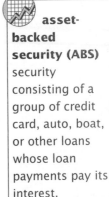

asset-backed security (ABS)
security consisting of a group of credit card, auto, boat, or other loans whose loan payments pay its interest.

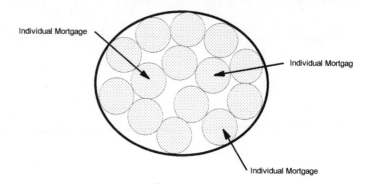

Individual Mortgage

Individual Mortgag

Individual Mortgage

FIGURE 4.1 Mortgage pool.

limited only by the imagination. In fact, David Bowie sold the rights to future royalties from his extensive collection of songs. All future sales of his work will be paid to the bondholders who in effect now own the rights to his music. Like your neighbor's teenager, this is a fresh and fast growing sector. In 1985 when asset-backeds arrived on the scene, a not-so-shabby $1.2 billion were issued. But 12 years later, more than $102 billion in new issues came to market in 1997 alone. Ninety percent of ABS are AAA rated because they are insured or have some form of credit enhancement such as overcollateralization, letters of credit, or reserve funds. Some have steady, predictable cash flows, but most have unpredictable cash flows like mortgage-backeds.

For our discussion, we will focus on MBSs since

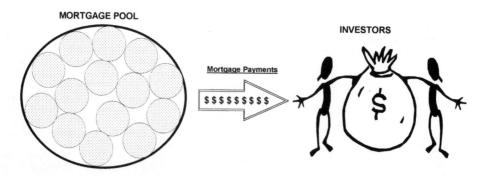

MORTGAGE POOL

INVESTORS

Mortgage Payments

$$$$$$$$$

FIGURE 4.2 Income passes through.

most of the mortgage-backed concepts also apply to asset-backeds.

MBSs are a popular target for techno-jargon obfuscation. For example, "Ms. Johnson, mortgage-backeds have negative convexity while most bonds have positive convexity." Sounds impressive. But, it's not so intimidating when you know that **negative convexity** is just a highfalutin way of saying that MBS prices tend to go up less when bond prices are rising due to falling interest rates and down more in price than other bonds when prices are falling due to rising interest rates. (See Figure 4.3.) Because they exhibit this less than desirable behavior, mortgage-backed bonds usually offer higher yields than comparable bonds.

The fact that MBSs are usually of the highest quality and yet pay relatively higher levels of income on a monthly basis is the main reason for this fixed income security's popularity. MBSs are *not* the investment of choice for investors who:

 negative convexity
a bond possessing this characteristic finds its price becomes more reactive when bond prices are going down and less responsive when prices are rising.

✔ Need a steady level of income.
✔ Are concerned about their investment's value in the secondary market.
✔ Are concerned about reinvestment risk.

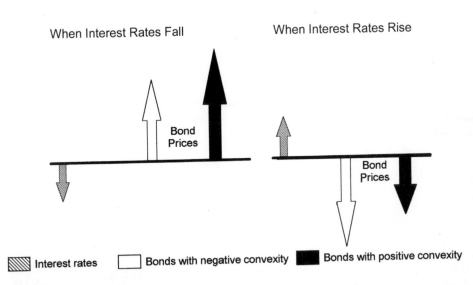

FIGURE 4.3 Convexity.

MBS CONCEPTION

Here's how a mortgage-backed security is made.

A soon-to-be homeowner goes to the bank and borrows money to buy a house. The bank lends him/her money at $8^1/2\%$.

Soon after, the bank sells its loan portfolio to mortgage brokers. The bank does this in order to clear the loans off its plate so that it'll be able to make new loans. Selling its loans is similar to when kids tell you that burping after a meal gives them more room for dessert.

The mortgage broker who bought the bank's loan portfolio then packages the loans and sells them to investors.

At each stage, a little of the cream is skimmed off. For example, say, the bank sells your mortgage with a number of similar $8^1/2\%$ loans. The mortgage broker pays the bank for the loan portfolio, takes a cut for its services, and sells the resulting 8% mortgage-backed bonds to investors. (See Figure 4.4.)

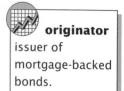

originator
issuer of mortgage-backed bonds.

Mortgage-backed issuers, aka **originators**, either issue "private" securities where mortgage payments are passed through directly to investors or issue securities that are backed by a guarantor such as a government

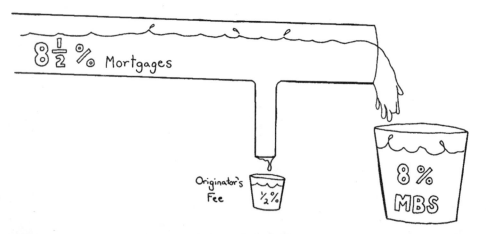

FIGURE 4.4 Flowchart of mortgage-backed security (MBS) creation. Drawing by Steven Saltzgiver.

agency. Private-label bonds are subject to the individual company's ability to evaluate the mortgage borrower's creditworthiness. Such bonds offer no guarantee of timely principal and interest payment, whereas MBSs issued by government agencies are subject to standardized underwriting requirements specified by the Federal National Mortgage Association (FNMA).

Private pass-through securities often do not have any payment guarantees; they are a pure conduit. The private-issue MBS investor receives only what the mortgage holders pay. These MBSs are issued by private companies, such as finance companies.

As another alternative the federal government created a number of agencies to facilitate mortgage lending. We'll look what makes each one unique.

Ginnie Mae

The Government National Mortgage Association (GNMA, affectionately pronounced "Ginnie Mae") is a corporation owned by the U.S. government and operating under the Department of Housing and Urban Development (HUD). GNMAs are made up of mortgages that are Federal Housing Administration (FHA) insured or Veterans Administration (VA) guaranteed. The government guarantees the timely payment of *both principal and interest* regardless of whether payment has been received from the mortgage borrower. Since they are backed by the full faith and credit of the U.S. government, they currently enjoy the AAA rating.

Fannie Mae

Federal National Mortgage Association (FNMA, referred to as "Fannie Mae") MBS pools are made up of conventional mortgages (not FHA-insured or VA-guaranteed). The agency, FNMA, guarantees timely payment of principal and interest, but the difference between these and GNMA is that these are *not* backed by the full faith and credit of the U.S. government. However, it is felt the government would bail out the agency if it were in danger of defaulting on payments so the securities are still AAA-rated. But, because the government guarantee is implied and not explicitly stated, FNMAs yield more than GNMAs.

Freddie Mac

Federal Home Loan Mortgage Corporation (FHLMC, called "Freddie Mac") also pools conventional mortgages. Their MBSs are known as participation certificates (FHLMC PCs). FHLMC guarantees the timely payment of interest and eventual payment of principal. This means it passes through whatever principal it receives and guarantees the MBS investor will receive scheduled but unpaid principal within a year. Like FNMAs, FHLMC PCs are *not* backed by the full faith and credit of the U.S. government; therefore, their yields are similar to FNMAs.

WHY MBSs YIELD MORE

1. Principal can be returned at any time.
2. Reinvestment risk is higher because principal is usually returned when interest rates are low.
3. The income you receive decreases over time as the face value erodes away.
4. The MBS's price in the secondary market does not go up as much and goes down more than traditional fixed income securities (negative convexity).

With all these disadvantages, you may be wondering why anyone would buy these bonds. The answer is the same as why investors buy bonds that have shaky credit: BECAUSE YOU ARE PAID TO. Your higher risk is rewarded by the potential for a higher return. Let's look at each of the four disadvantages in turn so you can decide whether they make a difference to you.

Return of Principal

You can see in Figure 4.5 that originally mortgage payments are primarily interest, and over time principal makes up a larger portion of the payment. As the mort-

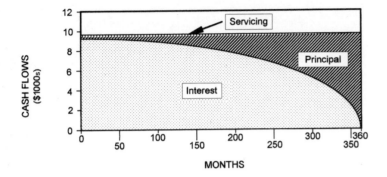

FIGURE 4.5 Life of a mortgage.

gages in the pool age, a higher and higher percentage of an MBS's monthly payment will be principal. Since there is less and less principal earning interest the income payments will decline.

Those of you who own houses know that with most mortgages you can prepay your home's loan principal at any time without penalty. For the MBS investor this means the face amount of the bond can be prepaid at the homeowner's whim. This means the MBS's natural acceleration of principal being returned to investors can be magnified by prepayments. In essence, the security is perpetually callable, and unlike traditional callable bonds that are called away at a premium on specific dates, bits and pieces of the MBS can trickle away at par, 100 cents on the dollar, at any time. This is **prepayment risk**. (See Table 4.1.)

Reinvestment Risk

What you homeowners also know is that you usually refinance when interest rates are low. So, when interest rates drop, this MBS principal prepayment trickle can turn into a deluge. What this means to the MBS investor is, "Oh, man, I get my principal back and have to reinvest it in lower-paying bonds."

Decreasing Income

What this mortgage prepayment also means to the MBS investor is that as the investment's face value declines

prepayment risk
the possibility that a bond owner will receive his/her principal back from the issuer before the maturity date.

TABLE 4.1 Mortgage Prepayments			
Month	Scheduled Principal	Principal Paid	Loan Face Value
			$25,000
January	$100	$125	24,875
February	100	100	24,775
March	100	200	24,575
April	100	1,000	23,575

over time, so the income it pays out also gets smaller. Even though the interest rate remains constant, the income paid to the investor declines. Mortgage analysts are constantly monitoring prepayment speeds. If prepayments pick up, yields to MBS investors decline; if they slow down, yields increase.

This is as if there were a beach where sunbathers have to lie a certain distance apart. Over time the ocean erodes the beach. Since the sunbathers must stay the same distance apart, fewer folks can soak up the solar rays. With the MBS, the amount of principal earning income gets smaller so the amount of income it produces diminishes. (See Figure 4.6.)

How about an MBS example of this concept? Let's say the MBS coupon in Table 4.2 is 10%. In January, the investor would earn $24,875 × .10 = $2,487.50; in April, $23,575 × .10 = $2,357.50.

An MBS pool that is made up of 30-year mortgages would have a stated maturity of 30 years. However, since principal is usually being paid out to the investor throughout the life of the bond, most of the investors end up owning only a small portion of the original face value at maturity. Therefore, with mortgage-backeds, rather than using maturity, a more meaningful measure of how long your principal will be outstanding is **average life**. Average life is the estimated time until half of a mortgage pool's principal has been paid off. The estimate is based on past experience with similar pools.

 average life
the time it is estimated that it will take a mortgage-backed security to return half of the principal to the investor. Also known as average maturity.

FIGURE 4.6 Principal erosion decreases income.
Drawing by Steven Saltzgiver.

TABLE 4.2 Decreasing Income		
Month	Loan Face Value	Income Earned
	$25,000	$2,500.00
January	24,875	2,487.50
February	24,775	2,477.50
March	24,575	2,457.50
April	23,575	2,357.50

A pool's average life can change with changes in interest rates. In the summer of 2002 the Lehman Brothers Mortgage index had an average maturity of 6.31 years. A 30-year MBS with a 6% coupon had an average life of 6.57 years, while a 30-year MBS with a 6½% coupon had a 4.2-year average life.

The longer the security's average life, the more price volatility it will have. The shorter the average life, the lower the security's price volatility for a given change in interest rates. This is like a diver bouncing on the end of a diving board. The shorter the board is, the smaller the arc from top to bottom of the board's bounce. The longer the board, the greater the distance between the tip of the board's high point and low point as the diver bounces on the end. (See Figure 4.7.)

volatility
the characteristic of having up and down changes.

Since how quickly homeowners prepay their mortgages changes with interest rates, so does the MBS's average life. As interest rates drop and homeowners refinance more often, the average life shortens because you are getting your principal back more quickly. So, the expectation about how long the time will be before half of the principal is returned to you is shorter. The expected yield drops because it is projected you'll have less principal remaining to earn you interest.

As interest rates rise, prepayments slow. The average life extends out into the future. It then is expected that it will take longer before half the face value is paid out to you.

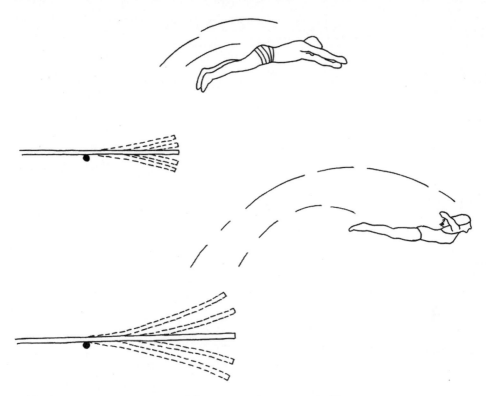

FIGURE 4.7 Longer average life (maturity); more volatility. Drawing by Steven Saltzgiver.

Negative Convexity

Besides the yield being affected, the problem with this shortening and lengthening is that the MBS becomes more responsive to interest rate moves when interest rates rise and bond prices are falling. Its price drop accelerates and falls faster than other fixed income investments. Then, when interest rates fall and bond prices are rising, the MBS becomes less responsive, and its price rise is slower relative to other fixed income investments.

An MBS is like a big rock. Its additional mass causes it to *fall faster*; and attaching a balloon to it will cause it to *rise more slowly*.

COLLATERALIZED MORTGAGE OBLIGATIONS (CMOs)

collateralized mortgage obligations (CMOs)
a security made up of mortgage-backed securities. It is split up into pieces called traunches that are designed to have specific volatility and maturity characteristics.

Wall Street loves to slice and dice securities, forever creating new entrants in the investment-of-the-month club: artificial financial alternatives.

In the 1990s the nouveau product du jour was the collateralized mortgage obligation (CMO). Before the CMO was conceived, institutional investors backed away from MBSs, complaining that the securities' negative convexity could cause them to underperform. So, Wall Street conceived and delivered the CMO.

The Making of a CMO

While an MBS is a pool of mortgages, a CMO is a pool of MBSs that is then cut up into component parts. Asset-backeds and corporates also package together their securities, slice and dice, and sell them as CDOs (collateralized debt obligations) in two types: CBOs (collateralized bond obligations) and CLOs (collateralized loan obligations).

You can think of a CMO as an apple pie. This pie is so skillfully cut that one piece would have all the choice apples, while another piece would consist of only butter and sugar, leaving yet a third piece with mealy, worm-infested apples. Woe to the diners who gave only a cursory glance at the crust before they swallowed.

traunche
division within a CMO that has its own unique characteristics and is sold as a separate security.

All of a CMO's pieces (aka **traunches**) are interrelated, so a change in one causes all the others to change as well. You need to understand how *all* the pieces behave, not just the one you're buying.

When CMOs first came to market, they often had only four traunches. (See Figure 4.8.) The face value of each traunche was paid off sequentially. Traunche A was paid off first, then traunche B, and so on.

As time went on CMOs got even harder to decipher because as the type of traunches got more complex, the number of traunches increased exponentially. Some CMOs had as many as 60 traunches, and it became next to impossible to figure out how all these funky traunches interacted. As you can see in Figure 4.9, we no longer have four neatly paying sequential traunches.

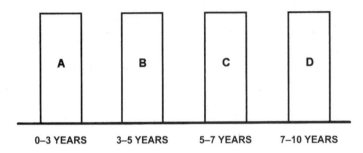

FIGURE 4.8 Collateralized mortgage obligation (CMO) traunches.

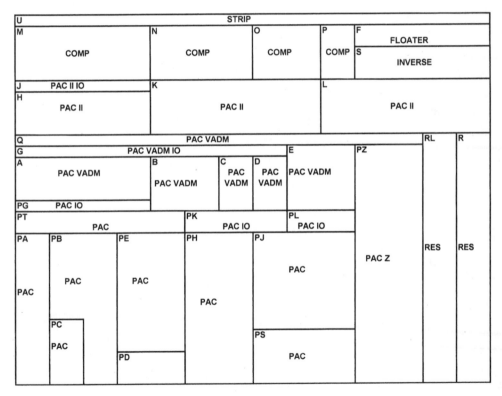

FIGURE 4.9 Complex collateralized mortgage obligation (CMO).

Some traunches would suddenly completely pay down. Some would lose half their value in a week. Some would decline in value instead of rising when interest rates fell. Some traunches jumped. It'd be like you were standing behind a wall and all of a sudden it jumped out of the way and there was a train bearing down on you.

We're not going to get into the complicated analytics involved in understanding a complex CMO's schematics here; that's another book. Suffice it to say that many investors were hurt by these bonds, and they now affectionately say that CMO stands for "Count Me Out." It's not hard to understand how CMOs got such a bad name. It isn't necessarily their fault—like any adolescent, they just aren't understood. Remember: Don't buy something if you don't fully understand it.

Going Global:
International Bonds

T his chapter travels beyond our country's borders. Throughout time, countries have cycled through different postures toward each other, such as isolationist or expansionist. Today's trend is globalization. This environment of openness is most obviously illustrated by the formation of the **European Union (EU)** alliance and its adoption of a single, common currency—the **euro** (€)—in 1999. At least economically, everyone around the world is trying to be one big happy family. Pools of capital are there for anyone who cares to take a dip. Investment opportunities of every type are available in every language. In 1993, 54% of the world debt was outside the United States, so certainly fixed income opportunities abroad abound.

When you invest outside the United States, you must account for the **currency risk** and **sovereign risk** involved. We will review some of the choices and risks involved in investing overseas, but our stay will be brief since this is an area where it can be best to have a professional as your guide. It is easier for these investment professionals who devote their resources and time to:

 European Union (EU) begun in 1950, the EU has 15 member states, with 13 others soon to be added. It includes countries that have not adopted the euro as their domestic currency.

euro (€)
common currency shared by 12 European countries that agreed to function as one economic and financial unit beginning in 1999. The monetary system is governed by one central bank. Trade and employment barriers have been dropped.

 currency risk
the risk that the currency your foreign bond is issued in will appreciate in value so your bond's proceeds will be converted back into fewer dollars than they would have been before.

✔ Track down elusive information.

✔ Decode foreign accounting practices and financial documents.

✔ Understand the intricacies of interrelated currency movements.

Even if international investing doesn't interest you, you should be aware that you may be investing internationally without realizing it when you buy domestic corporate bonds. Companies such as Ford, PepsiCo, and IBM have operations all around the globe. When you invest in such global conglomerates, your investment return is likely to be impacted by the same factors that affect international securities, such as currency exchange rates, health of the foreign economies, and trade relations with the countries where these companies do business.

If you are interested in investing in international bonds, bonds issued by foreign governments, or bonds of companies domiciled in foreign countries, it is probably for the unique opportunities they can offer you. A major consideration is the chance to diversify your portfolio. Diversification is most effective when your various investments are not highly **correlated**—they either react to different events or react differently to the same events. This is often the case with bonds issued by other countries. They can be impacted by events that our own bonds don't even notice. For example, our bonds have little if any reaction to France's employment figures, but their domestic bonds can react quite dramatically to the news. The less correlated a country's in-

The opposite of correlated is to be inversely related, which means to move in the opposite direction or behave in an opposite manner. For example, the behavior of a hungry cat and a hungry horse when they see food will be highly correlated (they'll both move toward the food), whereas the behavior of a rock and a balloon released from the top of the Empire State Building are inversely related.

vestments are with ours the more different their behavior will be. This means that the opportunity for diversification will be greater, but so too could be the opportunity for risk.

Another reason to buy bonds beyond our borders is for the chance to earn higher interest rates. Higher-quality issuers (developed nations, such as those countries in the G-8) tend to be more highly correlated with our economy (since we're considered a developed nation). Therefore, their interest rates tend to be highly correlated with our own. When you invest in securities issued in these countries the primary benefit you are looking for is currency diversification, whereas emerging markets (often known as **NICs** or **newly industrialized countries**) offer a wider range of diversification, as well as greater chances for income pickup and capital gains. However, this also means they offer a greater chance for loss.

INTERNATIONAL FIXED INCOME ALTERNATIVES

As for international bonds, investing in them is generally broken down into two categories: U.S. pay (dollar-denominated) and foreign pay (denominated in a currency other than U.S. dollars).

There is no currency risk with U.S. pay bonds for U.S. investors; however, you also lower the investment diversification impact because you aren't diversifying out of U.S. dollars. One of the most straightforward ways to invest in foreign entities is through **Yankee bonds**. Foreign banks and foreign companies issue Yankee bonds in the U.S. market. They are, therefore, registered with the **Securities and Exchange Commission (SEC)** and **underwritten** by a domestic syndicate. Because these bonds are listed and trade in our domestic market, they often offer more liquidity and easier access to information, making them an attractive alternative for individual investors.

There is a fairly new type of security known as **global bonds**. These bonds are issued in a number of different countries simultaneously. In each country they are issued in the country's own currency. They are registered

sovereign risk
the risk that the government where the bonds are issued will take actions that will hurt the bond's value.

correlated
objects are said to be correlated when their actions tend to resemble one another; objects that are not correlated react dissimilarly to events.

G-8
eight developed
nations that have
formed a loose
economic alliance
(formerly the G-
7). Their
economies and
interest rates
tend to move in
the same
direction. The G-8
includes: Canada,
France, Germany,
Great Britain,
Italy, Japan,
Russia, and the
United States.

**newly
industrialized
country (NIC)**
emerging
market; offers
diversification
and profit
potential but
also risk.

**Yankee
bonds**
dollar-
denominated
bonds issued in
the United States
by foreign banks
and corporations.

in each country where they are issued, so in the United States they are registered with the SEC. Securities have to meet certain criteria and standards in order to be registered with the SEC, so this gives investors a certain peace of mind.

You need to be aware that even though IBM is a U.S. corporation, IBM Netherlands could be a separate and foreign entity whose bonds would be held to standards that could be different from the SEC's. **Eurobonds** and **Eurodollar bonds** also are regulated by the issuing country's guidelines, not the SEC's. Those differences may or may not be important. To protect yourself when you are buying foreign bonds, there are several questions you need to ask yourself:

✔ Who issued the bond?

✔ What market is the bond traded in?

✔ Where is the entity that issued the bond domiciled?

Once you have answered these questions, you can use that information to delve deeper into what legal, accounting, and regulatory standards apply to this issue. The legal questions are innumerable:

✔ What happens if the issuer goes bankrupt?

✔ Is there a bankruptcy court to govern the process most profitably or will the assets just be sold at fire sale prices, leaving investors with next to nothing?

✔ Will the courts rule on issues that protect shareholder rights?

Regulatory standards refer to what the issuer's investment governing body, like our SEC, requires issuers to do and uphold. The standards may be much more lax than our own, leaving room for graft or misunderstanding.

There are other matters to grapple with. The length of the year you use to calculate the interest can be different. Taxation can be an issue. When do you convert back into dollars? Furthermore, you have to wait until the foreign bond is **seasoned** before you buy it. The quandaries go on and on. This arena can be fraught with painful leg traps for the unsuspecting individual investor.

RISKS OF INTERNATIONAL INVESTING

As mentioned at the beginning of our discussion about international investing, when you invest in foreign bonds (or stocks), you add two more types of risks to the menu: currency risk and sovereign risk. Because of the added complexity these risks introduce, many investors choose to engage professional financial advisers when they venture abroad to participate in foreign markets. Even if you do hire an expert, it is still important that you understand the risks involved so that you know what questions to ask and can guide your adviser toward what is appropriate for you.

Currency Risk

When you invest in securities that pay interest and principal in some currency other than the U.S. dollar, you take on the added uncertainty of currency risk. This is the risk that the foreign currency will **depreciate** (go down in value) against the dollar while you are invested there, which is the same as saying that the dollar will **appreciate** (rise in value) versus that currency.

If the foreign currency you've invested in depreciates versus the dollar, it would take more foreign currency to buy the same number of U.S. dollars, because the foreign currency is worth less (it has depreciated in value). (See Figure 5.1.)

As long as you stay in the foreign currency, there's no problem with the dollar appreciating. The problem comes when you try to convert your earnings back into U.S. dollars. For example, if you earned 12% interest but

Securities and Exchange Commission (SEC)
federal agency that regulates the securities industry. It makes rules to discourage fraud, and then polices, arbitrates, and punishes misconduct. It was created by the Securities Exchange Act of 1934 to enforce the Securities Act of 1933.

underwritten
when an investment bank buys a new issue, assumes the market risk, and attempts to resell it to the public; a syndicate underwrites the new issue.

global bond

bond issued in several countries' currencies simultaneously.

Eurobond

bond underwritten by banks and investment firms from several different European countries. Eurobonds can be denominated in any currency. They are sold to investors outside the country whose currency pays the issue's principal and interest.

the currency depreciated 10% versus the U.S. dollar, when you convert your earnings back into U.S. dollars, you find that you actually made only 2%.

Of course, the dollar can also depreciate (foreign currency appreciates). In this case, your investment return is increased because the interest or principal payment converts into more dollars. Let's say you earned 12% interest and the currency appreciates 10%; your total return would be 22%.

Currency Conversions

The exchange rate is also known as the FX rate (FX stands for foreign exchange). Fortunately for U.S. investors, all foreign exchange markets quote their currency in terms of the U.S. dollar. Unfortunately, they don't all quote it in the same way.

Almost all currencies quote their value in terms of how many currency units equal one dollar. For example, 7.5 deutsche marks (DM) = $1; 133 yen = $1. However, a few currencies quote their value in terms of how many dollars equal one unit of their currency, most notably the British pound and Australian dollar. For example, $3 = 1 British pound. The Canadian dollar is quoted in terms of both U.S. dollars per Canadian dollars and Canadian dollars per U.S. dollars. International traders look at cross

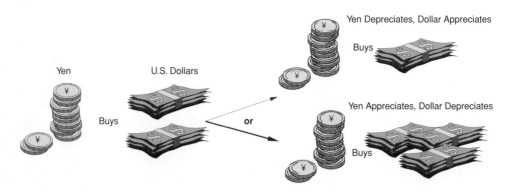

FIGURE 5.1 Currency risk.

If you own dollars and are looking to invest or travel abroad, you want either the dollar to appreciate/get stronger or the foreign currency to depreciate/weaken, so your dollars will have more purchasing power outside the United States. If you own foreign investments and would like to repatriate them back into dollars, you hope the dollar weakens or the currency you're invested in strengthens, so each unit of the foreign currency can buy more dollars.

 Eurodollar bond
a bond whose principal and interest are paid in U.S. currency held in foreign banks, usually European banks. They are not registered with the SEC.

currency rates, which show the exchange rates between a number of currencies (Table 5.1).

Let's say you own Anleihe der Bundesrepublik Deutschland (Bunds) 4¾% 7/4/08, which paid 4,750 DM annually—now 2,428.64 euros (€). When you decide to convert the July 4, 2002, interest payment on July 10, the FX rate is .9884 (that's dollars per euro). So, you will receive $2,400.47, found by multiplying €2,428.64 by .9884. When you convert your next interest payment, let's say the exchange rate is .9412 (do not use this as a forecast—I'm just randomly pulling numbers out of the air); so you would then receive $2,285.84. You can see how currency fluctuations can impact the U.S. dollar value of your foreign investments.

 seasoned
securities have been outstanding and traded in the secondary market for a while.

Computing currency exchanges can be confusing; it's easy to invert the calculations if you don't do it all the time. At Bloomberg.com there is a currency calculator, where you just put in the currencies you are concerned with and out pops the answer!

 depreciate
decline in value.

The monetary policy, economic environment, and political developments in a country all play a role in its currency's valuation. A high inflation rate can hurt a currency because investors don't want to own a currency whose value is being inflated away. Relatively high **real interest rates** can help a country's currency. There is also the risk that a country may institute capital controls. This means it decrees that the currency is no longer convert-

 appreciate
the investment value rises higher.

TABLE 5.1 Cross Currency Rates

	USD	GBP	CHF	JPY	CAD	AUD	EUR	NZD	DKK	SEK
SEK	9.3367	13.98	6.1777	7.7001	6.1406	5.3625	9.0631	4.6515	1.2193	SELF
DKK	7.6574	11.47	5.0666	6.3151	5.0361	4.3980	7.4330	3.8149	SELF	0.8201
NZD	2.0072	3.0060	1.3281	1.6554	1.3201	1.1529	1.9484	SELF	0.2621	0.2150
EUR	1.0302	1.5428	0.6816	0.8496	0.6775	0.5917	SELF	0.5132	0.1345	0.1103
AUD	1.7411	2.6075	1.1520	1.4359	1.1451	SELF	1.6901	0.8674	0.2274	0.1865
CAD	1.5205	2.2771	1.0061	1.2540	SELF	0.8733	1.4760	0.7575	0.1986	0.1629
JPY	121.26	181.59	80.23	SELF	79.75	69.64	117.70	60.41	15.84	12.99
CHF	1.5114	2.2634	SELF	1.2464	0.9940	0.8680	1.4671	0.7530	0.1974	0.1619
GBP	0.6677	SELF	0.4418	0.5507	0.4392	0.3835	0.6482	0.3327	0.0872	0.0715
USD	SELF	1.4976	0.6617	0.8247	0.6577	0.5744	0.9707	0.4982	0.1306	0.1071

USD	U.S. dollar	GBP	British pound	CHF	Swiss franc
JPY	Japanese yen	CAD	Canadian dollar	AUD	Australian dollar
EUR	Euro	NZD	New Zealand dollar	DKK	Danish krone
SEK	Swedish krona			

June 2002, Bloomberg.com.

ible. It is isolating its currency and financial system from everyone else because it is in big trouble and views this as the only way to protect itself. Spain instituted capital controls in the early 1990s. Russia seems to change the rules daily. Capital controls is actually an example of both currency risk and sovereign risk, which leads us to our next discussion.

Sovereign Risk

Sovereign risk is at work when the Peruvian government decides to nationalize the coffee operations you just invested in, leaving your investment worthless. Sovereign risk rears its head when the Russian government decides to print rubles as if they were manufacturing tissue paper. Sovereign risk ensnares you when militant factions topple the democratic government in order to institute anarchy.

Think back over the past hundred years at how many governments and companies have come and gone. Very few enterprises have been around for as long as their investors envisioned. With boundaries being constantly redrawn, trying to keep a current globe in your den has been an expensive task. The theme for humankind's recent history has certainly been "temporal." With all this unpredictable change, you can see how not understanding what's going on could be financially dangerous.

Sovereign risk can stalk the unsuspecting foreign investor because we are far away and aren't aware of all that is going on. Our naïveté is as ingrained as our way of looking at the world; we often don't have a full appreciation of the differences in culture and psychology. Principles we take for granted like freedom of expression and social justice may be unknown in that country.

In addition, the rules of business may be very different. That country's accounting practices may be so totally obscure to us that a company that looks solvent may actually be operating in the red according to our own standards. Contracts may not carry the same legally binding clout that they do in the United States and may be ignored on a whim. Unfavorable taxation could result in any income advantage being taxed away.

real interest rate what you're left with after inflation deflated your return (real rate of return equals nominal interest rate minus inflation rate).

Foreign investing can be a labrinyth of the unknown, rife with hidden pitfalls for the uninformed investor, and often the information needed to clear up the confusion is very hard to secure. Besides the economic dilemmas, you may also find it difficult to monitor social issues. Companies don't usually advertise in their reports that they use child labor or operate unsafe sweatshops. Other countries may not police or care about these issues. Unless you made a visit you might never know your money is supporting undesirable business practices.

Currency risk and sovereign risk are the reasons why the vast majority of investors choose to invest in countries with very similar cultures and those whose currencies tend to highly correlate with our own, like Canada. These risks are also why they choose to use investment professionals who dedicate their full-time efforts to understanding the nuances of foreign investment environments. There are myriad mutual funds, as well as investment professionals, that specialize in the global arena. This is one area where it can pay to hire a specialist.

Chapter 6

Paid to Wait:
Convertible Bonds

This chapter moves away from traditional bonds and explores a type of hybrid security. Like a mixed metaphor, convertible bonds look and act like a bond, but they can also look and act like common stock. Investors are attracted to convertibles because they pay an enticing and steady income while you wait for the stock price to move higher. If it does move, you've locked in a purchase price.

Convertible bonds (aka converts) are similar to traditional fixed income investments in that they pay income twice a year, have a maturity date, and are sometimes callable. In fact, in the *Wall Street Journal* they appear with the listed corporate bonds. They are different from traditional bonds in that they pay interest and offer the option to convert the bonds into a certain number of the issuer's common stock shares at a specified price. How many shares of common stock each convertible bond can be exchanged for when it is converted is set by the convert's **conversion ratio** when the convertible is issued.

Since convertibles are bonds that can become stock, the security's value responds to changes in the common stock's price and the credit quality of the company. Interest rates have little impact because convertibles tend to have low yields.

conversion ratio
set when a convertible bond is issued, this ratio calculates how many shares of common stock each convertible bond can be exchanged for when the bond is converted (conversion ratio equals par value divided by conversion price).

93

Xmart

Security	Yield
Stock	0%
Convert	6%
Bond	8%

call

an option contract that gives the buyer the right to purchase a security from the owner at a specific price before the contract's expiration date.

In the preceding example, you can see that converts tend to yield more than the common stock and straight debt tends to yield more than the convert. It also illustrates why converts are so popular. A convert gives you potential equity price participation and a higher yield. So if the common stock doesn't move you're still earning an attractive yield.

The convertible's long-term stock option (the option to convert the bond into shares of stock) is valuable, so the company can pay lower interest than on the company's straight debt (a traditional bond).

out-of-the-money

the futures or option contract has no intrinsic value; if it were exercised today the contract holder would lose money.

The conversion price is established at issue. It is usually much higher than the stock price is when the convertible bond is issued. For example, imagine that International Flag Inc. convertible bonds are issued on September 10, 2003, when the common stock is trading at $15 per share. Their conversion price is $25 per share. If you decide to convert, you trade in the convertible bond and pay $25 a share for the common stock; you then own the common stock instead of the convert. Converting into common stock is obviously not something you would do until the stock price rises higher than the conversion price of $25 per share.

strike price

price stipulated in a futures or option contract that the contract can be exercised at (i.e., the price the security can be put or called at).

If you are familiar with options, it may help to think of a convertible as a bond trading with an attached stock (**call**) option. When the bond is issued, the convertible's conversion price is like an **out-of-the-money** call option's **strike price**. (See Figure 6.1.) At this point the conversion option is not worth much because the likelihood of its being **exercised** is remote. The conversion option doesn't appreciate much in value until the underlying stock price gets closer to the conversion (strike) price, and it becomes more likely that the conversion option will be exercised.

When the stock's market price rises above the conversion price and the stock is now yielding more than the convertible, the convertible's option is **in-the-money**. As long as this is the relationship (Figure 6.1), the convertible price moves in lockstep with the underlying stock's value price. This is because now it is profitable to convert the bond into the common stock. The convertible has become a **proxy** for the stock and so will mimic the common stock's behavior.

Most convertibles are callable. When the company decides to call a convertible, it must notify you ahead of time so that you have time to convert the bond if you wish. Convertible bond calls may be expressed as a conditional statement. For example, "This bond is noncallable for four years from date of issue unless the common stock sells at 140% of the conversion price for 30 consecutive trading days." In other words, if the common stock's price trades at levels 40% above the convertible's conversion price for 30 trading days straight, the issuer can call the convert. So, if the conversion price is $25, and the stock price trades at $35 for 30 trading days, the company could call the bond.

If a company files for bankruptcy, convertible

exercise
to use the right you purchased in a futures or option contract.

in-the-money
the price of the underlying security has moved so that if you exercised the option you would make money. The contract has intrinsic value.

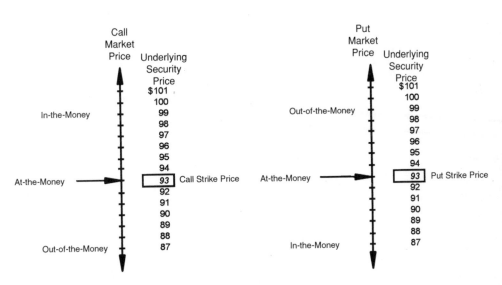

FIGURE 6.1 Options: in-, at-, and out-of-the-money.

proxy

stand-in for; e.g., an in-the-money convertible bond can be exchanged for stock, so it is considered to be an alternative and equivalent form of the common stock.

put

contract that enables the option holder to sell a security to the other party at a set price until the contract expires.

Options

When you buy an option, you are paying for the opportunity to do something in the future should you so choose. For example, when you buy a call, you are paying for the chance to buy a commodity like corn, or a stock, or a bond at a certain price. (We'll refer to just bonds here.) This price is called a strike price. You are hoping the price of the bond you've bought a call on will rise above the strike price, so you can buy the security at a lower-than-market price. If the price does move higher, you could immediately exercise the option, buy the bond, and sell it at the higher market price for a profit. Options have an expiration date after which the contract ceases to exist, so the market has to move higher before then for you to make any money.

So, when you buy a call, you are buying the option to purchase the bond at a certain price. When you sell a call, you receive a call premium (cost of the option) from the call buyer. You are giving that person the right to call the bond away from you. You are hoping the price doesn't move higher so the person won't call your security away at a lower-than-market price. You'll be able to keep the bond, and you'll have made money from having sold the now worthless call. Selling a call is also known as writing a call.

Call options involve the right to call the bond away from the owner. **Put** options involve the right to force someone to buy your bond at a higher-than-market price. When you buy a put, you are paying for the right to sell your bond at a certain price to the person who sells you the put. You are protecting yourself from having the price of your security drop. If the price does fall, you can sell your bond at a higher-than-market price, limiting losses. On the other hand, the put seller is hoping the price of the bond won't fall, so the premium you paid him/her will be clear profit without any consequences. The put seller doesn't want to have to pay above-market prices for the bond.

Options themselves can be traded in the secondary market once the contract has been written. Their value is based on how much time there is until the option expires (theta), how volatile the market is (vega), and where the market price is versus the strike price. The option is worth more the more time there is until expiration, the more volatility there is in the market, and the more in-the-money it is. This last point refers to the relationship between the strike and market price. The strike price does not change. When the contracts are written a call's strike price is lower than the market price, and a put's strike price is above the market price. The options are originally out-of-the-money. This means that if you exercised the option immediately (you said, "Yes, I want to call/put the bond"), you would lose the money you paid for the option. At-the-money means the market price equals the strike price. In-the-money means if you exercised the option, you'd make money. The option is said to have intrinsic value because it can be "converted" into cash. A call is in-the-money when the security's market price is above the strike price. A put is in-the-money when the security's market price is below the strike price.

bondholders are usually behind traditional bond investors and in front of preferred and common stock owners in the line of lien holders trying to claim a piece of the failing company's assets.

This seniority tends to provide convertibles with more downside price protection than the company's preferred or common stock because of its place in the capital structure—where it stands in its claim on company assets in the case of bankruptcy.

Convertibles are also an attractive common stock alternative for investors who plan to hold the securities in a **margin account**. The security offers participation in the common stock's upside while the interest earned helps to defray the margin interest expense. (See Figure 6.2.)

 margin account
investment account where the investor borrows money from the investment firm in order to buy securities, paying a higher interest rate on the money borrowed.

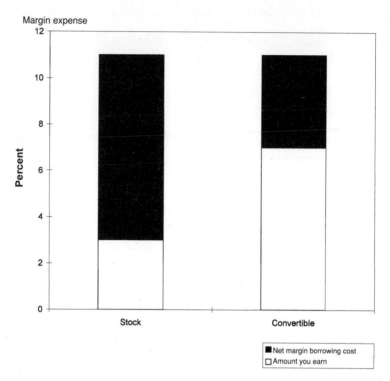

FIGURE 6.2 Convertibles help defray margin expenses.

WHEN TO BUY CONVERTS

If you don't think you'll ever buy convertibles, skip this section. But if the convertible concept intrigues you, read on. There's some math to follow. Plan on reading it a couple of times, and don't worry if it doesn't come clear right away.

It makes sense to buy a convertible that is not yet convert-able if either you think it will be in-the-money in the near future, or the yield is high enough to make it worth the wait to see if the convert will be in-the-money at some point.

To help decide if the latter is the case, follow these three steps:

1. Calculate the convert's yield advantage versus the common stock yield.

2. Calculate how much you are paying for the conversion option; it's the difference between the price you are paying and the price you would pay if the bond weren't convertible. It is known as the **(convertible) premium**.

3. See if the yield advantage (step 1) is greater than the premium you are paying (step 2) for the ability to convert the bond into stock.

Pretend today's date is 9/30/05. We're looking at Snafu Co.

Common Stock

Price: 31⅝   Annual dividend: $1.25

Convertible Bond

Issued in 2004   BB-rated
Coupon: 7½%   Maturity: 9/10/14
Current market price: 97   Callable 4/2/06 at 105.08
Conversion price: $44.25
Conversion ratio: 22.599

Remember, the conversion ratio tells you how many shares of common stock each convertible bond can be exchanged for when it is converted. If it is not given to you, you can calculate it:

$$\text{Conversion ratio} = \text{Par value} \div \text{Conversion price}$$
$$= \$1,000 \div \$44.25$$
$$= 22.599$$

This means each Snafu convertible bond can be exchanged for 22.599 shares of Snafu common stock. In order to make a buying decision, take the above information through the following steps:

(convertible) premium
how much more you have to pay for a convert over and above the price it would cost if it were a straight bond. The premium is expressed as a percentage of the convert's theoretical value. The reason for the premium includes such factors as the ability to convert the bond into common stock and the ability to buy it on margin.

Step 1: Find the Yield Advantage

Start by calculating the common stock's yield:

$$\text{Stock yield} = \text{Dividend} \div \text{Current price}$$
$$= \$1.25 \div 31.625$$
$$= 4\%$$

Then calculate the convertible's yield:

$$\text{Convert current yield} = \text{Coupon} \div \text{Current price}$$
$$= 7\tfrac{1}{2}\% \div 97$$
$$= 7.7\%$$

To calculate the convertible's yield advantage, subtract the stock's yield from the convert's yield:

$$\text{Yield advantage} = \text{Convert yield} - \text{Stock yield}$$
$$= 7.7\% - 4\%$$
$$= 3.7\%$$

Step 2: Find the Convertible's Premium

Start by calculating what the bond's theoretical price would be if you stripped off the conversion option, so it became a straight bond. This cannot really be done—it's just a theoretical concept, so that you can compare it with the convert's current price to see the value of the option. This theoretical price is known as **parity**.

 parity
a convertible bond's theoretical value if it were a straight bond without the conversion option.

$$\text{Parity} = \text{Current stock price} \times \text{Conversion ratio}$$
$$= 31.625 \times 22.599$$
$$= \$714.69$$

Then divide the current price by the theoretical price (parity):

$$\text{Premium} = \text{Bond's current dollar value} \div \text{Parity}$$
$$= \$970 \div \$714.69$$

$$= 35.7\%$$
$$= 1.357 = 35.7\% \text{ premium}$$

You subtract 1 from 1.357 and your result is the % change: 35.7%. You can also use this method to find percentage increases. Say you had $5,000 invested and it earned 5%. To calculate its value in one year you would multiply $5,000 times (1 + .05):

$$\$5,000 \times 1.05 = \$5,250$$

This premium shows you how much the bond is trading above the bond's theoretical value at the conversion price (Figure 6.3). The higher the percentage the bond's actual value is above the theoretical value (parity), the further you need the common stock's price to rise before you can convert the bond.

Be careful not to confuse this use of the word

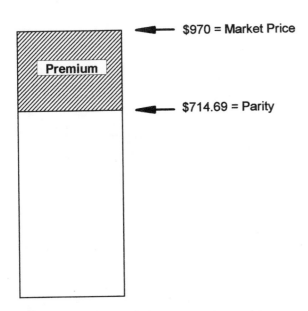

FIGURE 6.3 Market price/parity relationship.

"premium" with the other meaning: a bond selling at a price above par. Make sure when discussing converts and premiums you know which definition the other person is using.

There is an assumption in this calculation that the stock, stock dividend, and convert's market value do not change. This is an estimation and is used only as a benchmark to gauge your **premium recovery period** projections against. It tells you how long you'll have to earn interest in order to earn back the premium you paid over the bond's theoretical value (what the bond is worth without its conversion feature), in other words, how long it takes you to earn back the shaded portion in Figure 6.3.

premium recovery period
how long it is estimated it would take the convertible bond owner to make back the premium through the yield advantage.

$$\text{Premium recovery period} = \frac{\{\text{Premium} \div [(100 + \text{Premium}) \div 100]\}}{\div \text{ Yield advantage period}}$$

$$= \{35.7 \div [(100 + 35.7) \div 100]\} \div 3.7$$

$$= [35.7 \div (135.7 \div 100)] \div 3.7$$

$$= (35.7 \div 1.357) \div 3.7$$

$$= 26.308 \div 3.7$$

$$= 7.1 \text{ years}$$

With these calculations completed, you can compare the 7.1 years to the bond's maturity (or call date if likely to be called). If the premium recovery (break-even period) is longer than these dates, you would buy the convert only if you felt certain the stock was moving dramatically higher and would be likely to be profitably converted. Even then, it may make more sense just to buy the stock.

Chapter

7

Almost a Bond: Preferred Stock

Why are we going to talk about stock in a book about bonds? Well, this type of stock acts enough like a bond to make mentioning it briefly a good idea. In fact, at most financial companies, preferred stock is traded on the bond desk.

The reason it resembles a bond even though it is a type of stock is because, unlike common stock, it pays a fixed dividend. However, there are many significant differences between preferreds and traditional bonds. For example, preferreds:

✔ Pay dividends, not interest.

✔ Pay dividends quarterly, not semiannually.

✔ Can suspend or defer dividends in certain conditions.

✔ Are issued in smaller denominations than bonds.

Table 7.1 shows a fictitious example of a preferred stock and a bond investment where each pay $100 a year.

Preferred stocks have lower denominations than bonds—$50 to $100 denominations, whereas bonds are $1,000. Another attractive feature is most preferreds have cumulative dividends (check the security's description to

TABLE 7.1 The Preferred/Bond Difference		
	Bond	Preferred
Number of payments per year	2	4
Income payment	$50	$25
Annual income	$100	$100
Years to maturity	10	10
Compounding periods in 10 years	20	40

make sure). This means if the company should miss some dividend payments due to big financial trouble, when it gets its act together it will pay you all the missed dividends in arrears.

The fact that preferreds pay dividends, not interest, makes them of great interest to corporate investors. When domestic corporations invest in the stock of other corporations, they can exclude 70% of the dividends received from their own gross income. This is known as the intercorporate dividends received deduction (DRD). For a corporation in the 34% tax bracket, preferred income would be taxed at only 10.2% instead of 34%.

$$\text{Effective tax rate on dividends earned} = \frac{\text{Corporate tax bracket} \times}{\% \text{ of dividends not excluded}}$$

$$= 34\% \times 30\%$$

$$= 10.2\%$$

In the creditor hierarchy, preferred stock owners stand in front of common stock owners and behind the company's debt holders. A similar instrument called preference stock is junior to preferred stock.

There are a number of different types of preferreds.

PERPETUAL PREFERRED

Perpetual preferreds are the most common. The quarterly dividend can be fixed or it can float with changes in interest rates. While there's no maturity date, most are callable.

Companies are more apt to call the securities when interest rates drop significantly and they want to stop paying the higher rate of interest.

ADJUSTABLE RATE PREFERRED

Adjustable rate preferreds (ARPs) are a type of perpetual preferred whose dividend rate floats, resetting each quarter. The dividend rate resets at a specific spread over a chosen fixed-rate security's yield. For example, it could reset at 1% above either the 3-month, 10-year, and 30-year Treasury's current yield. Which Treasury is selected depends on which one has the highest yield at that time. (The issue's actual reset parameters are spelled out in the preferred's **prospectus**.)

There is usually a stated maximum and minimum rate known as the **collar**. (See Figure 7.1.) Between the upper

prospectus
document sent to people considering investing in securities such as stocks, bonds, mutual funds or unit investment trusts. It details what the investment objectives are, what it invests in, and how it has performed in the past.

  collar
an adjustable rate bond's maximum and minimum interest rate. The bond will not pay interest higher than the upper collar or lower than its lower collar.

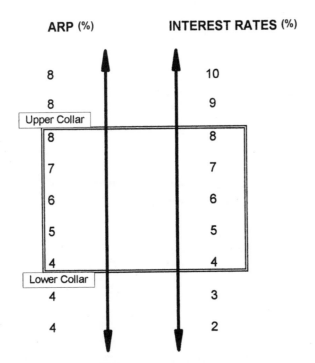

FIGURE 7.1   Adjustable rate preferred (ARP) collars.

and lower collars the preferred interest rate floats with current interest rates. At the maximum or minimum rate the preferred's rate stops floating and becomes fixed at that level.

So, between the collars when interest rates rise, you will happily watch the dividend rate adjust higher. You'll also notice that unlike fixed-rate securities the preferred's price tends not to decline as the preferred's interest rate rises with current interest rates. Since the security's rate rises with market rates there is no need to lower the price to entice investors to buy the bond. But, your happiness is limited by the upper collar. When the rate locks in, its interest rate becomes fixed, and the security's price is free to fall like other fixed-rate securities.

Conversely, when rates drop, so too does the ARP's yield as it resets quarterly with current rates. Not only do your dividends decline, but you also will not participate in any price appreciation until the lower collar locks in the yield and the preferred becomes a fixed-rate security. You obviously want to own ARPs when interest rates are rising, and you'd rather not own them when interest rates are falling.

CONVERTIBLE PREFERRED

Convertible preferreds can be converted into a specific number of shares of common stock. The conversion feature works the same as for convertible bonds. Investors would buy this type of convertible if they wanted quarterly payments or had less money to invest.

SINKING FUND PREFERRED

Sinking fund preferreds require that the issuer retire a certain percentage of the issue each year. This helps support the price of those left outstanding—a nice feature as long as you aren't one of the ones picked by the lottery to be retired sooner rather than later.

THE CHIMERA INVESTMENT: FIXED RATE CAPITAL SECURITIES

Fixed rate capital securities were developed in the early 1990s to provide borrowers with another inexpensive financing alternative. Since then, $145 billion worth have been issued.

Like the mythical Chimera, which was part lion, part serpent, and part goat, this investment combines the characteristics of corporate bonds with preferred stock. Interest payments are made either monthly, quarterly, or semiannually. They mature in 20 to 49 years, except for, some that are perpetual; and most are investment grade. Typical issuers include electric and gas utilities, industrial companies, telephone providers, banks, and financial companies. Most have a $25 liquidation value like preferreds; however, a few recently have been issued with a $1,000 face value. Also like preferreds, they trade on the major securities exchanges, so you can easily see what they are worth.

In the issuer's capital structure, the lien line, fixed rate capital securities rank senior to common, preferred stock and convertibles and behind subordinated debt securities. The result is they tend to yield more than the issuer's bonds. They also yield more than the company's preferreds because there is no dividends received deduction (DRD) tax benefit to corporations. The yield pickup is also a result of their being callable after 5 to 10 years. Remember to ask for the yield-to-worst (YTW is explained in Chapter 10) when evaluating these securities. Another reason fixed rate capital securities yield more than any other securities issued by a company is that the issuer can defer payments if it is in financial trouble.

Let's take a look at this nervy characteristic where the issuer has the option to defer payments. It can do it only if it has stopped paying all other stock dividends. The interest on the fixed rate capital securities continues to accrue even when not being paid, so hopefully the company will pay you in arrears. However, this leads to a little snafu with the IRS, in that you have to pay taxes on

original issue discount (OID)
the bond issue was not issued at par but instead came to market at a discount. If you sell the bond in the secondary market, you must check to see if the price is above or below the accrued amortization line to determine if you owe capital gains tax.

the income every year even if you haven't gotten it yet. In fact, due to any income deferral and the fact that some are issued as **original issue discounts (OIDs)**, the tax calculations on these nuggets can be pretty nasty. Hopefully, whomever you buy fixed rate capital securities through will do it for you.

There are three types that differ in how they are issued:

1. Preferred partnership securities.

2. Trust preferred securities (or capital securities).

3. Junior subordinated debentures.

And they are called by a boatload of acronyms:

MIDS	Monthly income debt securities
QUICS	Quarterly income capital securities
QUIDS	Quarterly income debt securities
QUIPS	Quarterly income preferred securities
SKIS	Subordinated capital income securities
TOPrS	Trust originated preferred securities
TruPS	Capital trust pass-through securities

Stay tuned for more witty creations. . . .

Chapter

8

It's a Wrap:
Wrapper Products

We're now moving from types of bonds to investment vehicles you can use to invest in bonds. Wrapper products are ready-made financial portfolios, packaged for individual investors. They're packaged by insurance companies, banks, investment firms, and mutual fund companies that fashion these portfolio packages-to-go for our convenience.

The problem with wrapper products is that there can get to be many layers (i.e., the financial intermediaries who produce these products). Each layer extracts its fees, muffling the investment's performance. (See Figure 8.1.)

For instance, I've seen a mutual fund (wrapper portfolio) that invested in collateralized mortgage obligations (a wrapper security: mortgages are packaged as mortgage-backed securities, and MBSs are then packaged as CMOs) held in an investor's wrapper account (explained later in the chapter). The resulting yield to the investors was about the same as if they'd gone out and bought a 3-month Treasury bill, but the risk was much greater.

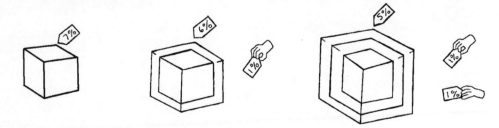

FIGURE 8.1 Wrapper products: layers of service fees affect yield. Drawing by Steven Saltzgiver.

BENEFITS

Even in light of the disadvantages, the advantages are very compelling.

Wrapper products offer:

- ✔ Low minimum investment.
- ✔ Diversified portfolio.
- ✔ Professional management.
- ✔ Ease of investment.
- ✔ Same advantages as institutional investors:

    Faster access to breaking news.

    Quicker trading.

    Better pricing because trading in size.

    Research and market reports from major wire houses.

    Pulse on big money's market temperament.

When we invest in most wrapper products, we pool our money together with a bunch of other folks and engage a full-time investment professional to manage our collective cash. The significant size of this pot enables the manager to benefit from institutional service, pricing, and access to information. These are advantages we as individuals could never hope to receive. We can buy into a well-diversified portfolio for as little as $500.

COSTS

Of course, there is a price for all of these inducements. The cost includes an annual management fee, 12b-1 fee, and in some cases an additional sales load. Management fees are annual payments charged to cover fund expenses. The 12b-1 fee is to support promotional activities; it is usually paid out to other firms—for example, broker sales concessions. The load is generally a one-time payment that is either charged when you invest, a **front-end load**; or charged when you sell, a **back-end load**.

Make sure the fees are reasonable. To help ensure these costs are reasonable, the ever-vigilant Securities and Exchange Commission (SEC) polices management companies to make sure they clearly disclose all investor costs in the prospectus which must be given to investors before they invest. So *read* your prospectus and make sure the charges look sensible to you.

When I started in the business, sales loads of $8\frac{1}{2}\%$ for stock funds and $4\frac{3}{4}\%$ for bond funds were not unusual. Now, 2% to 4% is more the norm, and there are many well-performing no-load funds available.

front-end load
mutual fund's sales charge that is added onto your purchase price.

back-end load
mutual fund sales charge that is subtracted from the price when you sell your fund shares; also known as a contingent deferred sales charge (CDSC).

PERFORMANCE

The SEC also regulates how wrapper products report performance so that they don't overstate their history in zealous marketing claims. When you evaluate a fixed income product's performance, you should look at both yield and total return. (See Table 8.1.)

During the 1980s, an outcry from unhappy investors got the SEC's attention. Thereafter, the SEC mandated that in addition to the current yield, funds had to include the **SEC yield** in advertisements. The SEC yield is calculated to prevent companies from falsely inflating the portfolio's yield by buying high-coupon bonds at a premium. This yield calculation subtracts the premium paid for the bond from the bond's higher coupon's income stream to give a more accurate reflection of the true yield earned. Otherwise mutual fund managers

SEC yield
standardized yield calculation established by the SEC that subtracts the premium paid for any bonds within the portfolio from their higher income stream.

TABLE 8.1 Performance Summary

Cumulative Total Returns (%)
as of 6/30/2002

	Merrill Lynch High Yield Master Index II
YTD	-5.57
1 Month	-6.27
3 Month	-5.89
6 Month	-5.57

Average Annual Total Returns (%)
as of 6/30/2002

	Merrill Lynch High Yield Master Index II	Merrill Lynch High Yield Master Index II
1 Year	-7.66	-4.36
3 Year	-8.22	-2.10
5 Year	-1.27	1.14
10 Year	6.10	6.28

Quarter-End Average Annual Total Returns (%)
as of 6/30/2002

	Return before Taxes	Return after Taxes on Distributions	High Yield Bond Average	Return after Taxes on Distributions and Sale of Fund Shares	High Yield Bond Average
1 Year	-7.66	-10.90	-6.77	-4.62	-1.92
3 Year	-8.22	-11.26	-5.68	-7.70	-3.22
5 Year	-1.27	-4.78	-2.61	-2.40	-0.76
10 Year	6.10	1.95	1.67	3.06	2.66

could buy higher-coupon bonds to boost the fund's claimed yield. This would artificially inflate the yield because they paid a premium for the bonds and the bonds would mature at par. The SEC recognized the economic effect that the premium has on the total return.

The best measure to use when you're gauging a fund's performance is its total return. This includes both the interest you earn and how much the value of your principal has changed in that time. Here's an exaggerated example: You could be attracted to a fund that is yielding 11%. Wisely, you look at the total return, which is –2% because the price is down 13%. While past performance doesn't assure future performance, it's smart to check a fund's long-term record, and not just invest in what has been the hottest performer during the last quarter.

BOND MUTUAL FUNDS

Mutual funds are the most popular type of wrapper product. There are more mutual funds than there are stocks listed on the New York Stock Exchange. In 1970, there were 361 mutual funds; in 2001, there were 8,255 (2,188 of these were bond funds, and many more had some of their assets invested in bonds).

In 1995, investors had $800 billion invested in fixed income mutual funds. And what do we bond fund investors look like? The **Investment Company Institute (ICI)** tells us that bond fund shareholders' median age is 44, median household income is $60,000, and median financial assets are $75,000; 20% of us are retired and 64% completed college. Whatever we really look like as individuals, there are two points that are very important for us to keep in mind when we're buying shares of a fixed income mutual fund:

Investment Company Institute (ICI) private company that monitors the mutual fund industry.

- ✔ Even though it buys fixed income investments, the fund's *dividend changes*.
- ✔ The fund *never matures*. Its principal value is always market-dependent.

Active portfolio management produces both of these characteristics. Since securities are constantly bought and sold and interest rates change, the fund's payout and yield are affected. And since mutual funds never mature, you are not guaranteed you'll ever get back the principal you invested. While the number of shares you own stays the same, the price you would get when you sell them fluctuates. These points should be carefully considered by investors who are counting on their interest and principal being there.

Even when you buy shares of a mutual fund, it is of premier importance to understand the securities it invests in. Do not buy a bond mutual fund based on its yield alone. The fund cannot act any differently from the bonds it invests in. Therefore, by understanding the risks and volatility involved in buying the type of bonds the fund is invested in, you will understand how the fund will respond to changes in the investment environment.

There are two general mutual fund classifications: open-end and closed-end. The first has no limits on how many investor shares there are in the fund while the second has a fixed number of shares.

Open-End Mutual Funds	*Closed-End Mutual Funds*
Fund has unlimited number of shares.	Number of shares is set at issue.
Fund size grows and contracts with changes in investor demand.	Fund share price rises and falls with changes in investor demand.
Investors buy shares from and sell shares back to company.	Investors buy and sell in secondary market like stocks.

Closed-end fund shares are bought from the fund company only in the original offering. After that they are traded on listed exchanges just like shares of stock. Fluctuations in investor demand don't affect the closed-end fund manager's investments. The overall size of the fund only changes with changes in the secondary market of the underlying securities' prices that make up the fund.

The number of fund shares never varies. Each share has two values. One is the market value that it is trading at on an exchange—the price we would pay for it. That value is determined by how much investor demand there is for the fund. The second value is determined by the price of the underlying securities that the fund is invested in. This is known as the share's **net asset value** (NAV). Because often a closed-end fund's market price is well below the NAV, there is a trend toward closed-end funds converting into or merging with open-end funds.

Open-end mutual funds are the most common type. Either you or your broker buys these funds directly from the fund company. The size of an open-end fund grows if investors are buying and declines if they are selling, as well as with security price changes in the secondary market.

Another way to think of the difference is to look at the equation:

net asset value (NAV) the dollar value of all the securities in a mutual fund at the close of the day divided by the number of outstanding shares.

$$\text{Total \$ in fund} = \text{Number of shares} \times \text{Each share's NAV}$$

With an open-end fund both factors change; with a closed-end fund only the second factor changes because the number of shares in the fund is fixed. You can imagine how the added uncertainty of the open-end fund's scenario can affect a manager's investment strategy. The ebb and flow can be dramatic. This unpredictable investor behavior, and therefore cash flow, can make a fund manager's job difficult. Often, disadvantageous buy and sell decisions can be forced on the manager since individuals tend to buy into the fund after prices have become high and to sell after prices have fallen.

Pricing

When you buy shares from or sell the shares back to an open-end fund company, the price is based on the net asset value, not on investor demand. The NAV is computed every night and is the total market value of all the securities within the fund plus any management fees. The NAV for most funds is available in the *Wall Street Journal* or on the Internet. If there is a front-end sales charge, it is added to the NAV when you buy it; and if there's a back-end sales charge, it is subtracted from the NAV when you sell it back. The NAV adjusted by the sales charge is called the public offering price, aka POP.

NAV + Front-end sales load = Buying POP

NAV − Back-end sales load = Selling POP

This pricing method has advantages over closed-end funds that trade on exchanges. What people think of an open-end fund has no effect on its share price because the fund will just get larger or smaller with investor demand or disfavor, whereas the market price of a closed-end fund is often based more on fickle investor sentiment than on performance. Like any listed stock, the price goes up or down depending on how much people want to own it.

Not understanding how funds operate can cause investors a lot of confusion and managers a lot of headaches. The following are examples of how this is so for closed- and open-end mutual funds.

Closed-end fund shares can trade at a premium or at a discount from the NAV, often for reasons that are not economically logical. When I worked on an investment team managing a number of closed-end bond funds, investors would call asking why a fund was trading at a discount. We had no idea, because the funds were performing beautifully. From an investment point of view, the funds should have been trading at a premium because they had an attractive payout and were outperforming the bond market. However, the fund's stock price was trading at a discount because of low investor demand that probably stemmed from not understanding how to evaluate the fund's performance. If you could have raised enough money to buy the entire fund and then sold the securities in the secondary market, you could have made a ton of money. But, since we don't have millions of dollars to buy out a fund, we are at the whims of other investors' demand.

In regard to our open-end funds, the question we'd get asked a lot had to do with a fund's share price dropping dramatically overnight. In fact, we were asked it at the same time every month. The answer was that the fund had just gone ex-dividend, meaning the dividend was paid out to investors and was no longer included in the fund. (See Figure 8.2.) The price of the fund would drop by the amount of the dividend paid out (plus or minus any market move). It confused people every month.

> A little investing tidbit: It's better to invest after a fund goes ex-dividend because you're investing in it at a lower price. If you invest just before it goes ex, you get the dividend; but you are also paying a higher price. You are paying the fund money that it then just hands back to you in the form of a dividend that you have to pay taxes on.

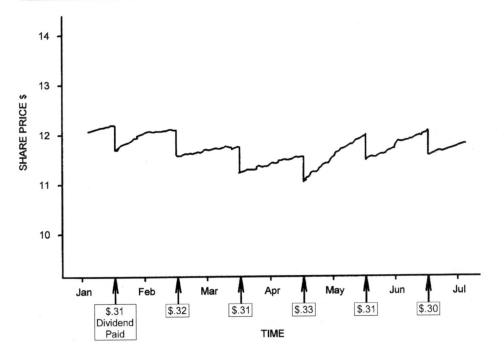

FIGURE 8.2 Open-end mutual fund price and dividend relationship.

In an open-ended fund the price is also affected by the changing market values of the securities owned within the fund. Every night the securities are valued. Figure 8.3 shows how both the price per share of the fund and the dividend change over time. This is in contrast to an individual bond, which has a fixed coupon (so the interest payout does not change) as well as a maturity (when you know you will get the face value back). There are no such assurances with a mutual fund.

Before you buy an open-end fund, the fund company must send you a prospectus explaining the fund's investment objective, how the fund invests, and its historical record. The trend has been to make prospectuses much shorter and easier to understand. It is in your best interest to read the whole thing to make sure it's really what you're looking for.

Performance

There are a number of tools you can use to judge a fund's performance. You can compare the fund's yield and total return to those of other funds and to appropriate indexes. Lipper ranks funds according to how they have performed within their competitive universe (funds with the same investment objectives and guidelines, such as high yield corporate bonds). Morningstar rates fund performance on

Prices & Distributions

Price History   as of 06/30/2002

12 Month Low-High	$ 7.41 - $ 8.83
Monthly Low-High	$ 7.41 - $ 7.93
On 06/01/2002	$ 7.93
On 06/30/2002	$ 7.41

Monthly NAV Chart
Chart Fund Price (NAV)

Distribution Schedule

Dividends: Monthly
Capital Gains: June, December

Distribution History

Dividends

Date	Per Share Amount	Reinvestment Price
03/31/2002	$0.051144	$8.01
04/30/2002	$0.049433	$8.08
05/31/2002	$0.043126	$7.95
06/30/2002	$0.041824	$7.41

Capital Gains

Date	Per Share Amount	Reinvestment Price
12/05/1997	$0.180000	$
06/05/1998	$0.300000	$
01/29/1999	$0.013000	$
06/30/1999	$0.093000	$12.50

FIGURE 8.3 Prices and distributions.

a star system, five stars being the best. (See Figure 8.4.) Both Lipper and Morningstar reports are available at most libraries. Your financial service should also have access to the information.

UNIT INVESTMENT TRUSTS (UITs)

Unit investment trusts (UITs) emigrated to our shores from Scotland in 1961. Like mutual funds, they enable smaller investors to buy into more diversified portfolios than they could buy on their own. UITs differ from funds in that they are not actively managed; a professional money manager is involved only at the beginning when the UIT is issued. The bonds are bought with the cash raised from selling the trust's units to investors. The bonds never change and are held until they mature. Up until 1995, most UITs were fixed income trusts. The most popular type of fixed income UIT has been municipal bond trusts.

A UIT's characteristics include:

✔ Fixed portfolio professionally selected.

✔ Steady payout.

✔ Known maturity.

Rankings/Ratings

Lipper Ranking	as of 06/30/2002
1 Year	#296 out of 372 High Current Yield
5 Year	#98 out of 166 High Current Yield
10 Year	#13 out of 51 High Current Yield

Morningstar Ratings	as of 06/30/2002
Overall	★★★
3 Year	★★
5 Year	★★
10 Year	★★★★

An overall rating is based on a weighted average of the fund's ratings for the 3, 5, and 10 year periods. The number of funds in the High Yield Bond category tracked by Morningstar was 286 for the 3 yr period; 166 for the 5 yr period; and 52 for the 10 yr period.

FIGURE 8.4 Rankings and ratings.

A UIT's prospectus stipulates what it can invest in, the maturity, the sales charge, and terms for redemption. It would be correct to say that UITs benefit from professional selection, not from professional management. Some investors like the fact that someone isn't meddling with their investment. There's no one trying to time interest rates or forecast market sentiment. Investors can go to sleep at night knowing exactly what securities they own.

The second benefit from a static portfolio invested in fixed income securities is that as long as none of the bonds are called or mature, the investors will receive the same income payout. This is unlike mutual funds, whose payout fluctuates depending on what is owned in the fund during that payment period.

Toward the end of the fixed income UIT's life, the principal is gradually returned to the investors as bonds are called or mature. Each unit receives back the same proportional amount of the principal. Since there is less principal earning interest, the income earned will drop commensurably.

If you are considering a UIT, it is very important to note the maturity dates and potential call dates to make sure the investment still makes sense in view of your long-term goals. Does the timing of the principal repayment fit your timetable? Also, keep in mind that callable bonds tend to be called when interest rates fall and reinvestment options are less attractive than the investment you were in.

The third benefit—a known maturity—means that, unlike with mutual funds, you know you will get your principal back by a certain date. UITs usually mature in 5 to 30 years. The minimum investment is generally $1,000. They are not sold on a yield-to-maturity (YTM) basis, but rather on a dollar price basis. Their return is estimated using the current return, as well as a more accurate long-term return number that takes into consideration the securities' market value, maturity, and discount or premium.

There is no annual management fee since the trust isn't actively managed; however, there could be a maintenance fee of $1.50 to $2 per $1,000 invested. In addition, UITs have historically carried sizable sales charges; but, as with mutual funds, the size of these charges has declined. They now typically run about $3^1/2\%$ to 5% of the total offering price for longer-term trusts. It is often difficult for investors to recognize the size of the sales charge because it is not broken out but is included in the purchase price, so ask what the charge is. Retail brokers are told by their management to make you aware of the charges. The charges are also stated in the UIT's prospectus. Since transaction costs are minimal after the trust is assembled and UITs don't continually market their units to the public, there are no ongoing management fees or marketing fees as there are with mutual funds.

A UIT's units can be sold back to the issuer at the public bid price at any time. That price is based on the value of the underlying securities and could be higher or lower than the price the investor paid. Most trust sponsors voluntarily maintain a secondary market for their trusts. The sales charge is paid when you buy the UIT, so there usually is no redemption fee.

ANNUITIES

Annuities are another packaged product, but this one has an advantage in that it allows your earnings to compound tax-deferred. As we have mentioned, this can have a dramatic impact on the growth of your investment. It is also likely that when the policy matures you will be retired and in a lower tax bracket. However, as with all packaged products, be wary.

A *Wall Street Journal* article, "Annuities 101: How to Sell to Senior Citizens" (July 2, 2002), chronicles how "Annuities U" offers courses on how to sell this vehicle. The course is popular since a salesperson who can get a prospect to transfer $50,000 to an annuity can make a commission of $3,000 to $4,000. The instructor is quoted as saying a number of insulting and misleading lines, including, "There's the technical answer and there's the senior answer. Tell them, it's like a CD—it's safe, it's guaranteed." In my experience, these words always warrant a closer look at what is being touted. Sure enough, the article goes on to caution that, "Annuities are actually a lot more complex and have downsides that the salesmen may not mention. The higher fees of most annuities can often cancel out their tax advantages; most annuities lock in investors for years, and annuities saddle heirs with higher taxes, unlike mutual funds or most other investments." Many annuities are mutual funds wrapped in a tax-deferred cloak. Just be careful, and don't be rushed into anything.

ASSET ALLOCATION AND WRAPPER ACCOUNTS

Many investment firms and mutual fund companies offer asset allocation services. Here professional managers decide how to allocate your money among different types of mutual funds within their family of funds. It's a service to make portfolio management easier for you, although with a little thought this is something you could do yourself. Some folks just feel more comfortable having a professional manager whose finger is closer to the markets' pulse make those decisions for them. Mind you, the decisions aren't made just for you but are made for the type of investor you classify yourself as (for example, conservative or aggressive, income or growth, etc.).

Another alternative is the wrapper account. It is different from the wrapper products previously discussed in that it is an individual's portfolio, not a pool of many investors' funds. A wealthy individual with a large portfolio ($100,000 minimum) has an investment firm hire an outside adviser. For this introduction, the investment firm receives part of the management fee. The investor gets a manager who manages the individual's money with his or her specific goals in mind.

CONCLUSION

Wrapper products offer the investor a turnkey investment alternative. Convenience, professional management, and institutional advantages are the services and benefits you receive for a price. Wrapper products charge additional fees for each wrapper service layered on top of the securities.

Investors who choose to invest via wrapper products do so for ease of investing and for professional investment input. It is up to the investors to determine if the additional cost brings with it benefits appropriate for them.

The next four chapters comprise probably the most important section of the book. This section will go over how bonds are traded, how they are priced, how to evaluate a bond's yield, and how price and yield are related.

PART TWO

FIXED INCOME FUNDAMENTALS

My Word Is My Bond

With fixed income investing, ignorance is not bliss; it's costly. To avoid being fleeced by un-ethical advisers or led astray by uninformed sources, read on.

There's some simple math with lots of examples to explain the concepts. Going through the examples and following along with a calculator may help you to understand and remember the material. Feel free to reread a section when it gets confusing.

THE PRIMARY MARKET

When a municipality or corporation decides to raise money in the bond market, it asks its **underwriter** to initiate an offering. The bank determines the economic feasibility of the issue, advises the issuer as to the size of the offering and the probable interest rate, and organizes a **syndicate** to underwrite the bonds.

underwriter
investment bank that agrees to buy a new issue and distribute it to investors. It assumes the risk and makes the underwriting spread on securities sold.

> *Steps of a Bond Issue*
> Issuer → Bank → Syndicate → Broker → Investor

$

syndicate
group of
investment firms
formed to
distribute a new
offering to
investors. Some
members take
market risk
because they buy
the issue and
own it until they
can sell it to
investors. Other
members only
sell the issue and
are not at risk.
The manager or
comanagers who
coordinate the
syndicate take on
the most risk and
allocate who gets
how many
bonds.

tombstone
newspaper
advertisement for
a new bond issue
that lists which
investment firms
are in the
syndicate, who
the issuer is, and
size of the issue.

The syndicate is usually a group of investment firms that sell the bonds through their distribution networks (institutional and/or retail sales forces). The syndicate pays the issuer's bank the face amount of the offering ($150 million in the issue pictured in Figure 9.1). The syndicate then owns the bonds and assumes the market risk until they can sell them. As you can see in Figure 9.1, there are a number of syndicate participants, and they participate in the offering's potential risk and profits to varying degrees.

It is important to understand where the firm you are thinking of dealing with is in this pecking order, so you can get an idea how likely it is you will get bonds. In today's marketplace, simply putting in an order doesn't guarantee you'll get the bonds you want. The healthy economy has boosted demand for all financial products, including fixed income securities. In this environment, it is not uncommon for even the comanaging firm (the #2 slot) not to get all the bonds it wants and for other syndicate participants to get totally shut out.

Big Oak Investments and Asset Managers Corporation are in larger print and are the deal's comanagers and lead underwriters. They decide who will get how many bonds. The other firms are part of the selling syndicate. If it's a popular issue, they may not get all the bonds they want. They may have their risk limited to the bonds they indicated for, or they may not have any risk and will just sell as many as they can.

This is an example of the **tombstone** that the selling syndicate places in the newspaper to announce the upcoming issue. This is part of the **due diligence** period when the market is tested to see whether the issue has been priced correctly. Potential investors are asked for **indications of interest**. Prices are not carved in stone until the end of the order period, so yield levels can keep changing right up until the deadline, which usually falls sometime between the late morning and midafternoon.

There are two ways to structure the offering. Some corporate bond issues have only one maturity date. This is known as a **term bond**. The alternative, a serial bond, has a series of sequential maturity dates and is more commonly found in the municipal market. When buying

This announcement is neither an offer to sell nor a solicitation of an offer to buy any of these securities. The offering is made only by the Prospectus.

U.S. $150,000,000

Creative Thought Incorporated

10% Senior Secured Notes Due 2005

Price 100%

Big Oak Investments   **Asset Managers Corporation**

CDBS Personal Consulting   Penrose Management

PereGrin Source   Hilltop Management   Douglas Partnership

The Kendall Advisor Group

April 30, 2003

FIGURE 9.1 Tombstone.

a serial you need to choose the maturities that best fit your needs.

The three most important points for you to remember when participating in a bond offering are:

1. Give your broker the minimum yield you will accept for each maturity you are interested in.
2. If you think you may sell the bonds before maturity, buy minimum quantities of $10,000 to $25,000. Ask the firm you are dealing with where its quantity price break is in the secondary market.

due diligence period when issuer is checked out to make sure what it asserts to be true is, and to make sure all the ducks are lined up for the new offering.

indications of interest
syndicate members canvas their major clients about their interest in an upcoming new issue to determine if the yield they are thinking about is too high or too low and whether they have to make adjustments.

term bond
bond where the entire issue's face value matures on the same day.

scale
list of a new bond offering's maturities and the expected yield at each level. Scales can be subject to numerous revisions before the offering and during the few hours the bonds are being offered.

Serial Bonds versus Sinking Fund Bonds

A serial bond is an issue made up of a series of bonds, each with a different maturity date. For example, a $1 million issue could have $250,000 5-year bonds, $250,000 6-year bonds, $250,000 7-year bonds, and $250,000 8-year bonds.

A sinking fund bond issue has one maturity date, but random portions are retired early on specified dates. For example, a $1 million bond issue with a sinking fund matures in 8 years, but the sinking fund is used to retire $250,000 of the issue in 5 years, $250,000 in 6 years, and another $250,000 in 7 years. You don't know which bonds of the $1 million face value will be retired early and which will be outstanding until maturity. If you own a sinking fund bond there is always the possibility a portion of your holding could be retired early on any one of the listed dates, because the bonds to be retired are selected randomly by lottery.

3. Understand you may not get all the bonds you want. Give your broker a range of the quantity you'll accept—for example, no fewer than $25,000 face value and no more than $50,000.

A new issue's yield adjustments prior to issuance are evident by the two cross outs seen in the **scale** pictured in Figure 9.2. These changes are why it is a very good idea to give your broker the minimum yield you'll accept when participating in a bond offering. This way your broker knows what to do if the level changes and the broker can't get back in touch with you. Sales commissions are fixed in an initial offering; a greedy broker can't charge you any more than an honest one.

In an initial offering the bonds can be priced at par, a discount, or a premium (see Chapter 10). If this makes a difference to you, be sure to mention it to your broker. In

COMPETITIVE RESALE WORKSHEET

AMOUNT	$19,459,756									
DATED	06/15/02									
DUE	06/15/03-17									

MUNICIPALITY, PURPOSE AND SECURITY
Our School District,
Some County, Massachsetts
School District (Serial) Bonds, 2002 (ULT)

1st INT DATE 06/15/03 (12Mos)
INTEREST J15-D15
REC. DATES Last business day of the
month preceding each interest payment date
DENOM $ 5,000
BOND FORM Book Entry
LEGAL OPINION
Wright, Saltzgiver & Billings, NYC 212-555-1234

6/15	CUSIP	$ AMOUNT	PRESALE	RATE	BASIS/YIELD	CONC.	ADD'L TKDN	RATE	BASIS/YIELD	UNSOLD BALANCE	6/15
2003		869,756		2½	1.99	1/8	1/4				2003
2004		915,000			2.15						2004
2005		965,000			2.45		3/8				2005
2006		1,020,000		3¾	3.05	1/4					2006
2007		1,075,000			.25						2007
2008		1,135,000			.50						2008
2009		1,195,000			.75						2009
2010		1,265,000			.80		½				2010
2011		1335000*		4½	4.15						2011
2012		1405000*			.30						2012
2013		1485000*			.35						2013
2014		1565000*			.50						2014
2015		1650000*		70	.65						2015
2016		1740000*		75	75 80						2016
2017		1840000*		80	85 90						2017
2018											2018
2019		* Callable									2019
2020											2020
2021											2021
2022											2022
2023											2023
2024											2024
2025											2025
2026											2026
2027											2027
2028											2028

OPTIONAL PROVISIONS:

Bonds due 2011-2017 are callable in whole or in part on any interest payment date on or after 6/15/11 at the followng prices
and accrued interest: 102% if called 6/15/11 and 12/15/11: 101% if called 6/15/12 and12/15/12: 100% if called 6/15/13 and thereafter.

NOTE 1: Any party executing and delivering a vid for a bond agrees, if its bid is accpeted, to provide to the District in writing,
within two (2) businesss days after the date of such award, all information which the District determines is necessary for it to
comply with SEC Rule 15c2-12, including all necessary pricing and sale information and underwriter identification.

*Winning Bid:*_____ *Gross Spread:*_____ *Other Bidders:*

FIGURE 9.2 Scale.

most cases you shouldn't care since it's the yield that
should be of concern, not the price.

Besides making your broker aware of the minimum
yield you'll accept, you will also want to establish the
minimum quantity acceptable. Too many small pieces will
probably be a bookkeeping nuisance and, more impor-
tantly, be highly illiquid. This is especially significant if
you plan to sell your bonds before they mature.

Small bond **positions** are illiquid because firms do

position
total holding of a
certain security;
the amount
invested in
something.

not want to get stuck with them—for reasons explained later—so they do not bid much for them. This means when you try to sell a small piece, brokers will charge you a much higher commission (i.e., offer you a much lower price) to buy it from you—that is, if they will buy it from you at all. Different firms recommend you buy minimum quantities of $10,000 or $25,000. If this is too rich for your blood, remember you can always buy bonds via mutual funds or unit investment trusts.

THE SECONDARY MARKET

Bond buyers often buy and hold their bonds; so, if you're looking for a certain security to meet a requirement in your portfolio, you need to be both patient and flexible because the exact bond may not be for sale when you are looking for it.

Between a bond's issue and maturity dates, it is bought or sold "in" the secondary market. The secondary market is not a physical place; it is an event. When you call a broker looking for bonds, there are three places the broker can look for bonds.

The first place brokers will check is their firm's inventory. As with any business, they want to move their own inventory. The quicker they turn over their inventory the more money they can make. Sometimes they will run specials on bonds they want to get rid of or bonds they were able to buy "cheap." If you are a big bond buyer, it will pay to shop different firms to see who has the best yield and price. In order to make a good judgment, compare bond yields for similar face values, maturities, and ratings and remember to ask for the **yield-to-worst (YTW)**. As mentioned before, when you're buying or selling smaller bond amounts, the prices are not as good (higher when you're buying and lower when you're selling), so keep to **lots** of $10,000 to $25,000 whenever possible.

If there's nothing of interest in their inventory, the second place brokers could look is a list of dealers' inventories from around the country. In the municipal market

yield-to-worst (YTW)
the lowest yield the bond you are considering could yield. When you compare the different types of yield (yield-to-call, yield-to-maturity), whichever is the lowest is the yield-to-worst and is the appropriate one to use to compare with other bond yields.

lots
created when you bundle together a bunch of the same security, usually done to take advantage of economies of scale.

the Blue List publishes this information. In other markets, traders have a network of other institutional traders and managers.

The third place to find bonds is in the portfolios of other people who are interested in selling. Most firms will do this, but not all. It is known as **crossing bonds**. The bonds are sold directly from one investor to another. The investment firm's trading desk is merely providing a service; the firm is not at market risk because it never owns the bond. Therefore, it charges only the cost of executing the trade plus a small fee, so usually both the buyer and seller get a better price.

Another point to keep in mind when buying or selling bonds in the secondary market is that you could create a taxable event. You have to pay taxes if you sell the bond at a price higher than what you paid for it.

If you hold a bond to maturity after having bought it in the secondary market at a discount, you'd owe taxes on the difference between the discount and face value. If you bought an original issue discount (OID) at a price below its amortized value and held it to maturity, you'd owe taxes on the difference between the purchase price and the amortized price. As I always suggest to investors venturing down the darkened corridors of the Internal Revenue Service labyrinth, check with an accountant or www.irs.gov.

 crossing bonds
the same investment firm acts as agent in a trade between two of its customers without the firm's trading desk ever owning the bonds.

Chapter 10

What Is It Worth to You?

When you're comparing bonds, it's the bonds' yields that will show you which is the better buy. The yield tells you what you will earn. However, while you use yield to determine which bond is the best deal, only OID securities that will mature in a year or less are traded using their yield. Most bonds are traded using their price. This section will help explain the difference; it will cover price, yield, and the relationship between a bond's price and its yield.

PRICE

Bonds are issued with different face values (e.g., $1,000, $5,000, $25,000). The face value is the lump sum you will receive when the bond matures. Since bonds have different face values, we cannot compare them using their dollar value. For example, two bonds in the secondary market with the same dollar value, $1,200, could have very different prices if one has a $1,000 face value (price: 120; capital gain: $200) and the other has a $5,000 face value (price: 24; capital loss: $3,800).

Par

All bonds mature at their face value and a price of **par** (100). Most coupon bonds are also issued at par. When

 par
price where the bond's dollar value equals the face value it will mature at ($1,000, $25,000, etc.). The price at par is 100 (i.e., the bond at par is trading at 100% of its face value).

the price is 100, the investment is "on par" with its face value. For example, a bond with $10,000 face value is worth $10,000 when the secondary market price is 100 (par). The current value is 100% of its face value when the bond is priced at 100.

Here is an example illustrating that par equals 100% of face value.

Bond A has a $25,000 face value, so when the bond is priced at 100, the bond is worth $25,000:

$$\$25,000 \times 100\% = \$25,000 \times 1.0 = \$25,000$$

Bond A

Face value: $25,000

	Price	*Value*
At issue	100	$25,000
Now	100	25,000
At maturity	100	25,000

If Not Par: Premium or Discount

premium
price above par;
price greater
than 100. When a
bond is trading
at a premium the
bond's dollar
value is higher
than its face
value (the
principal amount
you get at
maturity).

discount
price below par;
price less than
100.

When the bond is free to trade in the secondary market, conditions will cause the price to fluctuate. When the price trades up above par, it is said to be trading at a **premium**. When the price is below par, it is said to be trading at a **discount**. (See Figure 10.1.)

A price is the percentage of face value. If a bond with a $10,000 face value is priced at 90 (90% of face value), it is now worth $9,000. In the following example, a bond

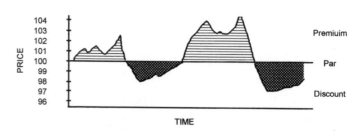

FIGURE 10.1 Premium, par, and discount.

To calculate percentage of something, multiply the percent in decimal form times the original number. Some examples of percents in their decimal form: 100% = 1; 50% = .5; 1% = .01; .01% = .0001; 140% = 1.4. To get the decimal form, remove the percentage sign and divide the number by 100 by moving the decimal point two places to the left.

priced at 102 means the current value of the investment is 102% of its face value.

Bond B

Face value: $1,000

Price: 102

$1,000 × 102% = $1,000 × 1.02 = $1,020

	Price	Value
At issue	100	$1,000
Now	102	1,020
At maturity	100	1,000

Let's look at Bond A at both a premium and a discount:

Bond A

Face value: $25,000

	Price	Value
At issue	100	$25,000
1 Year ago (premium)	103	25,750
Now (discount)	90	22,500
At maturity	100	25,000

Bond A's price one year ago was a 3% increase from face value:

$$\$25,000 \times .03 = \$750$$
$$\$25,000 + \$750 = \$25,750$$

The price now is a 10% decrease from face value:

$$\$25,000 \times .10 = \$2,500$$
$$\$25,000 - \$2,500 = \$22,500$$

As you can see, a bond's price between issuance and maturity moves all over the place in the secondary market. Here bonds are traded using their price, not their dollar value. Traders say, "The bid is $100^7/_8$." They do not say, "The bid is $10,087.50."

The reason the pricing system is based on par (i.e., percent of face value) is so that you can compare bonds with different face values. For example, it would be very hard to compare bond A and Bond B's value even at the same price:

point

if the price changes from 102 to 103, it has changed a point. A one-point change in the price affects the bond's dollar value by 1% of the face value. For example, a point is worth $10 when bond has a $1,000 face value; a point is worth $50 when a bond has a $5,000 face value.

Bond A

Face value: $25,000

Price	*Value*
$100^7/_8$	$25,218.75

Bond B

Face value: $1,000

Price	*Value*
$100^7/_8$	$1,008.75

If the bonds were traded in dollars, the trader would not be able to tell at a glance that both bonds were at a $^7/_8$ of a point premium.

What's the Point?

Bonds trade in 1/32 increments. Thirty-two thirty-seconds are known as "a **point**." 100 points equals par.

32/32 = 1 point

100 points = par

If a bond's price goes from 100 to 101½, the bond is said to have traded up one and a half points. Here's a trick to help remember this point is a percentage point (1% or .01) of the face value. Now, look at the last sentence expressed as an equation:

1 point = 1% of the bond's face value

There, that should be clearer. If not, here's an example:

Bond A

Calculate the value of a point:

1 point = 1% of the face value

Face value: $25,000

$$1 \text{ point} = 1\% \times \$25,000$$
$$= .01 \times \$25,000$$
$$= \$250$$

Now that you've calculated the value of a point, you can figure the dollar value of the bond at different prices. Calculate the value the bond priced at 103:

$$\text{Value at } 103 = \text{Face value} + 3 \text{ points}$$
$$= \$25,000 + (3 \times \$250)$$
$$= \$25,000 + \$750$$
$$= \$25,750$$

Calculate the value the bond priced at 90:

$$\text{Value at } 90 = \text{Face value} - 10 \text{ points}$$
$$= \$25,000 - (10 \times \$250)$$
$$= \$25,000 - \$2,500$$
$$= \$22,500$$

WHAT IS IT WORTH TO YOU?

Here are two final items to remember when trying to convert points into dollars.

The first is to remember that the dollar value of a point is different for bonds with different face values. For example, say two different bonds both fall 3 points. One bond ($10,000 face value) loses $300 while the other ($1000 face value) has just a $30 loss.

The second item is don't assume that a point always equals 1%, because this is true only if you start at par. A decline in price from 89 to 86 is 3 points but it is a drop of 3.37%. An increase from 104 to 107 is 3 points but is a rise of 2.88%. A drop in price from 85 to 70 is 15 points but is a drop of 17.6%. And so on. . . .

To calculate percentage change, remember "ebb": ending value minus beginning value divided by beginning value. For example:

$$(Ending - Beginning) \div Beginning = \% \text{ change}$$
$$(86 - 89) \div 89 = -3.37\%$$

Something Less than the Point

When the price of a bond includes a fraction of a point, it is broken down into 1/32 increments; 2/32 is referred to as 1/16, 4/32 as 1/8, 8/32 as $\frac{1}{4}$, and 16/32 as $\frac{1}{2}$.

In bond pricing notations, a price of 101-02 is $101^2/_{32}$ (i.e., $101^1/_{16}$, not $101^2/_{100}$ or 101.02). It is not the decimal system. In the price 101-02, the 101 part (i.e., the whole number) is called the **handle** in trading jargon. When institutional traders are trading, the handle is often known and not mentioned. For example, "We'll bid 02 for the bonds."

A bond priced at $99^1/_8$ whose price rises $^3/_4$ of a point would then be worth $99^7/_8$.

$$99^1/_8 + {}^3/_4 = 99^4/_{32} + {}^{24}/_{32} = 99^{28}/_{32} = 99^7/_8$$

 handle
trader lingo for the part of the bond's price that is a whole number. When a bond's price is $98^1/_4$, the handle is 98.

The dollar value of each 1/32 depends on the original face value of the bond.

Bond A

Face value: $25,000

1 point = $25,000 × .01 = $250

Bond B

Face value: $1,000

1 point = $1,000 × .01 = $10

plus
add $^1/_{64}$ to the price given.

To calculate the corresponding value of a 32nd, divide the point's dollar value by 32:

Bond A

$250 ÷ 32 = $7.8125

Bond B

$10 ÷ 32 = $.3125

Once in a great while you will hear someone speak of a **plus** (symbolized: +) as in $98^1/_8{}^+$ (i.e., "98 and an eighth plus").

A plus equals $^1/_{64}$. So, $98^1/_8{}^+$ is just another way of saying $98^9/_{64}$.

$$98^1/_8 + {}^1/_{64} = 98^8/_{64} + {}^1/_{64} = 98^9/_{64}$$

This shorthand expression developed in **institutional trading** where speed is often critical during **fast markets**. Since institutional traders are trading in size, the difference in the prices other traders offer them can be quite small. It is easier for the trader to quickly compare prices using pluses. Referring to the preceding example, you can see how $98^1/_8$ and $98^1/_8{}^+$ are much easier to compare at a glance than $98^1/_8$ and $98^9/_{64}$.

institutional trading
sector of the bond market where bonds are traded in very large size—for example, $1 million. The smaller-sized trades done by individuals are usually done on retail trading desks.

fast markets
when prices in the secondary market are rising or falling with extreme speed.

Accrued Interest

A bond investor earns interest every day; however, it is paid out only twice a year. Between payments interest accrues to the owner. The price rises by that amount every day and then drops by the total amount of interest when it is paid out (Figure 10.2). This price movement is sometimes hard to distinguish due to other factors in the secondary market that also affect the bond's price. Some of these factors will be reviewed in Part Three.

Here is an example of this phenomenon.

Data	*Calculations*
Bond's face value: $1,000	
Value of 1 point: $10	$1,000 × .01 = $10
Interest rate: 6%	
Semiannual interest payment: $30	$1,000 × .06 = $60 $60 ÷ 2 = $30
Interest's daily accrual: $.17	6 months × 30 days = 180 days $30 ÷ 180 days = $.17

Using these numbers, let's see in Table 10.1 how this daily interest accrual can affect the bond's price, assuming an original price of 104, no market moves during the six-month period, and that each month has 30 days. ($.17 × 30 = $5 monthly accrual).

COUPON ACCURAL

3-year Bond, 6% Coupon, $1000 Face Value

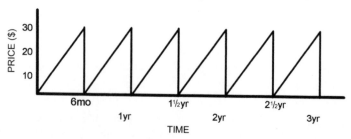

FIGURE 10.2 Coupon accrual.

TABLE 10.1 Coupon Accrual

	Last Coupon Payment	1 Month	2 Months	3 Months	4 Months	5 Months	6 months – 1 Day	6 Months*
Price	104	104.5	105	105.5	106	106.5	107	104
Value	$1,040	$1,045	$1,050	$1,055	$1,060	$1,065	$1,070	$1,040

*At this time $30 in interest is paid out.

When a bond is purchased in the secondary market, the new owner pays the previous investor the current market value of the bond plus any accrued interest the previous investor has earned but not yet been paid. In the previous example, if the bond traded the last day of month 4, the purchaser would owe the seller $20 per bond.

In other words, accrued interest is included in the price because the purchaser owes the previous owner the interest that she/he earned from the last interest payment until the trade date. Interest payments are made twice a year: on the anniversary of the bond's maturity and six months before. The purchaser will then receive the full coupon when paid by the issuer, so his or her net income (amount received from issuer minus amount paid to previous owner) is for only the period he or she owned the bond.

For example, assume it's now 2005:

Bond C: The Tree Corp. 7¹/₄% 8/15/15 N/C

Face value: $10,000

Trade date: 5/15/05

Settlement date: 5/18/05

Last interest payment: 2/15/05

Purchase price: 103¹/₄ ($10,325)

The new owner owes the previous owner the three months of interest from February 15th to May 15th.

How much is that? Well, the bond pays ($10,000 × .0725). $725 a year in interest, in other words, ($725 ÷ 2) or $362.50 per semiannual interest payment. Corporate bonds use a 365-day year, so this bond accrues $1.986 in interest a day ($725 ÷ 365). Since 92 days have transpired from the last interest date to the trade date, the previous owner is owed $182.71. This is added to the purchase price: $10,325 + $182.71 for a total price owed of $10,507.71.

Interest earned per day: $725 ÷ 365 = $1.986

Interest owed: $1.986 × 92 = $182.71

Price: $10,325 + $182.71 = $10,507.71

Pricing Zeros

This section is going to take the same concepts we've just gone over and apply them to pricing zero coupon bonds (zeros).

Zeros are issued at a deep discount from their face value. They don't pay interest until maturity.

For example, if you buy a 6% zero that matures in 10 years at $10,000, the bond would be issued at roughly 55, meaning you would pay $5,500 for it ($10,000 × 55%, or $10,000 × .55 = $5,500).

A zero with $10,000 face value:

	Price	*Value*
At issue	55	$5,500
At maturity	100	$10,000

The investor earns $4,500 in interest over the life of the bond. This amount actually assumes a constant annual reinvestment rate, and so it also includes the interest on your interest. (See Figure 10.3.)

You now know a little known fact, that zeros are like coupon bonds that automatically reinvest your interest for you semiannually. The benefit is you eliminate the coupon's reinvestment risk and don't have to mess with reinvesting it yourself.

After a zero has been issued, accrued interest is involved in determining its theoretical par value. Using our previous example, let's say the secondary market never moves during the 10 years that the bond is outstanding. During this time, the zero coupon bond's par value would rise by the same amount every day so that at the end it is equal to the maturity's $10,000 face value.

There are approximately 3,650 days in 10 years. (In real life, the calculation would take into consideration leap years.) After 3,650 days, the value of this zero would

10 years, 6% Yield

$10,000, Total face value

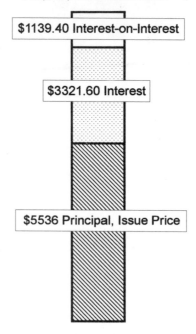

$1139.40 Interest-on-Interest

$3321.60 Interest

$5536 Principal, Issue Price

FIGURE 10.3 Zero's payout at maturity.

have risen $4,500 from the $5,500 purchase price to reach its $10,000 face value by its maturity date.

$4,500 ÷ 3,650 days = 1.233

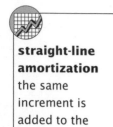

**straight-line
amortization**
the same
increment is
added to the
price every day.

So, if you screen out market gyrations, the bond's price would have to rise by roughly $1.23 a day. This is what is known as **straight-line amortization**: The original value increases by the same increment every day, eventually reaching the face value when it matures.

As mentioned before, a zero's face value also includes compounded interest-on-interest. The more accurate measure is not a straight line but a curved one that moves higher more quickly the closer you are to maturity because the compounding effect accelerates.

The government wants you to pay taxes on a taxable zero's interest every year even though you don't get the interest until the bond matures. Every year you take this amount of annual interest and add it onto your cost basis. If you sell before the bond matures at a price above this adjusted cost basis, you owe capital gains on the difference. If you sell below this adjusted cost basis, you have a capital loss in the amount of the difference. You need to calculate how much interest accrues daily. This can be a nightmare; it's best to call an accountant or the IRS for guidance.

Figure 10.4 illustrates the theoretical amortization line. Each day there is a theoretical price that falls along this line that can be thought of as the zero's par value. Any market price above this line is a premium, and any price below is a discount.

Investors must pay taxes on a zero's **accrued interest**. Even though zeros do not pay interest until maturity,

 accrued interest bond investors earn interest every day, but it is paid out only periodically; most pay semiannually, and a few pay monthly. Accrued interest has been earned by the investor but has not yet been paid out.

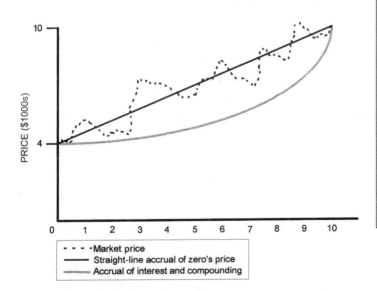

- - - - Market price
——— Straight-line accrual of zero's price
———— Accrual of interest and compounding

FIGURE 10.4 Zero coupon's price accrual.

investors owe taxes every year on the interest earned but not yet paid out. This is the amount the amortization line has risen during the past year.

Conclusion

There have been articles written about how difficult it is to price bonds since so few are traded on exchanges. The fact that most bond trading goes on over-the-counter (OTC) makes it difficult for the layperson to know where prices are. While you may not be able to find the price of your exact security, you may be able to find the price of a similar security on the World Wide Web or by using an investment firm's software. A great source of information and bond-related links is the Bond Market Association, at www.investinginbonds.com.

YIELD

As is probably obvious by now, nothing is straightforward when it comes to bonds. We've just discussed that a bond's price is measured in points. Well, just to further obfuscate bonds' helically entropic counterlogical labyrinth, yields are measured in points too—**basis points (bp)**; but basis points are very different from price points.

When a bond's yield moves from 5% to 6%, the yield has increased 1%:

5% + 1% = 6%

But the percentage change is actually 20%:

5% + (5% × 20%) = 6%

 basis point (bp) the smallest measure when discussing bond yields; 1 basis point equals .01%. Traders sometimes call them "beeps."

When we talk about yield, the confusion arises because "up 5%" can mean up five 1% units or up a 5% change from the first measurement. Even trying to explain the point of confusion is confusing. Let's see if an example helps show how this is confusing. You can say you gained 10 pounds or you can say your weight is up 8%; your apple harvest can be up 80 bushels or up 25%; your heating bill can be up $10 or up 5%. But, when you're talking about bonds, you can say the yield is up 1% or it's up 20% and be right both times, because the unit and the change are both referred to as percent; confusion abounds. (See Figure 10.5.)

In a bond trader's hectic world being clear is crucial since a misunderstanding can be costly to the tune of hundreds of thousands of dollars, so this potential area of confusion had to be eliminated. A term other than percent was coined for a unit of yield. So, a bond's yield is measured in basis points (abbreviated "bp"). When a bond's yield moves from 5% to 6%, it has risen 100 basis points.

A basis point equals .01%. There are 100 basis points in 1%. Here are some examples:

$$300 \text{ bp} = 3\%$$
$$100 \text{ bp} = 1\%$$
$$50 \text{ bp} = .5\%$$
$$1 \text{ bp} = .01\%$$

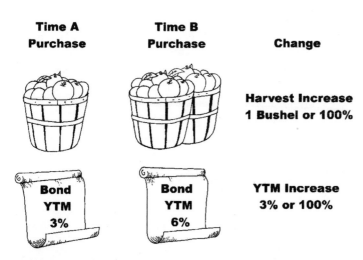

Time A Purchase	Time B Purchase	Change
		Harvest Increase 1 Bushel or 100%
Bond YTM 3%	Bond YTM 6%	YTM Increase 3% or 100%

FIGURE 10.5 Computing change can be confusing. Drawing by Steven Saltzgiver.

If someone tells you A-rated corporates are yielding 200 basis points more than A-rated munis and you know A-rated munis are yielding 7%, you can then figure out that A-rated corporates are yielding 9%.

$$200 \text{ bp} = 2\%$$
$$7\% + 2\% = 9\%$$

Here's another example: If a bond yielding 7.25% gained 7 basis points, its yield would rise by .07% to 7.32%. Another time you could hear basis points being used is in a sentence like, "The Fed's tight monetary policy could lower market interest rates 50 to 75 basis points."

Figuring Value

When you're trying to decide whether one bond is a better value than another bond, you do so by comparing their yields, not by comparing their prices. That means that understanding what different yield measures tell you is of premier importance. Each type of yield measure is unique and provides you with different information. Not knowing the difference between them is one of the most common and most dangerous information gaps bond investors share.

It is dangerous because investment professionals who are either unethical or uninformed can tell you the bond's highest yield instead of the most accurate. By most accurate, I mean the yield you are most likely to actually earn. You can check to make sure you were told the right yield by looking at your trade **confirm**. The Securities and Exchange Commission (SEC) requires that the yield disclosed on the confirm be the most conservative and the most likely to be received. If you don't like what you see, call back and cancel the trade. You don't "own" the bonds until the settlement date even though you earn interest from the trade date.

To avoid any misunderstanding or miscommunica-

confirm
short for "trade confirmation," this lists all the particulars of the trade.

The confirm is sent after a bond trade is executed but before the settlement date to the investor with a duplicate sent to his/her investment professional. The confirm details all of the trade particulars: security description, price, accrued interest, trade date, settlement date, dollars owed or to be received. The investor checks the details to make sure they are correct. If they are correct and the investor is buying, the investor sends in a check.

tion, let's take a little time now to become acquainted with the various yield types:

- ✔ Coupon yield.
- ✔ Current yield.
- ✔ Yield-to-maturity (YTM).
- ✔ Yield-to-call (YTC).
- ✔ Yield-to-worst (YTW).

Coupon Yield. The **coupon yield** tells you how many dollars you'll receive while the other yields tell you what your return on investment will be. The only time the coupon yield is your return on investment is if you pay par for the bond.

 coupon yield
the interest the issuer has promised to pay, an annual percentage of the face value.

The term "coupon yield" originates from the not too distant past when an investor who bought a bond actually received a printed certificate with coupons attached. When it came time for an interest payment, the bondholder would clip the coupon and redeem it for the cash due.

You can use the coupon yield to calculate the annual income and the interest payments you'll receive. For example, a bond that has a $10,000 face value and 7% coupon yield would pay $700 a year: 7% of $10,000 is $700.

$$\$10,000 \times .07 = \$700$$

Since the annual income is paid in two semiannual installments, the interest payments can be found by dividing the annual income in two.

$700 ÷ 2 = $350

Current Yield. When you go to the deli counter and ask for two pounds of salami, the white-clad butcher slices off a pile of meat and hands you a neatly wrapped package. The **current yield** is analogous to the two pounds you asked for; it is not the 2.17 pounds you actually get. It is only a rough estimate of what you received.

Think of the current yield as a thumbnail sketch of your future return on investment. It's useful for a quick return estimate when you're paying something other than par for the bond. However, when you're making a comparison and investment choice between different bonds, you should use one of the other types of yield we'll discuss.

Current yield is arrived at by taking the bond's annual income and dividing it by the bond's current price (value). For example, look at the same bond's current return at different price levels:

> **current yield**
> to calculate, divide the bond's annual dollar interest by the current market price.

Face value: $1,000

Coupon: 10%

Annual income: $1,000 × .10 = $100

Price #1: 97

Value: $1,000 × .97 = $970

Current yield: $100 ÷ $970 = .103 or 10.3%

Price #2: 104

Value: $1,000 × 1.04 = $1,040

Current yield: $100 ÷ $1,040 = .0962 or 9.62%

Price #3: 100

Value: $1,000 × 1 = $1,000

Current yield: $100 ÷ $1,000 = .10 or 10%

Note that when the price is par, the current yield equals the coupon yield.

While current yield is fine for a quick yield calculation, it misses some important nuances that are captured in the yield-to-maturity measure.

Yield-to-Maturity. The previous two yields are simple yields. They do not take into account that you can reinvest your income and the significant effect compounding coupons can have on you returns. When you own a bond with a larger coupon, you will receive your money sooner. This means you can reinvest this money and earn more money for a longer period of time. Yield-to-maturity (YTM) helps you account for this advantage. It allows you to accurately compare bonds with different coupons and maturities.

YTM does this by calculating what your return would be if you were able to reinvest your income at a rate equal to the YTM.

Luckily, logarithmic calculators can calculate a bond's YTM for you, because you don't want to do it by hand. That would take you what my grandmother called "a month of Sundays." For the masochists among you, the formula is in the accompanying sidebar.

Assuming the bond was priced at par when it was issued, when the bond is priced at 100, the coupon rate equals the current yield and it will also equal the yield-to-maturity.

At 100:

Coupon = Current yield = YTM

When a bond trades to a premium (price > 100):

Coupon > Current yield > YTM

The general formula* for the yield-to-maturity for a bond paying interest semiannually is:

$$P = \sum_{t=1}^{2n} \frac{C/2}{\left(1+\dfrac{r}{2}\right)^t} + \frac{R}{\left(1+\dfrac{r}{2}\right)^{2n}}$$

where

    P = price of bond

    n = number of years to maturity

    C = annual dollar coupon interest

    r = yield-to-maturity

    R = redemption value of bond at maturity

    t = 1

*Source: The Handbook of Fixed Income Securities, 2d edition, edited by Frank J. Fabozzi and Irving M. Pollack, Homewood, IL: Dow Jones-Irwin, 1987, p. 64.

You may ask, how do you find an answer when the answer is in the formula? You have to keep trying numbers until you narrow it down to the correct answer. People used to use the bond yield table to look up YTM approximations. However, with the advent of financial calculators and financial software that can give you the exact answer in nanoseconds, you can't even find a bond yield table anymore, because no one uses it.

For example:

UST 7⅞% Feb 21
(i.e., U.S. Treasury, 7⅞% coupon, due February 2021)

Price spread: 126-02 / 126-08

Ask yield: 5.78%

7⅞% > 6.2% > 5.78%

Coupon > Current yield > YTM

When a bond trades to a discount (price < 100):

Coupon < Current yield < YTM

For example:

FNMA 6.20% 11/03

Price spread: 98-25 / 98-31
Ask yield: 6.43%

Coupon < Current yield < YTM
6.2% < 6.3% < 6.43%

Yield-to-Call. As we have seen, some bonds can be retired before their maturity date. These are known as callable bonds. The issuer can call the bonds in, but only after specific dates at set prices. Callable bonds are usually issued by municipalities or corporations. There are still a few callable U.S. Treasury securities outstanding.

For example:

XOM 7⅝ 2/33 – 03 @ 102, 05 @ 100

This is an issue of Exxon Corp. with a 7⅝% coupon maturing on February 15, 2033; the first possible call date is on February 15, 2003, at a price of 102 until February 15, 2005, when it can be called at 100.

When a bond is likely to be called, you would want to know what the **yield-to-call (YTC)** is, not the YTM. A bond is most likely to be called if interest rates drop and the issuer wants to refinance its old higher-cost debt. This means that premium bonds are more likely to be **trading at** their YTC because the probability they will be called by the issuer is higher.

Yield-to-Worst. So, if a bond is callable, how do you know whether to use the YTM or one of the YTCs when comparing bonds? The rule here is: Always use

yield-to-call (YTC) estimated yield investor will receive if the bond is called before maturity by the issuer.

trading at the yield used to price the bond. The secondary market feels the bond should offer the investor this yield; thus, the bond's price adjusts so the investor receiving this coupon will earn this yield.

> If a bond is callable, trading at a premium, and the yield-to-call (YTC) is lower than the yield to maturity (YTM), you should use the YTC in order to appropriately compare it with other bonds. In this case, the YTC is the yield that the market deems as the most likely to be realized because it looks like the bond is likely to be called. So this is the yield, not the yield-to-maturity, that the market will use to price the bond. The price will adjust in the market so that the bond's YTC is equal to similar bonds and fits into the spectrum of other bond yields.

the lowest yield. This yield is known as the yield-to-worst (YTW).

For example:

BENCO 5¾ 8/15/09-04

Maturity	Yield
8/15/09	5.63%

Call Dates	Yield
8/15/04	5.60%
8/15/07	5.57%

For this bond, the second call date results in the YTW. Therefore, this bond should be sold at a 5.57% YTW.

Most investment professionals have a Monroe calculator or software on their computer that calculates the yield-to-worst, accrued interest, and so on. All you have to do is ask. If they can't give you these yields, you may want to suggest they read this book.

You may have noticed in the preceding example that as the price goes up, the yield goes down. This leads us to our next discussion.

PRICE IS INVERSELY RELATED TO YIELD

When I first started working at a large mutual fund company, I had a headset planted on my head and was answering brokers' inquiries. The company was known for its bond funds; so, since my previous experience included assisting two stock jocks and peddling copier equipment, I was desperately trying to sharpen my fixed income acumen before anyone discovered I had no idea what I was talking about.

I remember the guy in the cubical opposite patiently explaining to me how a bond's price is inversely related to its yield. To my mind, their moving in opposite directions seemed counterintuitive. I pretended to understand, politely giving him the old smile and nod but secretly wondering if he really knew what he was talking about—could bonds actually be so convoluted?

That night I kept thinking about what he'd said. The next day I asked him for clarification and hoped I was able to disguise the fact I had no idea what he'd been talking about the day before. He gallantly tried again. This time I glimpsed the concept a couple of times but the essential *why* still eluded me. Then on the third day my coworker's diligent labor paid off, and the heavy cerebral cloud cover parted as rays of enlightenment shone down—the Aha! experience.

Hopefully, it won't take you as long as it did me, but if it does, stick with it because everything else hinges on springing open this Pandora's box. Since different strokes work for different folks, there are a few different explanations to follow.

Take 1

The classic analogy for demonstrating the relationship between price and yield is a seesaw (see Figure 10.6). However, while this may be a useful image to help you remember the relationship, it does nothing in the way of explaining why. If you're like me (I'm like an interest rate atheist), you need to understand why before you'll accept

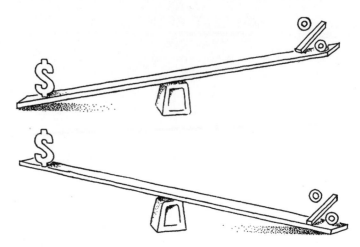

FIGURE 10.6   Price moves opposite yield.
Drawing by Steven Saltzgiver.

anything. However, if you don't care why, skip to the next chapter, "Riding the Curve."

Take 2

An analogy illustrating the price/yield relationship would be: buying oranges to make orange juice. You buy 10 fresh oranges for $2 to make 1 quart of orange juice.

However, after you buy your oranges a new shipment comes in. These oranges produce twice as much juice as yours: 10 new oranges make 2 quarts of juice. You want to sell your oranges for $2, but the buyers at the fruit market aren't interested in them. The new oranges are much more attractive to potential buyers because their juice yield is so much higher than yours. (See Figure 10.7.)

In order to attract buyers, you have to lower the price of your 10 oranges to $1. At this price, buyers can buy 20 of your less desirable oranges, which would bring their juice yield up. Since the orange investors' juice yield will be the same for the same cost—$2 for 2 quarts—they won't care which batch of oranges they buy.

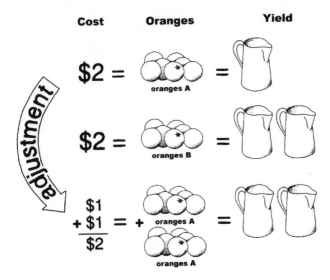

Cost   Oranges   Yield

FIGURE 10.7 Price changes with moves in current market yield.
Drawing by Steven Saltzgiver.

Take 3

As the name "fixed income" implies, most bonds have a fixed interest (coupon) rate that doesn't change. The fact that the coupon doesn't change while interest rates are constantly changing in the secondary market is what causes bond prices to move in the opposite direction from current interest rates. As interest rates go up, bond prices go down, and vice versa.

Think of it this way: Bond A comes to market. It's a popular offering, and investors snap it up.

Sometime later interest rates rise; Bond B comes to market and its coupon is higher than Bond A's. Older bonds with lower coupons are less attractive. New investors would rather buy Bond B than Bond A. Bond A's price has to fall to in order to entice investors. (See Figure 10.8.)

Since the market is efficient, Bond A's price should fall until the demand for it (an older, lower-coupon bond) is the same as the demand for the new, higher-yielding bonds. Investors will be indifferent as to which bond they own when the YTM is the same for both bonds.

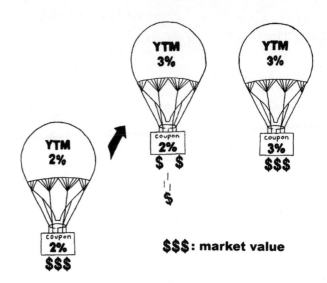

FIGURE 10.8   Price changes as yield adjusts to current market yield.
Drawing by Steven Saltzgiver.

Conversely, when interest rates fall, everyone wants older bonds instead of the new issue. The new Bond C is less attractive because it has a lower coupon. So, investors bid up the prices on older bonds in their hunt for higher interest rates. As older bonds' prices rise, their effective yields drop. The prices will continue to rise until Bond A's and Bond B's YTMs fall to Bond C's YTM.

Take 4

Let's look at a bond example with some numbers attached. When bonds first come to the market, they are sold for par (par = 100). Say a company issues a bond in January with a 10% coupon maturing in 5 years.

Bond A

Maturity:	January
Coupon:	10%
Price:	100
YTM:	10%

The company issues additional 5-year bonds in April when interest rates have risen to 12%. If any of the January investors now wish to sell, they will have to discount the price of their bonds since investors would rather be paid April's 12% than January's 10%.

But how far will they have to lower the price? Well, the price will fall until investors can earn the same amount of money regardless of which bond they buy. In other words, the price on Bond A will drop until its YTM equals Bond B's YTM.

Bond A			Bond B		
Maturity:	January		Maturity:	April	
Coupon:	10%		Coupon:	12%	
Price:	97		Price:	100	
YTM:	12%		YTM:	12%	

Now let's say soon thereafter current interest rates move back to 10%. Each bond's price would rise to the point where its YTM equals 10%.

Bond A			Bond B		
Maturity:	January		Maturity:	April	
Coupon:	10%		Coupon:	12%	
Price:	100		Price:	103	
YTM:	10%		YTM:	10%	

As you can see, bonds that have already been issued and are trading in the secondary market constantly readjust their market price in response to current interest rate moves. Since they can't change their coupons, they are always adjusting their prices so their YTMs are in line with current interest rates; that way buyers will still be interested.

As interest rates rise, bond prices in the secondary market fall so that their yields will move higher to line up with current interest rates and buyers will get a fair yield.

As interest rates fall, bond prices in the secondary market rise so that their yields will move lower to line up with current interest rates, and sellers will get a fair price for their bonds.

Riding the Curve

THE YIELD CURVE

"Reading" the yield curve will be one of your greatest aids when you're deciphering the fixed income market's future direction and formulating your investment strategy. It gives you insight into market sentiment and expectations. You can also identify value along the curve.

When you read the yield curve through a looking glass oriented toward the past, you can identify oddball behavior that's due for some corrective discipline. Our efficient markets will quickly apply a firm hand to any unwarranted aberration and will bring prices and yields back into a more normal pattern.

Catch the Curve: What Is a Yield Curve?

The yield curve plots the current yield-to-maturity for each maturity from three months out to 30 years. (See Figure 11.1.) The graph's "y" (i.e., vertical) axis plots the yield; the "x" (i.e., horizontal) axis marks the maturities.

The yield curve in Figure 11.2 is said to be positively sloped. This means the short-maturity end of the curve (3 months to 2 years) is yielding less than the long-maturity end (10 to 30 years). It is also a steep

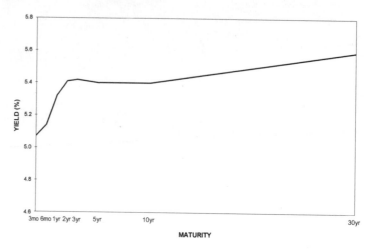

FIGURE 11.1   Yield curve.

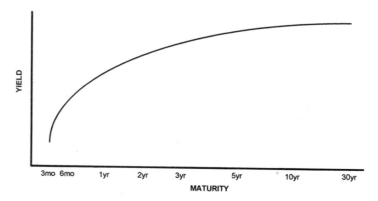

FIGURE 11.2   Positively sloped yield curve.

yield curve because the difference between the long end and the short end is quite dramatic.

The positively sloped curve has become known as the normal yield curve because of the widely held belief that this is its usual shape. When there is little or no difference in yields across the curve, the yield curve is flat (Figure 11.3).

When the short end of the curve yields more than the long end, it is an inverted, aka negatively sloped yield curve, as you see in Figure 11.4.

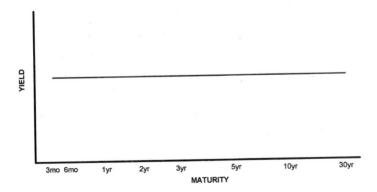

FIGURE 11.3 Flat yield curve.

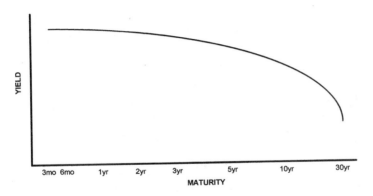

FIGURE 11.4 Negatively sloped yield curve.

What Does the Yield Curve Tell You?

Reading the yield curve tells you what the majority of players in the bond market expect interest rates to be in the future. Whether you agree or disagree will determine your investment strategy.

There are a number of ways to interpret the yield curve. Each contributes a piece to the puzzle. As usual the names are more daunting than their concepts: the term structure of interest rates, supply and demand, and the bipolar dynamic.

The Term Structure of Interest Rates

According to the term structure of interest rates, a bond's maturity and yield are tied together. There are three theories on how they are related.

Liquidity Hypothesis. This says that as time increases there is more market risk and less liquidity, so longer-term bonds should offer higher yields. This is not a complete explanation of the yield curve and so we venture on to the second theory.

Expectations Hypothesis. This explanation incorporates the implied forward yield curve, which is a theoretical yield curve. You find this curve by beginning with the actual yield curve as it is currently shaped. Let's say the 1-year is 5.00% and the 2-year is 5.05%. You can either buy a 2-year or buy a 1-year and when it matures in a year buy another 1-year. In order to be equivalent to the current 2-year's return, the 1-year interest rate you reinvest in would have to be 5.10% [(5.00% + 5.10%) ÷ 2 = 5.05%]; 5.10% is what is known as the implied forward rate. If you think the 1-year rate will be higher than 5.10% next year, you would buy the two 1-year maturities. If you think the 1-year rate will be less than 5.10% next year, you would buy the 2-year.

You can construct an entire yield curve using implied forward rates. Using this curve combined with your expectations for where you think interest rates will be in the future, you can determine what maturities you should be buying.

Since in modern history the yield curve is usually positively sloped, you can infer that interest rates are expected to go up over time. Coincidentally, the positively sloped curve is the shape you would expect when inflation is predicted to be heading higher. Perhaps this explains why, during the inflationary environment we've had since World War II, investors have come to expect a positively sloped yield curve. (If you don't believe we've been in an inflationary environment, just compare what you paid for your house with what your parents paid.)

Conversely, a negatively sloped yield curve would portend a deflationary environment with consumer prices and interest rates trending downward.

Market Segmentation. This assumes that the majority of market players are captive investors in one segment of the yield curve. For example, a pension fund may have to invest in the middle-range maturities. An insurance company may have to invest in specific maturities to match its policies' annuity structures. Indonesia may only be able to invest in the short end of the curve. Whatever their restrictions, this theory says the appetite these investors have for their targeted maturity at any one time will determine the interest rate. More appetite means the lower the yields for that maturity will move; the less interest there is, the higher the yields will be for that maturity. In my view, this explanation may occasionally contribute to the yield curve's shape, but it is too simplistic for the depth and sophistication that today's fixed income investors possess.

Supply and Demand

Another force that influences the shape of the yield curve is the now-familiar market participant: supply and demand. When an auction promises to flood the market with securities of a particular maturity, you may see a pop up in the yield curve's curvature at that point. Conversely, when a maturity is in great demand or experiences negligible new supply, the yield may drop at that point, giving the yield curve a bumpy countenance. So, high demand or low supply can cause a maturity's interest rate to fall, and lackluster demand or a flood of supply can cause a maturity's interest rate to rise.

The Bipolar Dynamic

You can also look at the yield curve as having two poles, each end of the curve being more responsive to different stimuli.

The short end of the curve is highly influenced by

tight policy

also known as being restrictive. The objective is to make it more difficult for people to get money. Since money becomes expensive it discourages borrowing. This tends to slow down the economy, so inflation doesn't get out of control.

inflation

when prices of goods and services are rising without any improvement in productivity or quality.

Federal Reserve actions. It's even affected by what Fed watchers say the Fed *might* do. Short rates tend to pop up if the Fed tightens or it looks like the Fed might tighten (**tight policy**). Higher rates help to let a little steam out of an overheating (very strong) economy and defuse a stronger economy's accompanying **inflation** fears. Conversely, short rates tend to drop when the Fed takes an easier stance—an **easy policy**. In this scenario, money becomes plentiful, and anytime there's a lot of something it tends to become cheaper. Since interest rates are the price someone pays to borrow money, when interest rates drop getting your hands on some money becomes less expensive. This encourages borrowing and helps to stimulate the economy.

When the Fed needs to rein in inflation, it tightens and short rates head higher. In response, long rates could head higher as well or they could head lower as investors are happy that the Fed is taking an aggressive stance against inflation. The second course would result in an inverted yield curve. Once inflation is felt to be contained, the curve tends to return to a slightly positive or flat slope.

The long end of the yield curve is more directly affected by inflation expectations. In the 1980s, **heavy hitters** in the long end of the yield curve were affectionately referred to as bond vigilantes. They were like disciplinary elves that invisibly sprang to action when interest rates seemed to ignore economic reality. The vigilantes were credited with pushing long rates over 10 percent in the spring and summer of 1987, which did indeed serve to discipline the overzealous financial markets. You may recall the stock market crash that followed in October.

SUMMARY

These various influences can take turns tugging the yield curve into different contortions, and at other times they can all pound on the curve at once. By using your expectations for future economic growth and inflation and by using the theories we've discussed as to what conditions change the yield curve's shape, you can decide where you think future interest rates will be, as well as the potential shape of the yield curve. If you're going to hold the bond until it matures, you can buy the highest point of the curve. If you're looking for capital gains to magnify your return, you could buy the area of the curve where you think that rates will be moving downward.

Here are some questions you can consider when you're using the yield curve to develop your investment strategy. If the yield curve is positively sloped and you think it will flatten, is the yield curve going to flatten by the short end moving up or the long end moving down? Or is the whole curve going to shift up or perhaps down? Are financial conditions going to instigate the need for cash and therefore a lot of selling in the secondary market? Are there foreign countries with large cash positions that may invest in our markets and, if so, what maturities do they prefer? Do you think the Fed may tighten due to inflation pressures? Or are the markets nervous because the Fed's not doing anything about inflation?

 easy policy
also known as being accommodative. The objective is to get more money into the domestic monetary system in an attempt to stimulate the economy.

 heavy hitters
big players, size traders, large investors.

12

A Volatile Relationship

When you're caught in an argument with someone, understanding what's motivating the other person often goes a long way toward resolving the conflict. After all, it's easier to defuse a bomb when you know where the fuse is. The same goes for bonds. If you know what causes fixed income volatility (i.e., what causes prices to bounce around in the secondary market) you have a better chance of defending against their negative moves.

Fixed income volatility can come from changes in the issuer's financial condition or from changing interest rates. For example, as an issuer's financial condition improves, its cost of borrowing declines because investors shoulder less risk. Any existing bonds the company had previously issued will appreciate in value, bringing those yields down to the newly appropriate level.

Conversely, if the issuer's credit is downgraded, existing bond values fall so that the yields will rise to levels that more adventurous investors will find alluring.

The features that make each bond unique shape a bond's volatility via their reactions to interest rate movements. A bond's:

✔ Maturity,
✔ Coupon, and
✔ Credit rating

affect the degree to which the bond will react to changes in interest rates. The level of current interest rates also affects how much all bonds will react to future changes.

The situation is similar to when you played with your Jr. Chemistry set. When you combined four different elements with nitrogen separately, you'd get four different reactions. Then if you combined all four with nitrogen at the same time, the sum total would be something different again with each element playing a part in the final reaction that sent the chemistry lab up in flames.

To understand how maturity, coupon, credit rating, and current interest rates contribute to a bond's volatility, let's examine how each one is affected by interest rate fluctuations.

MATURITY

The *shorter* a bond's maturity, the *lower* its sensitivity to interest rate changes.

The *longer* a bond's maturity, the *greater* its volatility.

A visual to help you remember this principle is a whip. When you crack a whip, the point that is the farthest away from you, the tip, travels the greatest distance. The handle you are holding onto moves the least.

The reason why bond volatility increases with time is reinvestment risk. Forecasting where interest rates will be in the future is like trying to read a street sign; our ability to see diminishes with distance.

It follows that as time elapses and the time until the bond matures becomes shorter, the bond will experience less volatility. For example, a 30-year bond that has been outstanding for 28 years and matures in 2 years will have the volatility of a 2-year bond.

COUPON

Bonds with *larger* coupons are *less* volatile.

Bonds with *smaller* coupons have *more* price movement for a given change in interest rates.

A bond with a larger coupon has a higher income stream that acts as a buffer to interest rate moves. You can use the image of a mattress to remember this principle. When you jump on a thicker mattress (bigger coupon) it absorbs more of the shock, so you don't bounce as much. In fact, bonds that are trading well above par are known as **cushion bonds** because their higher coupons offer a cushion against falling prices. These bonds are viewed as defensive securities.

A reason for this is because the larger the coupon is, the longer the bond will remain attractive in the face of rising interest rates. For example, say you own two bonds, a 6% coupon and an 11% coupon. Market interest rates rise from 5% to 7%. Your 11% coupon bond is still attractive relative to the new-issue 7% bonds and will still be selling at a premium. However, the 6% is less attractive and will sell at a discount now.

Here again, the mathematical explanation is the present value of money. When you own a bond with a larger coupon, you receive a higher percentage of your investment's total return sooner. And remember, a dollar today is preferable to a dollar tomorrow.

The time until you get half the money you are owed is shorter. The fact you are getting more of your money sooner decreases the bond's relative volatility. The sooner you get the money, the more apt you are to be right about where you can reinvest that money (see maturity factor).

In Figure 12.1, notice the triangle (which represents when you would have received half of your cash from the issuer) moving to shorter and shorter times as the volatility falls. Zero coupon bonds have the most volatility (all other factors being the same), because there is no coupon. All of your return comes at the end (the furthest point

cushion bonds

bonds trading in the secondary market that have coupons significantly higher than current interest rates. Their larger coupon offers a cushion against price fluctuations when interest rates move, so these bonds tend to experience less price volatility. Since they are trading at substantial premiums, many investors won't buy (they erroneously think they are expensive). Therefore, the YTM is often higher than similar bonds with lower coupons, offering an attractive yield pickup.

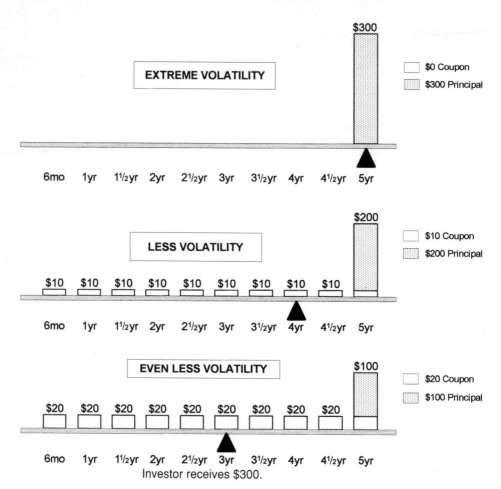

FIGURE 12.1   Money sooner: less volatility.

from the present) when the economic conditions are the least known.

CREDIT RATING

The *better* a bond's credit rating, the *less* responsive it will be to changes in interest rates.

The *greater* the credit risk, the *higher* the sensitivity to interest rate changes.

As you have probably noticed with the first two factors, uncertainty leads to increased price sensitivity. This is also true when there's uncertainty about an issuer's creditworthiness. Lower-rated bonds tend to be more volatile than their higher-rated siblings.

This is because companies with shakier credit are more likely to feel pain when interest rates rise. They usually have a greater need to borrow capital and thus are more at the mercy of interest rates. When interest rates go up, it costs them more because they need to borrow more. They also can't afford the luxury of a financial cushion, so there's nothing to fall back on when higher interest rates slow the economy.

But you've heard the expression, "nowhere to go but up." When interest rates decline, lower-rated bonds also tend to rebound higher than established companies with better credit because there's more room for improvement and therefore more upside potential.

CURRENT INTEREST RATES

The *higher* current interest rates are, the *less* sensitive bonds will tend to be.

The *lower* current interest rates are, the *more* volatile all bonds will tend to be.

This is because when interest rates are lower each move has a bigger impact. An analogy would be: If you have a tablespoon of yellow paint and a cup of yellow paint and then add a drop of green paint to each, the smaller tablespoonful turns greener than the larger cupful where the drop has less of an impact.

For example, when interest rates are at 4%, a 100 bp change in interest rates represents a 25% move. The same 100 bp change in interest rates represents only a 10% move when interest rates are at 10%. Since when interest rates are low, yields move to a greater degree, so too does the corresponding price. This is because price and yield are inversely and directly related.

BUT WHAT TO DO?

How can you predict a bond's volatility when there are so many different factors battling for control? For example, a bond with a short maturity could have more volatility than a longer bond, if the shorter bond is a zero coupon and the longer bond has a large coupon. The next section decodes the mystery of how to compare dissimilar bonds.

WE'RE HERE FOR THE DURATION

duration
the measure of
bond price
volatility in
years. Duration
equates the bond
to a zero coupon
bond (e.g., a
bond with a 4-
year duration has
the volatility of a
4-year zero).

Fixed income tacticians measure price volatility using **duration**. A bond's duration predicts how much its price should move for a 1% change in interest rates.

You calculate a bond's duration using three variables:

1. Maturity.
2. Coupon.
3. Current interest rates.

The duration formula reduces the bond in question down to a zero coupon bond equivalent. The result is measured in years. A 7% 30-year bond with a 7.2-year duration is expected to have the same volatility as a zero coupon bond maturing in 7.2 years. Furthermore, the price is expected to change roughly 7.2% when interest rates change 100 bp.

The formula set down by Frederick Macaulay in 1938 is a bit of a nightmare. Luckily, most financial software will do it for you with the press of a button. Man, do I love technology!

You don't have to try to compare apples with oranges, bananas, or apricots any longer. With duration, it's as if someone handed you a lens that makes this fruit salad look like it's all peaches, so that you can easily pick out the most luscious.

Duration is also helpful when trying to design your overall portfolio. Let's say you want your portfolio's target

The Macaulay duration formula, for you masochists, is:

$$D = \frac{\displaystyle\sum_{t=1}^{m} \frac{tC_t}{(1+r)^t}}{\displaystyle\sum_{t=1}^{m} \frac{C_t}{(1+r)^t}}$$

The formula is simply a weighted-average calculation. The time until the receipt (t) of each cash flow is multiplied by the present value of the cash flow ($C_t/(1 + r)_t$). The sum of these components is divided by the sum of the weights, which is also the full price (including accrued interest) of the bond.*

*"Understanding Duration and Volatility," Robert W. Kopprasch, PhD, CFA. In *The Handbook of Fixed Income Securities*, 2d edition, edited by Frank J. Fabozzi and Irving M. Pollack, Homewood, IL: Dow Jones-Irwin, 1987.

duration to be 5 years. Currently, you own 8- and 6-year-duration bonds. So, your next bond will need to have a 1-year duration in order to bring the portfolio's average duration to 5 years, assuming you have the same amount invested in each bond.

Duration is the quintessential tool in a professional portfolio manager's arsenal. Managers lengthen the portfolio's duration when they are **bullish** so that if bond prices do rise the portfolio will get "more bang for the buck." But, if they are **bearish** on bond prices, they shorten the portfolio's duration to protect the portfolio from losing as much of its value.

VOLATILITY'S VOLATILITY: CONVEXITY

There is another calculation that estimates how much a bond's duration should change when interest rates move.

 bullish
good; positive; up; increasing in value. In the bond market this means interest rates are headed down and bond prices are going up.

 bearish
bad; negative; down; decreasing in value. In the bond market this means interest rates are headed up and bond prices are going down.

convexity
Measures the rate of change in a bond's sensitivity to interest rate moves. It's the rate of change in a bond's duration (price volatility).

In other words, duration's volatility is measured by its convexity. Don't kill yourself trying to understand convexity; it's not a crucial concept. However, it does shed some light on why different bonds act the way they do.

Positive convexity is like having a bond whose price is attached to a balloon that gets bigger and moves higher more quickly as interest rates fall. Having a positively convex bond is also like having the bond's price attached to a parachute that gets bigger, slowing the price drop, as interest rates rise.

Most bonds that have a fixed coupon and maturity date have positive convexity. This means when interest rates fall and prices are rising, their durations get longer. The result is their prices rise at a faster rate of change than bonds with negative convexity. Conversely, as interest rates rise, their durations shorten, slowing the rate of price decline. Obviously, positive convexity is a nice thing to have.

Negative convexity, on the other hand, is not a desirable quality for a bond to have. Bonds that are negatively convex have prices that tend to go up less and down more than their positively convex brethren do. It's as if their price were attached to a balloon that gets smaller as interest rates fall, so the price rises at an ever slowing pace. When interest rates rise, it's as if their price is attached to a parachute that gets smaller and smaller, so the price falls faster and faster.

As we discussed in Chapter 4, mortgage-backed bonds (MBSs) possess negative convexity. As interest rates drop and other bond prices are increasing, these bonds increase in value at a slower rate. As interest rates rise, MBSs lose value more quickly than other fixed income securities with positive convexity. The reason is that principal prepayments return your investment at disadvantageous times; for example, you may have to reinvest the returned principal at lower rates. Callable bonds also exhibit some negative convexity since they can be called by the issuer when interest rates drop.

Since they tend to go up less in price and down more, securities with negative convexity should pay higher yields than similar bonds with positive convexity.

PART THREE

FACTORS
AFFECTING
BONDS

Chapter

13

Is It the Moon, the Fed, or Your Mother-in-Law That Gets Bonds to Move?

FUNDAMENTAL FACTORS

Legions of financial professionals and devoted investors dedicate countless hours to **fundamental analysis**, interpreting data in hopes of discovering future trends for the economy and financial markets before others do. This section covers many of the fundamental factors that can affect the fixed income market and reviews what those effects tend to be.

It is important to remember that the relationships described are only market tendencies. Our ability to predict interest rates is clouded by the fact that all these factors are pushing and pulling on interest rates at once. For example, a strong dollar that exists in an environment where there are falling imports and low inflation can be seen as bullish for bonds, while when imports are surging and consumer sentiment is high a strong dollar can be viewed as bearish for bonds.

Throughout its history, the bond market has tended to

fundamental analysis
researching economic indicators, financial statistics, and issuer's financial position in an attempt to predict the future direction and behavior of the economy, interest rates or a certain bond issue.

181

focus on a couple of indicators, and has awaited their release with suspended breath. But, regardless of what numbers are currently in vogue, you're best served by looking at all of the factors in order to get a general sense of the market's psychology and to develop your own economic projections.

To identify trends, look at how the data's monthly changes have progressed over time, say the past 3 to 6 months. It's also helpful to look at year-to-date figures, year-over-year statistics, and the moving average for the trailing 12 months. You can find such figures in the *Wall Street Journal*, *Investor's Business Daily*, and the weekly paper, *Barron's*.

Another thing to watch for is revisions, especially with volatile indicators. For example, if last month's **producer price index (PPI)** was first reported as +.2% and this month's is +.3%, you might start to worry about inflation, until you notice that last month's reading was revised from +.2% to −.1%.

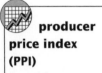 **producer price index (PPI)**
monthly measure of the change in wholesale prices as calculated by the U.S. Bureau of Labor Statistics.

"Buy the rumor; sell the fact." The bond market's reaction is more dramatic when it is surprised by an economic indicator. This is because financial markets are very efficient, and prices move quickly in response to signs, even rumors, of what may happen. So, any numbers that confirm what's already believed are greeted with a hearty ho hum. The news is said to be already "in the market" or to have been already "discounted" by the market (i.e., prices and yields have already moved). Sometimes when the numbers are released, the market actually trades in the opposite direction from what you'd expect because the previous reaction to the rumor was so overblown. However, if the data that's released indicates a bigger effect than expected, the markets immediately move further to include the new information.

Table 13.1 lists many of the indicators that financial analysts, traders, and managers study to help them frame where the economy and interest rates will be in the future.

When you are buying bonds, you should look at where interest rates are and what the bond is yielding. When you are selling bonds, you are more interested in where bond prices are. So, if you are buying you will look at the column furthest to the right in Table 13.1, and if you are selling you will look at the column second from the right.

TABLE 13.1 Economic Indicators

Indicator	Release Date	Period Covered	Data	Probable Direction of Bond Market Prices	Probable Direction of Interest Rates
U.S. dollar	Traded 24 hours	N/A	←	←	→
Initial unemployment claims	Every Thursday	Week ending previous Saturday	←	←	→
Car sales	1st to 3rd business day of month	Previous month	←	→	←
Purchasing managers' report	1st business day of month	Previous month	Moving up to 60 / Moving down to 40	→ / ←	← / →
Payroll employment and unemployment rate	1st–7th day of month	Previous month	←	→	←
Producer price index (PPI)	9th–16th day of month	Previous month	←	→	←
Retail sales	11th–14th day of month	Previous month	←	→	←
Industrial production and capacity utilization	14th–17th day of month	Previous month	←	→	←

(Continued)

TABLE 13.1 Continued

Indicator	Release Date	Period Covered	Data	Probable Direction of Bond Market Prices	Probable Direction of Interest Rates
Consumer sentiment	13th–20th day of month	Previous month	↑	→	↑
Housing starts and building permits	16th–20th day of month	Previous month	↑	→	↑
Consumer price index (CPI)	15th–21st day of month	Previous month	↑	→	↑
Durable goods order	22nd–28th day of month	Previous month	↑	→	↑
Gross domestic product (GDP)	21st–30th day of month	Previous month	↑	→	↑
Personal income and consumption spending	22nd–28th day of month	Previous month	↑	→	↑

Indicator	Release date	Report month			
Leading indicators	Last business day	Previous month of month	←	→	←
New home sales	28th day of last–4th day of this month	Previous month	←	→	←
Construction spending	1st business day of month	Two months ago	←	→	←
Factory orders	30th day of last–6th of this month	Two months ago	←	→	←
Business inventories and sales	13th–17th day of month	Two months ago	←	←	→
Trade balance	15th–17th day of month	Two months ago	Deficit Surplus	→ ←	← →
Nonfarm productivity and unit labor costs	7th–14th day of quarter's middle month	Previous month	←	→	←

An indicator's importance can be related to when it is released. Indicators that come earlier in the month can get a bigger market reaction because they represent new information, whereas data that's released later may only serve to confirm what's already been seen. An indicator's volatility or susceptibility to revisions can also diminish the market's reaction to its release.

All of the relationships and effects we'll discuss are only tendencies. The final outcome is the result of countless factors. The nuance involved in predicting future interest rates comes from intuiting which indicators will exert the strongest influence on the markets, which are best correlated with future interest rate moves, and which will give you the earliest read. Then you need to be watching for trends in these indicators. Are they showing momentum in one direction or another? Are they pointing to a shift in direction?

The key of course is to be able to predict accurately what will happen before everyone else realizes what is going to happen. Hey, no one said predicting interest rates is easy, and many have said it's impossible. As always, keep your ears open, and let common sense be your guide.

The Economy

Economic strength and expectations for future growth are major influences affecting where interest rates will head.

Calm pervades the fixed income market when there is steady, moderate growth that won't stimulate inflation above an accepted comfort zone (about a 3% inflation rate).

If the economy looks to be revving its engines to take off at top speeds, interest rates usually move higher in an attempt to discourage borrowing and brake the economy to a more restrained pace.

When prospects for the economy are dreary, companies become conservative, so there is less business activity, building, hiring, and so on. Interest rates drop in response to the demand for money drying up—remember, interest rates are the cost of borrowing money. As fewer people want to borrow money, the competition for each greenback declines and the cost to acquire (borrow) it also drops. In a minute we'll talk about how the Fed attempts to jump-start this process.

Gross Domestic Product (GDP)

The most comprehensive measure of our domestic economy is gross domestic product (GDP). GDP measures the value of items produced within the United States' borders. GDP is a more accurate measure of our country's productivity than gross national product (GNP), which was used before December 1991. GNP measured the output of U.S. individuals, companies, and the government—even when their activity was outside the United States. Adopting the GDP measure meant we now measure our output the same way as almost every other country in the world, so it became easier to make international comparisons. (See Figure 13.1.)

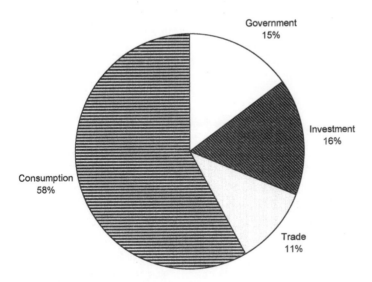

FIGURE 13.1 Composition of gross domestic product (GDP).

Gross domestic product (GDP) used to be calculated using a fixed-weight index, meaning it measured our goods and services using prices from the index's benchmark year. The index and benchmark would be updated about every 10 years. This led to a problem known as the substitution effect, which also affects other fixed-weight measures indexed from a base year. Over time the growth rate becomes overstated. People tend to substitute cheaper competitors for more expensive goods (e.g., generic shampoo), but the index still uses the old higher prices. The more time since the base year, the greater the distortion. The Commerce Department, which calculates GDP, converted to a "chain-weighted" GDP late in 1995. In the new chain-weighted method, the change in GDP is calculated between two successive years using contemporaneous prices, not using prices from some arbitrary index year.

$$GDP = C + I + G + (X - M)$$

Gross domestic product = Consumption
+ Investment + Government spending
+ (Exports − Imports)

The average GDP (economic) growth rate that won't freak out the financial markets seems to be between 2.5% and 3%. The Commerce Department releases three different versions of each quarter's GDP reading; the subsequent readings become more accurate as more data is incorporated. The first is the GDP Advance Estimates, which are released the month after the quarter being measured ends. The GDP Preliminary Estimates arrive a month later, and the GDP Revised Estimates arrive the month after that.

As mentioned before, bonds like a weak economy, and therefore a low GDP reading is bullish for bonds. On the other hand, a higher GDP reading sends bond yields higher and prices lower.

Many other economic indicators that we look at are important because they are components of GDP and give us a glimpse into what GDP could be before the number is actually released. Since being able to accurately assess what shape the economy is in and predict where interest rates are headed means being able to make money in the bond market, interpreting economic indicators is a valuable and elusive art. To help you cultivate this art we'll now look at many of the factors that players in the bond market watch, analyze, and trade off.

When nominal GDP is adjusted for inflation, it becomes the more meaningful real GDP reading. There are two deflator measures—implicit and fixed-weight—that are released with GDP which we'll cover next in our discussion of inflation.

Inflation

Inflation is defined as too many dollars chasing too few goods. This competing demand for scarce products or services pushes prices higher. Inflation leads to higher interest rates because it erodes the value of money. Borrowers love inflation because they can pay off their debts with dollars that are worth less. Investors hate inflation because they can't buy as much with the dollars they receive back.

In an inflationary environment, today's dollar may be worth only 33 cents next year. So, before clever investors will lend their money, they will demand more interest to ensure an acceptable *real* rate of return. For example, if you earn 4% over five years when inflation has been 6%, you have actually lost 2%! Therefore, if inflation is expected to be 6% and investors want a real return of 3%, they will demand to be paid around 9% before they'll lend their money.

In times when inflation is not a concern or **deflation** is expected, interest rates will drop because investors are not requiring this inflation premium. Another reason interest rates drop in a deflationary environment is because the economy is usually slow, and when the economy is slow, the demand for money is scant.

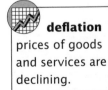 **deflation**
prices of goods and services are declining.

As mentioned before, we're pretty used to 3% to 4% inflation, but the bond market will begin to get hot flashes and act pretty miserably when inflation moves higher than this comfort zone. When inflation gets on towards 6%, panic mode will begin to set in. Interest rates will begin to spiral higher. For example, in 1981 inflation was at double-digit levels and the rate for a 30-year mortgage was around 18%.

When evaluating how inflation is going to affect the bond market, what is causing the inflation is often more important than the inflation indicator's actual reading. For example, if the reason for this month's higher reading is that bad weather caused a poor harvest, the inflation impact could be temporary. Or is the higher reading due to higher wage costs and lower productivity enabling inflation to settle in for an extended stay?

The primary inflation measures are the Commodity Research Bureau (CRB) index, the producer price index (PPI), the **consumer price index (CPI)**, and the GDP deflators. (See Table 13.2.) Each measure has its strong points and can make a valuable contribution to the inflation picture.

consumer price index (CPI)
prices of domestic and imported goods and services purchased by U.S. consumers as calculated by the Bureau of Labor Statistics.

TABLE 13.2 Evaluating Inflation Measures			
Measure	Includes	Positives	Negatives
CRB index	19 commodities, futures prices	Traded daily on exchanges, constantly revalued	Narrow sample
PPI	3,450 commodities, wholesale prices	Broad-based measure	Goods only
CPI	364 goods and services	Also includes services and some imports	Narrow sample
Fixed-weight deflator	5,000 goods and services	Broadest inflation measure	No imported goods
Implicit deflator	5,000 goods and services	Captures changes in spending patterns caused by reaction to inflation.	Not a pure inflation measure

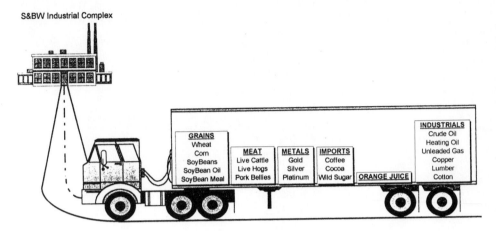

FIGURE 13.2 Commodity Research Bureau (CRB) futures price index.

Commodity Research Bureau. The CRB index is a basket of commodities that are raw materials. Many components are agricultural, so bad weather can distort the reading month-to-month. It's best to look at this reading's trend over time: moving averages, past few months, and year-over-year statistics. (See Figure 13.2.)

Producer Price Index and Consumer Price Index. These indexes both measure goods made here in the United States. PPI (Figure 13.3) measures the prices domestic producers pay for the goods they buy (crude, intermediate, and finished indexes). CPI (Figure 13.4) measures the prices consumers pay for the things they buy and the services they use. CPI includes imports, as well as domestic products.

Bond market investors often take note of what PPI and CPI are **ex-food and energy** because food and energy are very volatile components that can distort the reading from month to month. Analysts are trying to eliminate the noise so that it is easier to identify the trend in the core inflation rate.

PPI measures what businesses pay for the capital goods (machinery, computers) they buy; this information

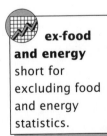

ex-food and energy short for excluding food and energy statistics.

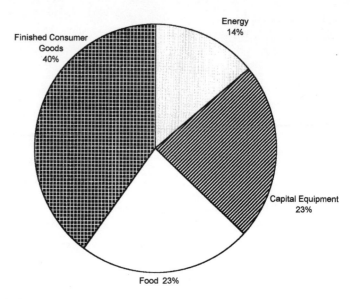

FIGURE 13.3   Composition of producer price index (PPI).

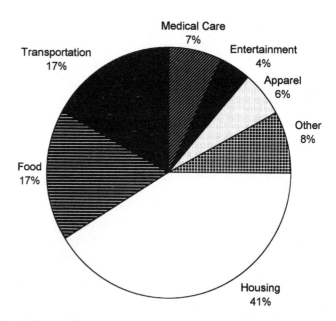

FIGURE 13.4   Consumer price index (CPI) weighting.

is not included in CPI. The index is seasonally adjusted (unlike the CRB index) and released for both crude and finished goods. As you can guess, the prices for crude goods foreshadow what will happen to the prices of finished goods.

The fixed-income market views CPI as the best inflation measure. It is released for urban workers (CPI-U), covering about 80% of us working folk, and for wage earners and clerical workers (CPI-W), about 40% of us. The markets prefer to look at the more comprehensive CPI-U, but CPI-W is the one used to adjust collective bargaining agreements, income tax brackets, and cost-of-living allowances (COLAs). Go figure! CPI's advantages include its counting goods and services, both domestic and imported. The problems with CPI include its small sample size and its being a fixed-weight measure. In addition, CPI doesn't measure quality improvements.

GDP Deflators. Two other inflation barometers are released with the GDP numbers: the implicit deflator and the fixed-weight deflator. Either of these can be used to deflate inflation out of nominal GDP to arrive at real GDP.

Each deflator measures a different type of inflation. Each is valid and valuable to look at. Both deflators survey over five thousand goods and services produced here in the United States. Economists admire the broad sample size, but are wary of the fact it does not include the foreign goods we buy.

The fixed-weight deflator prices a set basket of goods. This constancy provides us with the best gauge of pure inflation, but you give up some relevancy.

On the other hand, the items within the implicit price deflator's enormous basket of goods change as our buying habits evolve with technology advances, fads, seasons, tastes, and prosperity. Since it reflects our times, many feel the implicit price deflator provides the most relevant measure of inflation.

The Federal Reserve

Economists and Fed watchers used to evaluate every move the Fed made and interpret whether an action it took was a run-of-the-mill adjustment or a change in monetary policy (beginning to tighten or ease). That changed in February 1994, when the Federal Reserve began telling everyone exactly what its objectives, policies, and actions were going to be and why. Less mysterious perhaps, but a lot saner.

The Federal Reserve is charged with regulating our banking industry and with the health of the economy. It is responsible to but not directly controlled by the Congress.

One of the first things the Fed does is look at the output gap. This is the difference between what GDP actually is and what it would potentially be at **full employment**. When the output gap widens because actual GDP exceeds potential GDP, it means most everyone who wants to work has a job and factories are putting in overtime. The Fed attempts to slow down the economy. When the output gap widens because actual GDP falls below potential GDP, they try to pump up the economy.

Under Chairman Alan Greenspan, the Federal Reserve has been preemptive for the first time in its history, so it now makes adjustments before the output gap critically widens. This is helpful (as long as they continue to read the economy correctly) because it takes the economy about 9 to 12 months to respond to monetary policy, so early action prevents a lot of whipsawing. In its forecasting the Fed evaluates the level of economic activity, the future output gap, and the leading indicators of inflation. Using these inputs the Fed arrives at the desired GDP growth rate. From this rate the Fed then figures its monetary targets—how much the **money supply** needs to grow in order to create the desired economic growth rate. The Fed measures money supply by **M1**, **M2**, and **M3**, and targets the M2 and M3's growth rates. The money supply's target growth rates that are established are then used to determine how much money is required in the banking system.

If the Fed feels the economy is lethargic and needs a boost, and inflation isn't a threat, then easy money is the aim of the day. It is hoped this will stimulate business activity. When the economy is gaining too much momen-

 full employment considered to be around 5.5% unemployment, a level of unemployment that is felt to be transitional (people temporarily out of work or between jobs). If unemployment falls below this level, it is felt inflation pressures will begin to heat up.

tum and looks to begin careening out of control, possibly igniting inflation's destructive forces, money is made scarce in the hope that interest rates will rise, thus discouraging additional business investment.

In Economics 101 we learned that the Fed has three methods of influencing how easy or difficult it is to get the money:

Leading Indicators of Inflation*

✔ Wage pressure.

✔ Commodity prices.

✔ Gold prices.

✔ Capacity utilization.

✔ Institute for Supply Management (ISM) Report.

✔ Exchange rates (dollars tend to fall when there's inflation).

✔ Shape of the yield curve (a steep curve could mean inflation).

*Stan Carnes and Stephen Slifer.

---

money supply

total amount of U.S. currency or money equivalents in the domestic economy, primarily the currency that's in circulation plus deposits in savings and checking accounts. There are four measures of money supply: M1, M2, M3, and L (the last includes longer-term liquid assets).

1. Open market operations.

2. Changing the **discount rate**.

3. Changing reserve requirements.

But since the Fed now tells us what it's doing, it no longer needs to have its actions make its policy statements. So, changing the discount rate or reserve requirements have lost their importance and are no longer monetary policy tools. The Fed finds that open market operations effectively adjust the system.

What do open market operations entail? If the Fed wants to add money to the system (easy policy), it will buy U.S. Treasuries—temporarily or permanently, depending on the add need. Since the Fed pays the sellers for the securities, this adds money to the system. If the Fed needs to re-

M1

currency in circulation, commercial bank demand deposits: NOW (interest-bearing checking) and ATS (automatic transfer from savings) accounts, credit union share drafts, and mutual savings bank demand deposits.

M2

includes M1 plus: overnight repurchase agreements issued by commercial banks, overnight Eurodollars savings accounts time deposits under $100,000, and money market mutual fund shares.

move money from the system (tight policy), it will sell U.S. Treasuries out of its portfolio—temporarily or permanently, depending on the drain need. The buyers pay the Fed money for the securities, thus removing it from the system.

The Fed uses these techniques to establish the **Fed funds rate**, the rate at which banks lend each other money overnight. Most other rates, including fixed income yields, are determined by the Fed funds rate. Short-term rates (maturing in a year or less) are directly affected, while long-term rates are more indirectly affected. This influence is why still keeping track of what the Fed is thinking and doing is of critical importance to fixed income investors.

When a bank needs money to meet its **reserve requirements**, it borrows overnight funds at the Fed funds rate from a bank that has excess reserves. This rate is set by market forces daily, unlike the prime rate and the discount rate, which are reviewed periodically by committees (banks and the Federal Reserve Board, respectively). The Fed funds rate is the parent of all interest rates; all either reflect or respond to it. For this reason the Fed funds rate is viewed as the most sensitive barometer forecasting the future direction of interest rates.

Supply and Demand

No need to beat a dead horse here; we've talked about the supply and demand effect a lot. If there are a lot of bonds floating around (supply ↑), or if folks just don't want them (demand ↓), then interest rates tend to go up in an effort to tempt investors back into the bond market. However, if everyone is scrambling after a handful of bonds, prices will be bid up, and interest rates will fall.

The Dollar

The basic reason the dollar gets stronger is that more people around the globe want to own dollars instead of other currencies, so the price gets bid up. These same people will want to earn interest on their dollars and so demand goes up for dollar-denominated bonds. This influx in demand could push interest rates lower.

A weak dollar means investors are less interested in our currency than they are in other currencies. Demand for dollar-denominated bonds subsequently declines, and interest rates could head higher.

As we mentioned earlier, import and inflation levels also affect interest rate reaction to the dollar helping to boost our economy.

M3
includes M2 plus: time deposits over $100,000 and term repurchase agreements.

discount rate
(1) An annualized rate of return based on the par value of a T-bill. (2) What the Federal Reserve charges member banks on a collateralized loan. It is the base rate that all other interest rates are pegged off.

In the United States we benefit from a maverick factor that can strengthen the dollar that is not enjoyed by other currencies. It is the crisis component. If there is an international crisis or disaster (war, stock market crash, real estate bust, etc.), people tend to run to gold, the U.S. dollar, and U.S. Treasuries because these are viewed as "safe haven" holdings. This psychology helps to give our currency and our bonds a boost often when it is badly needed. It also tends to lower interest rates some at these times.

Employment

Investing in fixed income is kind of perverse because you cheer when people are out of work and cry into your cappuccino when employment is up. This is because unemployment indicates a slow economy, which can lead to lower interest rates and higher bond prices, while high employment screams that the economy is robust and that interest rates will probably head higher with bond prices careening lower.

Fed funds rate
the interest rate a bank will charge another bank that needs an overnight loan.

There are three measures of employment: initial jobless claims, payroll employment, and the unemployment rate.

Initial jobless claims are released every week. Claims tend to foreshadow the other employment measures as

reserve requirement restriction set by the Federal Reserve's Board of Governors that regulates how much of a bank's money can be lent out and how much must be kept on hand in the form of cash and liquid assets. It is a percentage of demand deposits and time deposits.

lagging indicator economic measure that tends to show how the economy was doing a while ago.

coincident indicator economic measure that tends to give readings that reflect how the economy is currently doing.

well as future economic conditions. Due to weather, as well as big corporate or seasonal layoffs, these data can be very volatile; so it is important to look at how claims have trended over time. A rise in jobless claims is bullish for the bond market because it indicates a slowing economy.

The government's monthly employment report—payroll employment and the unemployment rate—is probably the most important piece of information the bond market hears. Combined with the fact that the employment numbers are difficult to predict and are often subject to big revisions, the bond market is poised for some wild rides when this report hits the airwaves. *Note:* The bond market likes a high unemployment rate and a low payroll employment number.

The unemployment rate, a **lagging indicator**, is arrived at through a household survey. It includes groups such as the self-employed and domestics that are ignored in payroll employment. Economists feel the economy is "happy" with 5% to 6% unemployment. If it drops below this level, inflation becomes a concern and the bond market gets real gloomy. Most economists look at the civilian unemployment rate because the military, which has a zero unemployment rate, can distort the reading.

The summer of 1998 experienced 4.5 percent unemployment while inflation remained low. Improvements in productivity contained wage costs, and cheap imports (look at how much you own is "Made in China") helped stifle inflation pressures.

Payroll employment, a **coincident indicator**, is often felt by many to be more accurate because it is compiled from a business survey. It is believed that businesses aren't motivated to embellish reality (i.e., lie) about the employment picture. However, payroll employment can give too strong a reading since people who work at more than one job are counted more than once. The payroll employment release also provides data for different types of jobs, tells us how many hours on average people worked (more hours, more overtime—stronger economy; bad for bonds), and what people were paid per hour (higher average hourly earnings—stronger economy; bad for bonds).

Institute for Supply Management Report on Business (ISM—formerly NAPM)

The report from the Institute for Supply Management (ISM)—formerly the National Association of Purchasing Management (NAPM)—is my favorite indicator because it includes information about a lot of different rates and is more of a **leading indicator**. It tells you what purchasing agents think they will be doing in the near future. It's also very timely, coming out the first working day of the month. This makes the numbers very difficult to forecast, so the bond market can have a dramatic reaction to the ISM release. There are a lot of nuggets of information within this report, and it is highly correlated with GDP growth. (See Table 13.3.)

A reading above 50 indicates an expanding economy, and below 50 indicates an economic contraction.

leading indicator economic measure that tends to presage what the economy is going to do in the future.

TABLE 13.3 Institute for Supply Management (ISM—formerly NAPM) Report of Business, February to May 2002

	February	March	April	May
ISM Survey	54.7	55.6	53.9	55.7
New orders	62.8	65.3	59.0	63.1
Production	61.2	57.8	58.0	58.5
Backlog orders	53.0	62.5	56.0	56.5
Supplier deliveries	52.3	53.1	53.7	53.9
Inventories	39.5	41.2	42.9	45.6
Prices	41.5	51.9	60.3	63.0
Employment	43.8	47.5	46.7	47.3
Export orders	51.1	51.0	51.9	53.3
Import orders	52.0	53.4	55.7	53.6

Source: www.napm.org/ISMReport.

The further you get away from 50 the faster the rate of the expansion or contraction. As the index approaches 60, the bond market becomes very concerned about an overheating economy. When it drops toward 40, it is felt a recession is imminent.

Trade Balance

This indicator was in vogue during the 1980s when we realized our economy was not a closed system. The trade balance shows us how the United States stands versus our international competition. It answers the question, "Are we importing more or exporting more?"

Trade balance = Exports – Imports

Currently, we are in a merchandise trade deficit (about $35 billion a month) and a service trade surplus (about $5 billion a month).

The value of our dollar has a profound effect on this indicator. If the dollar is strong, our trade balance (now a deficit) tends to get worse because the goods we manufacture become more expensive, so exports fall; furthermore, foreign-made products become cheaper, so imports increase. A weak dollar gives domestic companies an edge because our goods become less expensive and more competitive on the international marketplace, thereby helping to swing the trade balance more in our favor.

Business cycle differences between countries can also have an impact on the trade balance. If our country's economy is stronger than our trading partners', we will tend to import more and export less.

Data is also available for our trade positions with individual countries. In case you're curious, Canada is our largest trading partner (23% of U.S. trade), followed by Mexico (14%), Japan (11%), China (8%), and Germany and the United Kingdom (both at 5%).

There are two other trade reports that are released quarterly instead of monthly. One is net exports, which is included in the GDP report and is valuable because it gives us the only inflation-adjusted reading. The current account balance is given scant market attention, but this oversight should be reconsidered because this is the most comprehensive trade measure. It includes goods, services, and financial flows. This last bit is crucial information that's not found anywhere else.

The bond market's reaction to the trade balance release can be a bit schizophrenic. A smaller deficit can strengthen the dollar, which is good news for the bond market. But, a smaller deficit also adds to GDP which is bad news for the bond market. How the bond market will interpret and respond to a shrinking deficit is often more a reflection of the current state of mind than anything else. Bond analysts will often look to see whether the deficit was narrowed by imports slowing (viewed as bullish for bonds), or exports burgeoning (more negative than positive for bonds).

Personal Income and Consumption

In our current "gotta have it all now" cultural milieu, a spike in personal income usually leads to a rise in personal consumption. This is bearish for bonds since it fulfills the classic definition of inflation: too many dollars chasing too few goods. By contrast, a drop in the savings rate is bullish for bonds because it is interpreted to mean that the economy has slowed, causing people to dip into their savings.

Disposable income = Personal income
– Tax payments

Savings rate = Disposable income
– Personal consumption

If, however, the current paradigm shifted and the majority of people started saving instead of spending, a rise in personal income could be bullish for both bonds and stocks as demand for them increased. While this scenario becomes more likely as the bulk of our population ages, it still seems to be far from our current experience.

Consumer Sentiment

The theory goes that if consumers are optimistic they'll spend more, boosting the economy (bond investors hiss). If consumers are pessimistic about the future, they tend to curtail spending, putting brakes on the economy. It's interesting to note that consumers' perceptions mold their actions, so in effect they can make their own predictions come true. This is why gauging how consumers feel about the future is of significant interest to the market.

The University of Michigan Institute for Social Research polls consumers as to how they feel about their current financial position and the future. Since three of the five questions people are asked deal with the future, this is felt to be a leading indicator. The better consumers feel about their finances, the more likely they are to spend money and fuel the economy, and the worse the bond market feels.

Industrial Production/ Capacity Utilization

Industrial production measures how many things were made during the month by U.S. factories, mines, and utilities. (It does not measure services.) It counts the quantity of items produced, not how much they are worth. Since it measures the number not the price, the reading is not distorted by inflation noise; it is a pure measure of economic growth, and accounts for about 42% of the economy.

Capacity utilization tells us how busy our industry is—how much of our sustainable production level is being used. Since sustainable production is lower than the total possible production, capacity utilization could be above 100%. If there is excess capacity, meaning a lot of industry is idle, then the fixed income market doesn't worry. But, when capacity utilization starts cranking along at 82% or higher, the fixed income market senses inflation pressure in the wind. When factories are straining at their top production rates in order to meet strong consumer demand, then producers are able to raise their prices. The bond market, of course, views this with great loathing.

> Industrial production and capacity utilization could increase without injury to the bond market, if productivity expanded or labor costs fell.

Durable Goods Orders

This is an extraordinarily volatile number since civilian aircraft and defense orders are so large and sporadic that they can knock this number all over the place. Many market watchers view these components as noise that doesn't contribute to identifying the underlying trends in the general economy; therefore, they look at durable goods orders ex-transportation and defense. They also average out the past few months' revised numbers in order to get a relevant reading, because revisions can be huge. Economists note that durable goods orders tend to turn down about 8 to 12 months before an economic downturn and turn up about a month or so before the bottom of a recession.

Also released in this report is data on durable goods shipments and orders backlog. An increase in shipments (synonymous with sales) could mean the economy is heating up (bad for bonds). A big orders backlog can be inflationary (bad for bonds). Note that if these readings become higher because of increased productivity or because more production capability has come on line, this would decrease inflation pressures, so bonds would not be concerned.

Other Indicators and Reports

Corporate Profits. A rise in corporate profits is usually good for stocks and bad for bonds. However, since this is a lagging indicator, its usefulness is limited since the news is probably already reflected in the financial markets. It really has an effect only if it doesn't confirm the accepted economic wisdom.

Housing Starts/Building Permits. New construction is affected by the economy and mortgage rates. Since this is the factor that hits us closest to home, it tends to be one of the first indicators that tells us when the economy is falling into or pulling out of a recession. Building a house also has a multiplier effect because of all the big-ticket appliances (furniture and stuff) one has to buy for the place. For these reasons, the bond market finds this data very interesting. A significant rise in this indicator can lead to a sell-off in the bond market because it could indicate that the economy is on the upswing, which could lead to higher interest rates. The market views the single-family data as a more trustworthy indicator than the multifamily numbers because single-family data is less volatile. Building permits give a good clue as to what next month's starts will be.

> A single-family house is counted as one start. One 100-apartment building is counted as 100 starts.

New Home Sales. This is another very volatile number. Contained in this report is the average and median sale price. This tidbit is interesting to look at because the trend gives a good inflation reading. The report also mentions how many houses are for sale and how long it's taking houses to sell; the more months it takes for houses to sell, the slower the economy. It's also fun to look at the geographic breakdown to get a feel for what's going on in other parts of the country.

Beware: New home sales can be subject to heavy revisions. Because of the data's volatility and revisions, the bond market reaction tends to be muted even when the market is surprised by the data.

Construction Spending. This data recounts what happened two months ago. Since it is such old news, the financial markets largely ignore this reading. It's viewed more as a confirmation and has an effect only if it doesn't line up.

Retail Sales. A jarring increase in retail sales doesn't bode well for the bond market because it means folks are spending money, which indicates a strong economy. Slow sales would tend to be bullish for the bond market. This number is usually looked at **ex-autos** because this is the data that the Commerce Department uses in the GDP consumption calculation. The number is hard to predict, and watch out for the revisions to previous months' releases. This number is also not adjusted for inflation and doesn't include services. Even with all its problems, the market is quite interested in this number; and since there can be big surprises, the market reaction can be pronounced.

> **ex-autos** short for excluding automobile sales.

> Retail sales data is about 60% durables and 40% nondurables.

Car Sales. This report counts the number of new and used cars/trucks sold during the month. The report's timeliness gives it punch. Data is given for total domestic sales and is broken down by manufacturer. It also presents the sales figures' year-over-year increase/decrease. The Commerce Department publishes seasonal factors before this release, so you can correct for any seasonal distortions. For example, in northern regions, winter sales could be down not because of any economic slowdown, but because snow buried the cars on the lot and kept folks home in front of the fire.

A pickup in car sales can indicate a strengthening economy that could pose a threat to the bond market. But, a pickup in used car sales that is not seen in new car sales can mean a slowing economy.

Factory Orders, Shipments, and Inventories. This report measures durables and nondurables goods. This is a lagging indicator since it takes companies, manufacturers included, a while to recognize and respond to a new trend in the economy. So this number tends not to change until general sentiment has already swung around and been digested by both the business and financial markets. Furthermore, most of this data has been seen already in the durable goods orders release. Therefore, the bond market doesn't react much to this release. Some economists like to calculate the inventories/sales ratio (use the shipment number for sales); if the ratio rises, the economy is felt to be slowing.

Business Inventories/Sales. This report contains mostly known information by the time it comes out. The only real new piece of information is retail inventories. Therefore, this indicator doesn't get much notice or reaction from the financial markets.

Index of Leading Economic Indicators. A school of thought holds that when the Index of Leading Economic Indicators (LEI) data changes in the same direction for three consecutive months, it signals a shift in the economic tide. The individual components making up the index have already been released and factored into the market. Therefore, use this number as a summary that's put together for your convenience. The components are:

- ✔ Average workweek—manufacturing.
- ✔ Building permits.
- ✔ Change in unfilled orders—durables.
- ✔ Consumer expectations.
- ✔ Initial unemployment claims.
- ✔ New orders for consumer goods.
- ✔ Plant and equipment orders.
- ✔ Real M2.
- ✔ Sensitive material prices.
- ✔ Stock prices (S&P 500).
- ✔ Vendor performance.

Historically, the LEI has turned down about 10 months before economic tops and turned up a month or two ahead of economic recoveries.

There is also the Index of Coincident Indicators and the Index of Lagging Indicators, neither of which individually merits much more than a passing glance; old news usually isn't pivotal news in the markets. What is of interest to economists is the ratio of coincident to lagging indicators. This often registers economic shifts even before the LEI series does. This is because the coincident index will show change several months before the lagging index changes. Therefore, the coincident/lagging ratio will tend to rise at the beginning of an economic expansion and fall near the peak.

TECHNICAL FACTORS

For those of you who love details, live to draw graphs, thrive on the quantifiable, or tend to overanalyze, **technical analysis** is for you. You'll want to delve in a lot deeper than the smattering we'll cover here.

Technicals are analogous to betting on baseball using only stats. There are a million ways to approach technical analysis. There's always some new funky technical that's supposed to give you an edge over the rest of the market because it's a nuance no one else has thought of yet. You can use technicals to follow anything that's quantifiable: copper prices, muni bond futures, car sales, corporate new issue volume. . . . The procedure remains the same regardless of what you're looking at. It's yet another example of humans' irrepressible urge to find order in chaos. Technicians graph the data they are interested in to identify trends in the visual representation. This type of analysis is employed to help the investor time the market. In other words, technicians are hoping to uncover signals that indicate that it is time either to buy or to sell a type of investment.

Technicals provide you with "if, then" statements that fundamental analysis does not. It tells you that if you experience a quantified amount of pain or pleasure (losses

technical analysis
studying graphic patterns of financial data (prices, yields, averages, trading volume, etc.) in an attempt to predict future patterns and trends.

> When I was an analyst, I referred to myself as a techno-fundamentalist (I think I made this up). What I meant was that I analyzed the fundamental data to generate my market forecast, and then would use technicals to confirm or deny my read. It was my attempt not to get too emotional about a point of view and to stay disciplined.

or gains), then bail out. By establishing buy and sell levels, technical analysis can help protect you from emotional reactions and discipline you from relying on the subjective point of view. Technicians feel their approach provides you with a systematic way of skewing the risk/reward trade-off in your favor.

Fixed income investors often use technicals to help identify patterns that may point to where interest rates are going. One way charts are used is to show the market's momentum. Has the market shifted from bullish to bearish? For example, in the equity market, if price/earnings (P/E) ratios have gotten historically high and a look at the advance/decline ratio begins to show more declines than advances, technicians could read this as an indication to sell. This example also shows how you can combine fundamental and technical analysis to get a reading. In addition, people overlay the patterns from different types of technical charts to see how the pictures support or refute each other. It's similar to looking through a stranger's photo album and then trying to surmise the story of that person's life from the pictures.

Here's an example of how it can pay to be well read in the fundamentals when you're trying to piece together the pictures and come up with a prediction for interest rates. The economy is muddling along at a comfortable pace, but one day you notice that housing starts have jumped higher and gold prices have broken out (moved above resistance—to be explained shortly). Hmm, you say; the economy may be heating up, sparking inflation and sending interest rates higher. You begin to get excited about selling your bonds and then buying them back when interest rates are at higher levels. Then you remember reading about how lumber prices have fallen, and that combined with lower mortgage rates could be the reason for the housing start increase. You also recall that South African miners are out on strike, thus boosting gold prices. You calm down and put your broker's number away.

A word to the wise about the strategy being considered to sell bond holdings and buy them back when interest rates move higher. Only do this when you are convinced the market will be moving considerably higher soon. The reason is there is a cost to being out of the bond market; you will not be earning the interest during this period. The longer it takes for rates to move higher, the higher rates will have to go to compensate you for the interest you lost while being on the sidelines. When you decide to put on this trade, make sure you are being cautious and have conviction. Also, while sidelined, reinvest the proceeds in an interest-bearing cash equivalent, such as money markets or **commercial paper**.

commercial paper
short-term securities with maturities from 2 to 270 days; issued by banks, insurance companies, and corporations that have cash to lend out.

When "reading" technicals, use caution and common sense. Look at a lot of data. Can you come up with a solid story that supports your prediction? This is truly a realm that is more art than science. All the patterns and relationships we're going to discuss are only generalities and possibilities and should be viewed as such and within the context of what else in going on in the world. People develop their own rules and gimmicks when playing this game. I like to look at the Treasury bond futures, CRB index, **spot** dollar, and gold, but every technician develops personal favorites. In technical analysis, people usually graph (aka **chart**) the high price and low price of the day as well as where the price

spot
current price.

chart
graphing data to create visual representation of trends; used in technical analysis.

close
price of the last trade for the day.

futures
a contract agreeing to buy or sell a certain amount of something (e.g., bonds, gold, cattle) at a set price on a specific date.

support
price level where in the past a security has tended to stop falling and rebound to higher levels; acts as a floor.

resistance
price level where in the past a security has tended to stop rising and then falls to lower levels; acts as a ceiling.

was when the market **closed** at the end of the day. Since bonds trade over-the-counter (OTC) 24 hours a day, the close is considered when Treasury **futures** close in Chicago (2 P.M. Central Time, 3 P.M. East Coast, 12 noon West Coast, etc.).

Okay, let's look at a few of the well-known patterns.

Moving Averages

One of my favorites is moving averages. It's a way to smooth out the noisy blips and bumps in the market so that it's easier to see the trend. You look at the average data for the trailing (past) 30 days, 90 days, 6 months, 12 months, and so on. You can look at this type of average for just about anything that's quantifiable.

As you can see in Figure 13.5, when the actual data crosses through the moving average it can signal a change in the trend.

Trend

Technicals can help you identify when a trend is being established. A rising trend line (Figure 13.6) connects the bottoms, and a falling trend line connects the tops. When a trend line is penetrated it can mean the beginning of a reversal.

Support and Resistance

Another useful and simple trend finder is establishing **support** or **resistance**. When a price breaks through resistance, it could be time to buy; and when it breaks through support, to could be time to sell. (See Figure 13.7.)

For example, if the market's heading up and you want to see if it'll keep heading higher, draw a straight line that connects the tops. This is known as ascending tops. When you extend the line connecting tops into the future, the prices it intersects become resistance. On any day when the market price (usually the closing price) goes above the resistance line, it's said to be a

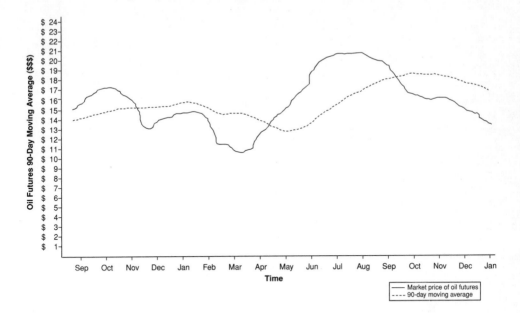

FIGURE 13.5 Moving average.

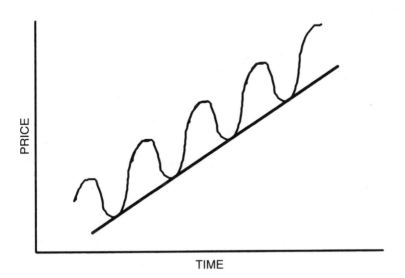

FIGURE 13.6 Rising trend line.

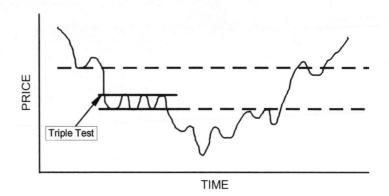

FIGURE 13.7   Support and resistance.

breakout. This means the price has cut free of its trading range and could gain momentum and move significantly higher.

If you think interest rates may be heading higher, pushing prices down, and you are looking for a signal to sell, you can draw a line connecting the bottoms. If the price doesn't move below the support line, it may bounce off and head higher and you can stay put and keep watching. It could continue up, or it could go lower and test the support line again. However, if the price violates support and moves below it, it may have broken out of its trading range and may continue to move lower. It could be a signal to sell.

Triple Test

You can also try using the triple top or bottom pattern to establish support or resistance. If a price tests the same spot three times and can't get above the top or below the bottom, then this theory says it won't. But if it does break through, supposedly it's a breakout and it could either skyrocket or plummet depending on the direction it's headed. You can see this in Figure 13.7. It tested the level three times and couldn't get through; but then it did and fell to much lower levels.

This discussion reminded me of a conversation I had during the summer of 1998 with a brilliant, fringe-thinking friend of mine, Rodney Brown, a bond trader and salesman who also is very into patterns. He felt we were experiencing what he termed a *Great Gatsby* phenomenon. The late 1920s were characterized by a technological abundance (industrial revolution) that created an environment of material prosperity and spiritual poverty. He saw parallels between Hoover's unwillingness to save Australian banks and the United States' current reticence to contribute to the International Monetary Fund (IMF). He was using this repeated pattern to support an extremely bearish outlook for the financial markets. This example demonstrates how technicians can also look for patterns in cultural and psychological behavior. Nothing is off-limits to technicians. Turned out Mr. Brown was right.

Double Tops and Bottoms

This is similar to the triple test. A double top consists of two tops that are separated by a valley. The second top is characterized by lower volume. The breakout usually has stronger volume than the second top.

Rounding Pattern

Another standard pattern is the rounding top or bottom (Figure 13.8). This pattern generally takes a long time to get established. When you want to identify this pattern is just over the crest or through the trough as it begins to shift its momentum and move in the other direction. Just over a crest would be a signal to sell and just through the trough would be a signal to buy.

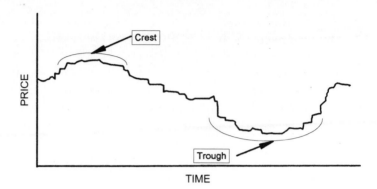

FIGURE 13.8   Rounding top and bottom.

Head and Shoulders

The pattern in Figure 13.9 is known as the head and shoulders for obvious reasons. Some technicians feel this is one of the most reliable patterns. It can appear at both market tops and bottoms. The number of shoulders and slope of the line can vary (the slope in Figure 13.9 is horizontal). Head and shoulders patterns are indicators of trend reversals.

The volume is usually quite heavy in the formation of the first shoulder. The tip-off is when volume

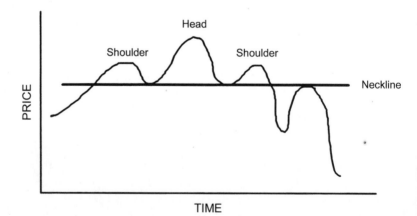

FIGURE 13.9   Head and shoulders.

falls off as the second shoulder is being formed. The neckline connects the bottom of the two shoulders. It is generally felt the line must project at least 3% through the neckline before it indicates a market reversal. The deeper the incursion the more profound the reversal. For a market bottom, the pattern looks as if it is standing on its head and is known as an inverse head and shoulders.

Relative Strength Index (RSI)

The relative strength index is also used to indicate trend reversals. It is found by dividing one index by another. So, a rising line indicates the numerator is outperforming; a falling line indicates the denominator is going to outperform. If you are looking at an RSI for a particular indicator, you can assume that it is in the numerator and the direction of the line shows its strength.

Dead Cat Bounce

I love the pattern known as the "dead cat bounce" (Figure 13.10) if for no other reason than for its imaginative moniker.

It means that it looked like the price would head higher, but it just fizzled and went *pluuhhh*. . . . I guess its originator felt dead cats wouldn't bounce very high. Let's hope she or he didn't test the theory. This technical pattern is used more to confirm what has already happened, although looking at it you might say, "Oh, yeah, this baby's run out of steam. It's not heading higher for a while."

If this technical appetizer has whetted your appetite for more, go for it. There's more information at your library. Many big cities have business libraries that have even more information. The World Wide Web is another resource with a lot of information. It's a great place to learn how to subscribe to a bunch of technical gurus'

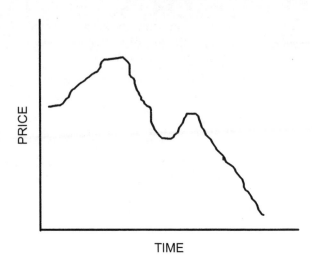

FIGURE 13.10 Dead cat bounce.

newsletters. On the Internet you can also get hooked up with an investment club that specializes in technicals.

Technicals can be a lot of fun. Some see it as absolute dogma; others see it as being as effective as blowing into a hurricane. If you can keep your perspective, technical analysis can be another useful tool in your investment garden shed.

PART FOUR

FIXED INCOME INVESTMENT STRATEGIES

Chapter

14

How to Buy

Before we get into investing strategies, we need to cover some trading tactics you can use in the fixed income secondary market. (For information about buying in the primary market see Chapter 9.) You can avoid a number of costly mistakes and also sound really smart by absorbing the next few paragraphs.

When you want to know a stock's price, you get a quote. However, with bonds you don't ask for a quote; instead, you ask for the bond's **bid/ask spread**. The **bid** is always lower than the **ask**.

Bid		Ask
101	/	101¼

The bid is on the left.   The ask is on the right.

The bid on the left, 101, is the highest price that someone is willing to pay for that bond. The ask price on the right, 101¼, is the lowest price that any current bondholder is willing to sell that bond for. Table 14.1 shows a sequence of bid/ask spreads.

You may be told a spread like:

$$\frac{1}{8} \; / \; \frac{1}{4}$$

This is traders' shorthand. They do this to save time by not having to say the whole numbers that usually both parties know anyway. The whole numbers are called the price's handle. In this case, if you don't know where the bond's

> **bid/ask spread**
> difference between what someone wants to buy the bond for and what someone wants to sell it for. An example of a bid/ask spread is 100-29/101-01. The ask is always higher than the bid. When the buyer and seller agree on a price, there is a trade—the bonds are sold and ownership transferred.

bid

the highest price anyone is willing to pay for a security in order to buy it. For example, you may say, "I want to earn $7^{1}/_{2}\%$," which for the bond you're interested in might mean a price of 101. Your bid for the bond is 101. That is the price you propose to the present bond owner.

ask

the lowest price anyone who owns the security is willing to accept as the selling price. It is the price the bond owner is "asking" for the bonds. This is also known as the offer because it is the price the owner is offering the bonds for to potential buyers.

TABLE 14.1 Bid/Ask Recap			
U.S. Treasury $5^{5}/_{8}\%$ 5/15/08			
July 1, 2002			
11:02	106-18 / 106-18+	11:01	106-17+ / 106-18+
11:02	106-17+ / 106-18+	11:01	106-18+ / 106-19
11:01	106-17+ / 106-18+	11:00	106-18+ / 106-19
11:01	106-17 / 106-19	11:00	106-19 / 106-20
11:01	106-18 / 106-18+	11:00	106-18+ /106-19+
11:01	106-17+ / 106-18+	11:00	106-18 / 106-19
11:01	106-18 / 106-18+	11:00	106-18+ / 106-19
11:01	106-17+ / 106-18+		

been trading, you'll have to ask what the handle is. If they say the handle is 99, that means the spread is:

$$99^{1}/_{8} \quad / \quad 99^{1}/_{4}$$

If you need a refresher, this was covered in Part Two.

The bid/ask spread can be as wide as 3 points or more; for example, $103^{1}/_{4}$ / $106^{1}/_{8}$. A wide spread indicates the bond is illiquid and is inactively traded. Conversely, highly liquid bonds like U.S. Treasuries can have a spread as small as a plus ($^{1}/_{64}$): $99^{11}/_{16}$ / $99^{11}/_{16}{}^{+}$.

If you decide to buy the bond, you can either **hit** the ask or you can put in a bid at the price you would like to pay. Conversely, if you're going to sell your bond, you can either hit the bid or you can submit an asking price. Don't waste people's time by putting in a ludicrous bid or ask. It should be somewhere near the market price.

Here's an example of how this works: The bond you are interested in is $101^{3}/_{4}$ / $102^{1}/_{4}$; but you are willing to pay $101^{7}/_{8}$, so you put in the bid at that price. The spread is now $101^{7}/_{8}$ / $102^{1}/_{4}$. Your bid is now the highest. Table 14.2 is a snapshot of all the bids and asks at the time you put in your bid.

In the table, the bid and ask are the bold prices. They are the highest bid and lowest ask of all the inquiries en-

tered. If the bond is listed on an exchange, then all entered bids and asks are kept there. If the bond is traded
over-the-counter, each trader that trades the bond keeps
his or her own bid/ask ledger. Note that listed bonds can
also be traded OTC.

When you are given a bid/ask spread, the prices are
for normal-sized trades, meaning trades of $20,000 face
value or more. If you are interested in prices for lots
smaller than this, you'll find they're different than the
bid/ask indicates. You'll have to pay a higher price than
shown in the bid/ask spread when you're buying, and
you'll receive a lower price when selling. Remember, if
there's a chance that you might have to sell your bonds before they mature, try not to buy small lots because they are
illiquid. Investment firms do not want to get stuck with
diddly little pieces, and since they don't really want to own
them, traders offer significantly lower prices for them.
However, if a firm does get stuck with a dinky bond-o-let,
sometimes you can get really good deals on them (check

hit

trader slang
meaning you
accept the price
and agree to
exchange money
for the bond.
Short for saying,
"Yes, I will
buy/sell at that
price. Let's trade
the bonds."

More Bond Lingo

A bond's description refers to the month it matures.
The month is abbreviated:

Month	*Abbreviation*
January	Jan
February	Feb
March	Mar
April	Apr
May	May
June	Jun
July	Jul
August	Aug (pronounced Augie)
September	Sep
October	Oct (pronounced Ocht)
November	Nov (pronounced Novie)
December	Dec (rhymes with niece)

Bids				Asks		
TABLE 14.2 Trader's Bond Ledger						
				103	for	$25,000
				102 7/8	for	$50,000
				102 3/4	for	$30,000
				102 5/8	for	$15,000
				102 5/8	for	$110,000
				102 1/2	for	$20,000
Current bid/ask spread→	**$25,000**	@	**101 7/8**	**/ 102 1/4**	**for**	**$40,000**
	$25,000	@	101 3/4			
	$25,000	@	101 1/2			
	$50,000	@	101 1/2			
	$125,000	@	101			

the yield-to-maturity). Go ahead and buy these tasty morsels, as long as you plan to hold them to maturity.

This brings us to another point. Sometimes investment firms will have positions in their inventory they want to unload. This is called having an **axe**. It could be they've owned the bonds for a long time, or they own too much of that type of bond (maturity, coupon, sector, etc.) in their **book**. Perhaps they have to move the bonds to make room for something else. You see, a dealer's inventory is like when you put your belongings in U-Store-It. There's a limited amount of space, and it's costly to keep stuff there. So, both you and the trader want only the most valuable things in there.

Whatever the reason, the bonds are **on special**. Since the trader is highly motivated to sell this position, he or she may let them go cheap. Just make sure the reason that the bonds are cheap isn't because the issuer's in trouble; do your research before you buy. Specials are often gone quickly, so you don't have a lot of time for research. That's why it's good to stay up on what's going on in the economy and bond market, and to specialize in a type of bond or bond sector; then you can quickly use your common sense and experience to make a judgment call on the bonds. Even when you use an investment adviser it's important to understand the investment enough so you

axe

trader jargon (short for "axe to grind"). It means traders have something they want to get rid of.

book

record of the bond trader's positions—what bonds are owned (long) and what are short. Similar to your portfolio statement.

know what questions to ask to make sure the investment is right for you at this time. It makes your adviser's job easier and will give you added peace of mind.

When a price is finally agreed to, don't whip out the pen and start scrawling a check just yet. First, the accrued interest needs to be calculated; the investment firm will do it for you and will include the accrued interest in the purchase price on your confirm. (See Figure 14.1.) This is the interest the former owner earned, but that hasn't been paid yet. Since the new owner will receive the undeserved interest in the next semiannual interest payment, the buyer pays the seller the interest earned to the point when the bond trades hands.

The confirm should arrive sometime during the settlement period. This is the time between the **trade date** and the **settlement date**. Different types of bonds have different settlement periods. What is normal settlement for that type of security is known as a regular way settlement. (See Table 14.3.)

Unlike stocks, when you trade bonds you don't pay a commission. Instead, in the bond market, when you're buying the price is marked up. When you're selling, the price you receive is marked down. This markup or markdown is how the broker/dealer is paid. Often this payment is transparent to the investor because it is included in the price.

Also unlike stocks, bonds aren't always available when you want them. With listed stocks, there are always shares available to buy. With bonds, it's best to be open and

on special
the bonds are cheap because the owner is desperate to unload them.

trade date
when the seller promises to sell the bond to a buyer, at an agreed price.

settlement date
when the money for the trade is due. If it is not received, the trade is canceled.

Transaction(s)	Trade Date	Branch	Account	Type C	IR No.	CUSIP No.	Market	Cap S/U	PE	Due Date
YOU SOLD	5/22/199	358	99999	1	2	146|1159611195-SB-2	6|E	|S		5/22/06
Quantity	Price		Description				Reference No.			Amount
10,000	82 3/4		SAM AND BEN ENTERPRISES INC				61249			8,338.83
			SUB DEB REG DTD 3/12/1992							
			YIELD 9.526MTY							
			DUE 03/01/2002 06.500% MS 01							
			NEXT CALL: 03/01/01 AT 104.550							
			SAME DAY SETTLEMENT							
Total Quantity	Gross Amount		Commission or Mark-Up/Down		Accrued Bond Interest		SEC Fee	Service Fee		Amount
10,000	8,275.00				59.98			3.85		8,338.83

FIGURE 14.1 Confirm.

TABLE 14.3 Regular Way Settlements	
Type	Settlement Period
U.S. Treasuries	Next day
Municipals	3 Business days
Corporates	3 Business days
Convertibles	3 Business days
Mutual funds	Next day

look for a type of bond and an acceptable yield. If you're looking for a specific bond and won't accept a similar alternative, you may be disappointed. Much of an issue's securities are squirreled away in accounts, and there's no way to find out where they are. So, when you're looking for an issue, there simply may not be any available at any price.

An investment firm may present an interesting bond to you, and you will probably find it difficult to locate the same bond at different firms to compare yields. What you can do is ask the firm that has the offering (and if you're buying in size inquire at other firms) if it has bonds with similar ratings and maturities and what their yield-to-maturity is (yield-to-worst if it's callable).

Let's say you're looking for a specific type of bond for your portfolio. There are three places investment firms can look for bonds to fulfill security requests:

1. Their own inventory.
2. Other firms' inventories.
3. Client accounts.

If you're selling a bond, it is a good idea to get multiple bids. (I probably wouldn't go to the trouble for small trades. You'll probably spend more on phone calls than you'll save.) You can get very different bids from different dealers. There are many reasons for the discrepancy. One is that one dealer may already own a lot of bonds like yours and not want any more; or a different dealer may really want your bonds and be willing to pay up for them. A third explanation could be a greedy broker.

There have been a number of articles written about how difficult it is to price bonds since there is no exchange where they trade. You can call a number of investment firms or look in the newspaper at benchmark Treasuries and the few listed bonds. Recently, another alternative has become available, and it could prove to be a boon for individual investors. Online trading, which was only the realm of institutional traders, is now becoming available to the rest of us. These online services offer another resource to get pricing information.

In conclusion, when you are buying bonds you need to evaluate yields; when you are selling a bond you want the highest price.

DO I BUY A PREMIUM OR A DISCOUNT?

There is an opportunity in the bond market I call the Premium Paradox. It is a result of how bonds are priced and demonstrates how the mass psychology in the bond market drives most bond investors.

Almost all investors approach buying bonds quite literally, meaning they refuse to pay a premium for a bond. In a cloud of missed opportunity and misunderstanding, they feel paying a premium means you paid too much for a bond. You and I know that all a premium price tells you is that interest rates have fallen since that bond was issued.

Because so many investors have their ignorance lead them away from premium bonds, sometimes these bonds will have higher yields than other similar bonds. So, keep your eyes peeled and you may find a good deal. As always, if the yield seems unusually high, double-check the financial health of the issuer just to make sure that shaky credit is not the reason for the additional yield. If it's not and the only reason the yield is higher appears to be investors' reticence to buy premiums, snap it up. And don't forget premium bonds offer investors another benefit: Their higher coupons can help protect their price from falling as much as other bonds when interest rates rise. Bonds with large premiums are known as cushion bonds because the extra coupon size significantly buffers the price. The Premium Paradox means that while a premium bond's price may make it appear more expensive to the untrained eye, it can actually be cheaper (i.e., offer more yield) and be less volatile.

So, the next logical question is: Should you buy discount bonds? The answer is yes. Discount bonds offer you a nice way to buy a larger face value for the amount of money you are investing.

For example, you could buy $20,000 face value for $8,000. Remember, this does not mean you're getting a great deal. You have to look at the yield, not the price, to determine that. But it does mean that you can buy a significant face value even if you don't have piles of cash lying around. Discount bonds enable you to plunk down a smaller amount and still get into the game.

Deep-discount bonds are also more price-sensitive to interest rate moves. This is a desirable trait when interest rates are headed lower because discount bonds will appreciate more in value. Of course, the trait is rotten when rates are rising because discount bonds lose more value, so you may want to avoid deep-discount bonds when interest rates look to be heading to higher ground—unless, of course, you are going to hold the bond until maturity; then price moves in the secondary market don't concern you.

I think that bonds are kind of like people. The discount bonds are the kids; they look attractive, and have a lot of appeal. Having a lot of energy, they tend to jump around and overreact to a lot of what life throws at them. Premium bonds, on the other hand, are the old folks. They react slowly and a bit more wisely to events. To some they may not appear that alluring at first glance, but a sharp eye sees that a superficial look can be deceiving. They've got a lot of appeal and much of interest to offer.

Chapter 15

What to Buy

A s the self-help gurus say, "You have to know your-self first." This sage mantra holds true for invest-ing, too.

The first thing you have to do when you're formulat-ing an investment plan is identify:

- ✔ **Risk.** How much risk am I comfortable with?
- ✔ **Goals.** What am I saving for?
- ✔ **Situation Now.** What am I currently invested in? What are my fixed and my variable living expenses?

You can start with a grid that includes all of the fixed income alternatives. (See Figure 15.1.)

Once you identify your investment needs, use them as a filter to screen out inappropriate alternatives. (See Figure 15.2.)

You can then use the projection you have formulated for where the economy and interest rates are headed to identify the **asset classes** you should be invested in: stocks, bonds, or cash; short or long end of the yield curve; fixed coupon or adjustable rate; and so on. (See Figure 15.3.)

It is like overlaying transparencies in biology class— the skeletal system, the circulatory system, the digestive

 asset class
grouping of like securities. Tax-exempt securities, floating rate notes, zero coupon bonds, and international bonds are examples of asset classes.

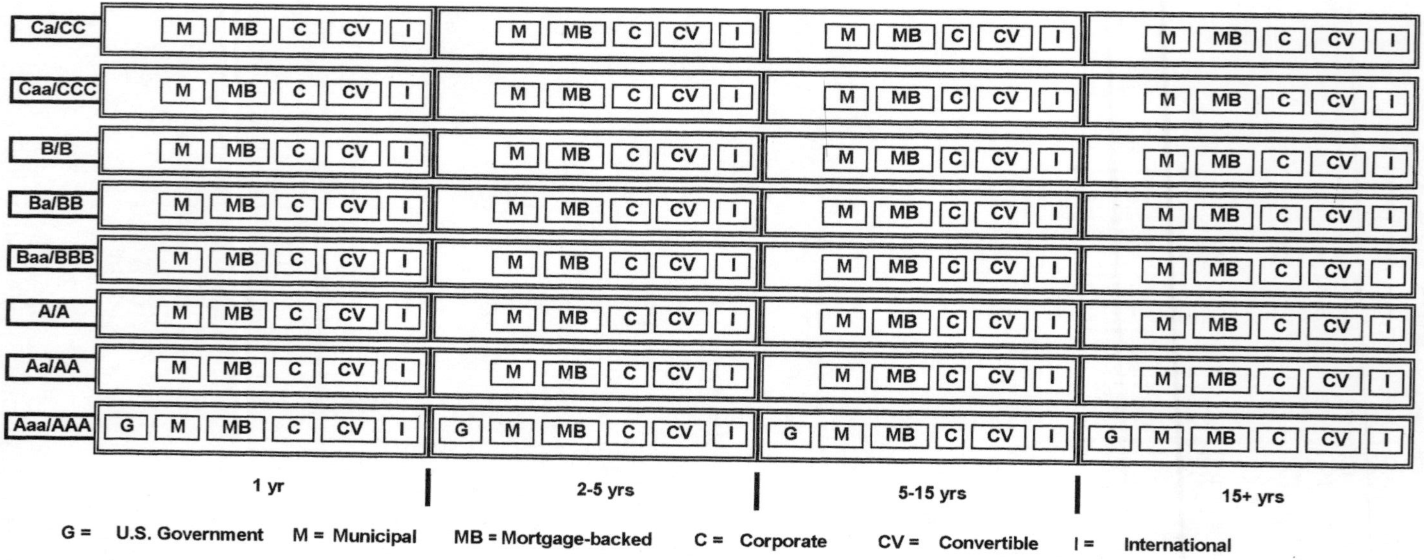
Ca/CC
Caa/CCC
B/B
Ba/BB
Baa/BBB
A/A
Aa/AA
Aaa/AAA
G
M
MB
C
CV
I
1 yr
2-5 yrs
5-15 yrs
15+ yrs
G = U.S. Government
M = Municipal
MB = Mortgage-backed
C = Corporate
CV = Convertible
I = International

FIGURE 15.1 Bond alternatives grid.

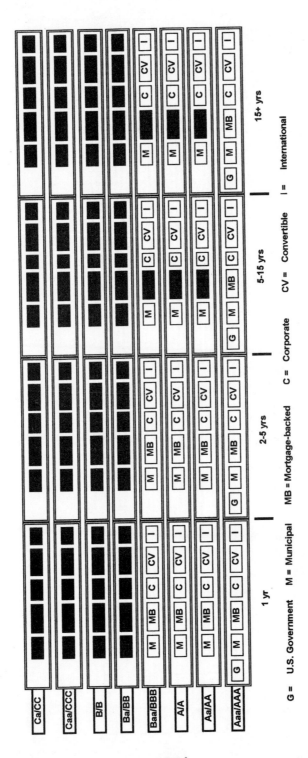

FIGURE 15.2 Needs filter.

G = U.S. Government   M = Municipal   MB = Mortgage-backed   C = Corporate   CV = Convertible   I = International

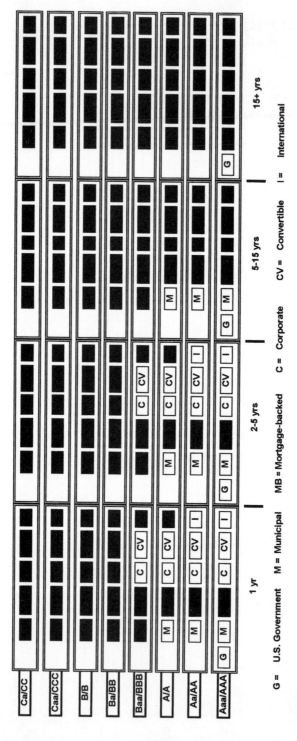

FIGURE 15.3 Economic filter.

G = U.S. Government   M = Municipal   MB = Mortgage-backed   C = Corporate   CV = Convertible   I = International

system, and so forth—only here you use your investment profile and economic projections to eliminate inappropriate investments until you are left with the best alternatives for you to pick from. Looking at the remaining types of investments, use your common sense to determine how much should be invested in each type. Then select the individual securities that will fill in these blanks.

You can answer the following questions to help you create your own investment matrix.

- ✔ What do you currently own and are there holes you need to fill?
- ✔ When do you need this money?
- ✔ Are you going to hold the bonds until they mature?
- ✔ How much money do you need to earn?
- ✔ What kind of risks can you take?
- ✔ How much volatility in the secondary market are you comfortable with? (This question is relevant only if you'll need to sell.)
- ✔ Do you want some participation in the equity's price movement?
- ✔ Do you need tax-free income?
- ✔ Do you want to diversify outside this country or does that pose too much risk for you?

I am pretty risk-averse. In order to literally sleep at night I need to have enough cash saved to be able to pay the mortgage for a year. Then, I have friends who are comfortable spending everything and living paycheck to paycheck, so that they have to borrow money in order to pay their taxes.

Would you be comfortable with an investment that could double your money but could also go down to "pennies on the dollar"? Or would you prefer an investment that pays less income than others but the income is more assured?

I approach each different type of savings with a different temperament. Our rainy-day mortgage fund is stashed in a money market fund. Our ordinary savings is in stock and bond funds, cash, and occasionally gold. The mix depends on my economic outlook. Our retirement savings and the kids' college funds are currently all in stocks, high-yield bonds, and international funds. I feel I can be more risky in these last savings categories because we have more time to ride out the peaks and valleys. However, as time marches on and we get close to retirement and college bills, I will retrench and become a lot more conservative with these accounts.

My dad, who is one of the only people who invested in IBM in the 1960s and lost money (right idea, bad timing advice), always told me, "Only invest as much as you can afford to lose." I agree this is true when you're considering investing in risky ventures.

How do you know how risky a bond is? Well, look at the duration. A bond with a 10-year duration could decline in value 30% if interest rates rise 300 basis points. (By this I mean a change from 7% to 10%; see page 149.) If you're risk-averse, buy bonds with lower durations. However, if you're not averse to risk and think interest rates are going down, buy bonds with longer durations.

If you are a very risk-averse investor, perhaps you should plan to invest only money that you won't need. Then invest this money in bonds that fit your risk and financial profile and hold the bonds until maturity.

As we went over in Part Three, bonds tend to be riskier if they have lower ratings, lower coupons, and longer maturities. You also assume additional risk when you invest in nondollar investments. If you are risk-averse, limit your exposure in these categories and focus on bonds with higher ratings, larger coupons, and shorter maturities. These tend to be less risky, more defensive alternatives. Active management can add another dimension of uncertainty and potential misjudgment. But this leads our discussion into a conundrum, because inaction is also an action. By not doing anything, you can miss opportunities which can be costly. So, don't become paralyzed by the possibilities. Think about the risks you are comfortable with, assess the risks involved with different alternatives, use your own common sense, and then diversify.

Our experience during this century has shown it is better to take a long-term view. If Sally had bought a 30-year Treasury for $30,000 in January 1987, that July after interest rates had risen substantially the investment would have been worth only $20,000. If she sold then and reinvested the proceeds in a money market earning a constant 2%, her investment would be worth $24,916.97 in July 1998. If she had ridden out the price collapse and stayed invested in the Treasury, her investment would have been worth $36,159.38 in July 1998.

If you are a risk taker and like to trade actively, be disciplined. Have trigger points where you will sell a portion of the investment. For example, sell 25% of the holding when the bond falls 10%, sell another 25% when it falls 20%, and buy it back if the technicals are positive when it's fallen 75%. Again, set these parameters based on your own risk tolerance. The more conservative you are, the sooner you will begin selling and the more you will sell of the position.

When setting the trigger points, think about how much you are willing to lose. This will dictate what price levels you should sell at. It's a good idea to flag a point about 10% higher than your selling levels to call your adviser and discuss what is going on. Talk about what is causing the market's fall and different scenarios for the future. Is this a short-term correction? Will prices rebound? Or is this the beginning of an extended bear market? At 5% above your drop-out rate, you could call and put in a stop loss order. This means you set a price or yield level (your adviser can calculate the price) where you want the broker to sell the bonds. The bonds will not be sold until the market price hits your mark, triggering the sale. Investors put in stop loss orders so they don't miss the market. They may be going on vacation or just not paying attention. It'd be too bad to miss the market just because your broker couldn't find you.

WHAT ARE YOUR GOALS?

The possibilities here are endless. Brainstorm and then prioritize the goals you come up with. Then estimate when you'll need the money and how much you'll probably need. Here are some of the items you may want to save for:

- ✔ Retirement.
- ✔ Education (career development, private school, college).
- ✔ House (primary, vacation, investment property).
- ✔ Unemployment.
- ✔ Eldercare (taking care of parents).
- ✔ Starting a business.
- ✔ Charitable trust.
- ✔ Travel.
- ✔ Cars.
- ✔ Wedding.
- ✔ Hobbies (boats, horses, collecting exotic butterflies).

WHERE ARE THE ECONOMY AND INTEREST RATES HEADED?

Evaluate the factors covered in Part Three. Keep up on current events. Stay alert. As with most areas of life, look and listen about three times more than you talk.

Remember that a stronger economy tends to lead to higher interest rates, which is bearish (not good) for bonds, and vice versa.

ALLOCATION/DIVERSIFICATION

Once you have answered these questions and are thinking about what investments to make, you need to think about your investment portfolio as a whole. Think about how you can integrate the individual securities so that your portfolio's overall shape will fit the mold your parameters set. When you have a well-designed portfolio, you can make adjustments in your asset allocation that will alter your portfolio's behavior should your needs change or the investment environment alter course.

For example, if you are risk-averse and designing your portfolio, you can decrease your aggregate risk by spreading your money around in different types of securities. By allocating various pieces of your investable assets into securities that are substantially different and react to different stimuli, you help guard against your whole portfolio getting hit hard all at once. This is called diversification.

There are different ways you can diversify your bond investments. You can invest in maturities that fall along different places on the yield curve. You can buy bonds with substantially different coupons. If you are not risk-averse, you can invest in bonds with different ratings. You can also diversify among different types of issuers.

You can spread your assets out among some of the different fixed income sectors reviewed in Part One.

Fixed Income Sectors

✔ U.S. Treasuries.

✔ Municipals.

✔ Corporate bonds.

✔ Mortgage-backeds.

✔ International bonds.

✔ Convertibles.

If you want to concentrate in the corporate or convertible sector, you can still diversify by varying the types of businesses the bond issuers are involved in. For example, you could buy bonds of airline, technology, utility, and retail companies; or you could buy those of oil, finance, and construction companies. If you're heavily invested in tax-exempts, you can diversify by buying out-of-state municipals that present good value.

EENIE, MEENIE, MINIE, MOE

Okay, once you've figured out what your parameters are, where the economy is headed, and what fixed income sectors you need to include in your portfolio, how do you decide which specific bond is the cheapest?

When traders ask how a bond is "priced," they are actually asking what the bond is yielding compared with other bonds. They don't at all mean what the bond's dollar price is. This is because it is a bond's yield, not its price, that determines its relative value. All a bond's price tells you is whether current interest rates are higher or lower than they were when the bond was issued.

So, how does the market assign value to fixed income securities and determine what their yield should be? Market participants look at the bond's fixed characteristics: coupon and maturity. It then evaluates how these characteristics could be affected by the market's outlook for interest rates, as well as the sector's and issue's financial prospects. All of these factors work together to determine the bond's relative value. The market is incredibly efficient. If a bond's yield is too low, demand for the bond will dry up until the price falls far enough so that the yield rises to a more tempting level. If the yield becomes too high, investors will swoop down gobbling up the issue until the demand forces the price higher and the yield falls to a point where it makes sense in light of what other bonds are yielding.

It is helpful to think of all bonds as being on a grid. Their characteristics, such as type, rating, and coupon, place their yields in a certain relationship to other bonds. As interest rates move or the outlook for a certain sector changes, all the bonds on the grid shift around until their yields settle into a new equilibrium relative to each other. For example, GNMA 7's may yield 25 bp more than 5-year T-notes, and if interest rates fall 150 bp, they may yield 32 bp more. In fact, this is called **matrix pricing** and it's precisely the method that's used to price **illiquid** bonds. Since illiquid bonds don't trade often, there may not be a recent trade to use to base the bond's price on. The procedure for pricing illiquid bonds begins by finding a bond that is similar; perhaps just the rating is different. Take that bond's yield and add to it a reasonable spread, usually established by specialized bond analysts. Once you arrive at the bond's appropriate yield, you can back out the projected price. Let's look at a fictitious example to illustrate

 matrix pricing
assigning an inactively traded bond a value by comparing it to other bonds that have a known price and adding an appropriate yield spread.

 illiquid
the lack of interest in the bond makes it very difficult to sell, because finding buyers is so tough.

this procedure. Say you are interested in finding out what an illiquid bond in your portfolio is worth. The actively traded bond that serves as a benchmark for this type of issue is currently yielding 4.23%; since analysts have calculated that your illiquid bond should yield about 210 basis points more, your bond's yield should be around 6.33%. Its price will be calculated using a YTM of 6.33%.

Mutual funds have to calculate the fund's net asset value (NAV) every day. They use matrix pricing to price bonds that didn't trade that day. This method is also used to help traders come up with reasonable bids for illiquid bonds that investors are looking to sell.

Some investors choose investments based only on their needs and stay with their holdings for the long term. Other investors like to match wits with the market and try to add to their return by moving their assets around. They are trying to buy at low prices and sell high.

SPREADS TO VALUE

When you are trying to decide between buying two different investments, you can look at the **spread**. The spread is the difference between their prices (price spread) or yields (yield spread). It is a way of tracking historical relationships between the two items in question.

When the difference between the prices or yields becomes larger, the spread has widened. When the difference lessens, the spread is said to have narrowed. (See Figure 15.4.)

Looking at what the spread is now, relative to where it's been in the past, gives you an idea whether today's pricing is out of whack. If the spread is vastly different from the norm and it doesn't make sense to you, investigate further. If it seems unwarranted, perhaps there will be a correction in the future. You may remember this from courses you've taken in your past as the concept of "regressing toward the mean." If that doesn't ring a bell, think of it as an oak tree growing in a ditch. Most of the acorns will fall close to the tree. The few that fall up the hill tend to roll back down toward the tree.

spread
the difference between the yields (yield spread) or the difference between the prices (price spread) of two securities. It is used to compare the past behavior of similar bonds with different maturities, different bond sectors, or bonds of different ratings.

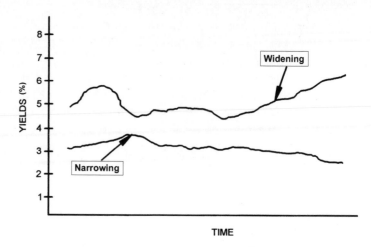

FIGURE 15.4 Yield spread.

MOB spread
spread of muni futures over bond futures.

Let's look at an example: A popular spread is the MOB **spread**. This is the difference between the price of municipal and Treasury bond futures. In fact, traders even trade futures on the MOB spread itself. If the spread widens it means the yield differential has also widened so the taxable Treasuries are probably more attractive. If the spread narrows more than the norm, the yield differential has narrowed and munis may be the better buy.

Classic Portfolio Strategies

T he following strategies are not mutually exclusive. You can mix and match them as they appeal to you and make sense for your situation.

INACTIVE APPROACH

By "inactive" I mean that you're not interested in trying to time the market. Instead, you want to put a disciplined investment procedure in place to guide your investing. The following strategies can help you do just that.

Ladder

This strategy is referred to as laddering maturities. You construct your fixed income portfolio by staggering the maturity dates, so the principal will be returned to you at different times. (See Figure 16.1.)

This helps decrease reinvestment risk because you receive money back to reinvest during different interest rate environments. In Table 16.1, you can see how rates move over time and how that would affect your reinvestment rate.

239

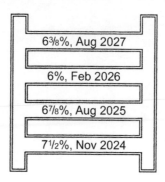

FIGURE 16.1 Treasury ladder.

Because this strategy lowers reinvestment risk, it is very popular with investors who are living off the income their portfolio generates. For example, I suggested this strategy to my grandmother. We put together a portfolio that had bonds maturing every year. This meant once a year she'd have some principal available to pay for the unexpected, and then she could reinvest what she didn't use. (See Figure 16.2.)

When a bond matures, you reinvest the principal in a security whose maturity is longer than the longest maturity you previously owned. You can tailor a bond ladder to fit your needs. For example, having money coming due every year, every 5 years, or every few months—whatever maturity staggering makes sense for you. Let's say you decided to

TABLE 16.1 U.S. T-Note 5³/₈% 6/30/03					
Date	*Yield*	*Date*	*Yield*	*Date*	*Yield*
12/93	5.21%	12/91	5.93%	12/89	7.84%
9/93	4.78	9/91	6.91	9/89	8.33
6/93	5.05	6/91	7.88	6/89	8.02
3/93	5.24	3/91	7.76	3/89	9.47
12/92	6.00	12/90	7.68	12/88	9.14
9/92	5.33	9/90	8.46	9/88	8.69
6/92	6.28	6/90	8.34	6/88	8.47
3/92	6.93	3/90	8.64	3/88	8.04

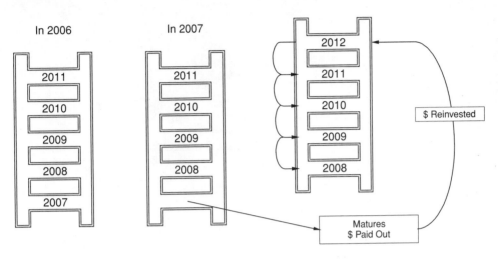

FIGURE 16.2 Reinvesting in the ladder.

have money come due every 2 years. You just received a lump sum payment, so you now own bonds maturing in 2, 4, 6, and 8 years. To continue building the ladder you would reinvest the money you just received into a 10-year bond.

Monthly Income

This is an excellent strategy for people living on a fixed income who need money to pay their monthly expenses. This strategy is similar to laddering maturities, but here you are laddering interest payments, staggering the interest payment dates to match your monthly expenses. Since there are 12 months in a year and bonds pay interest twice a year, you can put this strategy in place with only six different bonds. (See Figure 16.3.) Of course, if you have enough money, you can buy more bonds for further diversification.

Another option for monthly income is to buy mutual funds. But remember, the income can change over time as interest rates move, and the change in income can be dramatic. By buying individual bonds, you lock in the fixed income until maturity, so the payments stay the same. Investment advisers and brokers can be very helpful in assembling this type of portfolio. Also, some unit investment

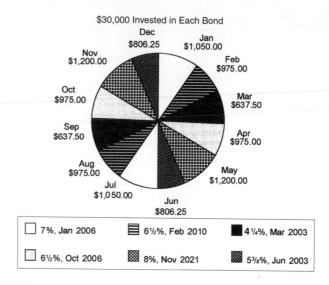

FIGURE 16.3 U.S. Treasury monthly income.

trusts (UITs) are structured to provide monthly income that remains constant for much of the trust's life; but remember, with a UIT you pay a substantial fee. Mortgage-backed securities (MBSs) also provide monthly income, but again the income level will change as homeowners pay off the principal.

90–10 Strategy

This is an excellent strategy for someone who is interested in riskier investments but also wants the principal to be secure.

It entails using zeros to anchor your return. Since zeros are bought at a discount, buy a zero whose face value equals the amount you originally had to invest, so you know that you'll have at least what you started with at maturity. Once you've bought the zeros, you can invest what's left over in other riskier investments.

For example, Rick, your postmaster, has decided to employ the 90–10 strategy. He has $100,000 to invest, even though every time you go in to buy stamps he complains how he's underpaid. He decides to take half and buy zeros that will have doubled in value when they mature in 20 years. This way he's sure to end up with the $100,000 he began with. Then with the other $50,000 he feels free to invest in riskier investments hoping to magnify his return. (So, now we know how Rick saved so many greenbacks; he's a smart fellow.)

Some of the traders I worked with called this second $50,000 "play money." This is not to say that you don't continue to take this money very seriously. You still have to do your research and identify opportunities that make good financial sense.

In our example, Rick invested 50% of his money in zeros, leaving 50% for other alternatives. These percentages can be altered to fit your investment profile. The more conservative you are the more you'd put in zeros, and the more aggressive you are the less you'd put in zeros. This investment strategy was originated by **hedge funds**; they would invest 10% in zeros and 90% in really aggressive gambles (thus the strategy's name).

Doubling Your Money

We touched on this while talking about the last strategy. Rick, your postmaster, bought zeros that would double his money. How'd he do this? Well, it is a straightforward formula known as the Rule of 72. You know what the interest rate is, and you know you want to double your money. What you don't know is how many years it will take to double your money given those two criteria. To get that, divide 72 by the interest rate:

72 ÷ Yield to maturity = Time to double your money

Systematic Investing

This strategy is great for those of you who, like me, aren't detail-oriented. It is also good for folks who have trouble saving, and for people who want to harness the power of compounding. This approach takes advantage of a number of market principles and gets them working for you instead of against you.

 hedge fund originally used to mean any mutual fund that uses futures and options defensively to limit risk. Hedge fund now usually refers to speculative funds that use these same techniques as an aggressive tool to compound their investment returns. These funds are known for their excessive volatility; they can give their investors incredibly stellar returns or they can lose most of your money for you.

Systematic investing, aka dollar-cost averaging, means you invest the same amount at set time intervals—for example, $20 every week. This strategy keeps you disciplined and helps you to avoid becoming overly emotional. As I've mentioned before, watching the cash flows in and out of mutual funds, you quickly recognize that the individual investor is a great **contrarian** indicator. We tend to panic and sell at the lowest prices and get sucked in after the market's soared and then pay top dollar.

The best way to avoid this and to get into the habit of saving is to scuttle away a piece of your paycheck every month. I don't care how small it is; just do it. Invest a percentage of your earnings. That way it grows as your salary grows. As you make more, you may even be able to afford a higher percentage.

I use this strategy in my kids' college savings account, but it is a great strategy for any long-range financial planning. Every month, I have a mutual fund company automatically debit our checking account and put the money into mutual fund accounts. Having the fund do it automatically is great for those of us who have trouble refraining from spending money that's there and for folks like me who aren't terribly organized.

contrarian

doing the opposite of what the majority is doing. It is kind of similar to using reverse psychology on your kids. A contrarian indicator is an indicator that you'd think would mean the market is likely to move in one direction, but the market actually moves in the other direction. A contrarian investor is one who does the opposite of what the investing masses are doing. If the majority is buying, he/she is selling and vice versa.

The Power of Compounding

Time is money. A head muni bond trader I worked with touted one of the greatest lines I've ever heard: "The time to invest is when you have money." He meant: Don't try to time the market; get in there, and get your money working for you. The power of compounding is like a snowball rolling down a hill. It gains momentum and size exponentially as it goes. (See Figure 16.4.)

The reason you want to get your money working for you as soon as possible is the power of compounding. When you invest in bonds, the interest you earn can be reinvested and begin earning you interest. Then the interest on your interest can be reinvested to earn interest. Soon not only is your principal earning you money, but so is your interest and the interest on your interest and

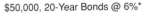

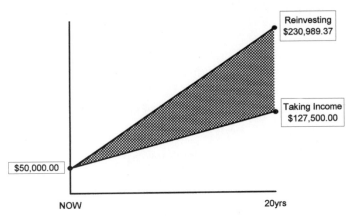

* Ignores taxation

FIGURE 16.4 Compounding makes a BIG difference.

your interest's interest is earning interest and on and on it
goes. It's the only legal pyramid scheme you can start,
and with this one you get all the benefit from every level.

Here's an example that shows how compounding can
amplify your investment returns. Tom and Mike each will
invest $120,000 in a bond paying 8%. They will reinvest
their income, so it compounds semiannually. The difference is Tom will invest $1,000 a month for 10 years, bring-
ing his total investment to $120,000. When Tom invests his
last installment, Mike will invest a lump sum of $120,000.
At that point Tom's investment will have already grown to
$184,165.68. Then they will both allow their investments
to roll until they retire in 20 years. Even though both Tom
and Mike invested $120,000, when they simultaneously re-
tire Tom will have $884,183.23 and Mike will have
$576,122.48. You can see how getting your money working
for you sooner can have a *dramatic* effect on your return.

You can estimate an investment's compounded value
using the following formula. It is only an estimate because
it assumes you reinvest the interest at a constant rate,
which obviously is not real life, where interest rates are
constantly changing.

The Land of Opportunity: Retirement Plans

I've never understood why people don't participate in 401(k) programs. Your company and the government are offering to give you money. If you were guaranteed to make 20% to 30% with the possibility to make more, wouldn't you do it? Well, that's exactly what you're being offered.

With a 401(k), the money is taken out of your paycheck on a pretax basis, so if your tax rate is 28%, you automatically make 28%! Plus, many employers will match what you put in with 25%, 50%, even 100% of what you contributed; this means if you put in $2,000 over the course of the year, they'll put in another $500, $1,000, even $2,000! Then you invest all this "free" money to make even more money for you! The topper is all this money compounds tax-deferred; you don't even have to pay taxes on the interest and capital gains until you take them out! It's the sweetest deal I've ever heard of.

On a similar note, many people don't contribute to their IRAs anymore because the contribution is no longer tax-deductible if your employer offers a retirement plan. But they're missing the boat. The capital gains and interest is still allowed to compound tax-free, and with more money working for you it grows faster. In a traditional IRA, you pay taxes on the account's growth when you withdraw money later in life. The assumption is that you won't be working, so you'll probably be in a lower tax bracket. It gets even better: In 1998 the Roth IRA was born. Here, not only are after-tax contributions allowed to compound tax-free, but no taxes will ever be owed on the compounded interest. (Okay, I'll get down from my soapbox now.)

Compounded growth = Amount invested $\times (1 + i)^n$

where

n = Number of compounding periods

i = percentage interest paid

For example, if it's a 10-year bond, there are 20 compounding periods because the bond pays interest twice a year (i.e., $n = 20$). The percentage interest paid each time is half the annual coupon rate. If the bond has a 7% coupon, then $i = 3.5\%$. With preferred stock, which pays income four times a year, $n = 40$ for 10 years. Preferred stock's interest per payment period is found by dividing the annual income by 4.

Let's do an example using the above bond and investing $25,000.

$$\$25,000 \times (1 + .035)^{20} = \$49,744.72$$

So, the investment would grow to $49,744.72. If you don't have a financial calculator that will raise 1.035 to the 20th power, you have to multiply it times itself 20 times before you multiply it by $25,000.

Tax-free and tax-deferred compounding—for example, within a retirement account, where you don't have to pay taxes on the reinvested interest—keeps a lot more of your money working for you, dramatically accelerating your account's growth. (See Figure 16.5.)

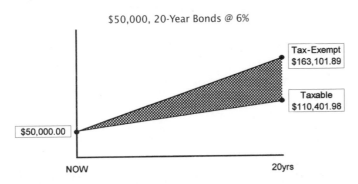

$50,000, 20-Year Bonds @ 6%

Tax-Exempt $163,101.89

Taxable $110,401.98

$50,000.00

NOW   20yrs

FIGURE 16.5 Tax-free compounding makes a difference, too.

The Barbell

This strategy involves averaging out risk while picking up some yield and/or the opportunity for capital gains.

This strategy is useful if:

✔ The maturity you are interested in is in short supply, thus making it more expensive.

✔ You think interest rates are heading lower and want to extend further out the curve than your risk tolerance will bear.

✔ You don't know where interest rates are going and you want to decrease reinvestment risk by diversifying your maturity exposure.

✔ There is a steep yield curve and the average yield of the two maturities is higher than if you bought the one maturity.

Let's say your ideal risk level is a portfolio duration of around the 7-year level. To fit this profile, you could buy all 7-year zeros. This is called buying a bullet maturity. Figure 16.6 illustrates where this term came from. You can see the bullet maturity has a higher yield than the average of the 2- and 12-year maturities.

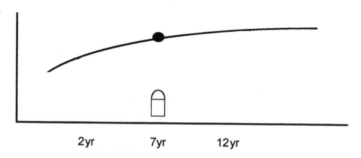

	2yr	7yr	12yr

FIGURE 16.6 Seven-year bullet.

Figure 16.7 shows what a barbell looks like when you put half of your assets in each end. You can see the average yield of the 2- and 12-year is higher than the 7-year yield. Depending on the shape of the yield curve, you may want to weight the barbell unevenly to take advantage of some opportunities in the yield curve.

For example, if the yield curve looks like Figure 16.8, you may want to take advantage of the blip in yields at 20 years. At the other end of the barbell, you probably wouldn't want to go any shorter than 2 years since T-bill yields are so low. Now that you've identified that 2 years and 20 years are cheap, you weight the barbells so that the average would be 7 years.

You can use this approach to balance your portfolio's coupon or rating distribution as well. Whatever your target coupon or rating is, straddle your assets so they average out to your target.

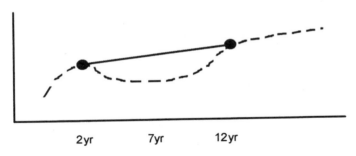

2yr   7yr   12yr

FIGURE 16.7 Two-year and 12-year barbell.

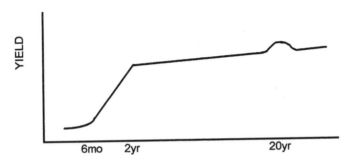

YIELD

6mo   2yr   20yr

FIGURE 16.8 Six-month to 2-year attractive and 20-year.

Reading the Yield Curve

We covered the yield curve in Part Three and touched on it in the barbell strategy. Reading the yield curve can be used to identify where is the best place to invest along the curve. For example, if you were investing when the curve looked like the one in Figure 16.9, it would make sense to **stay short** because **moving out the yield curve** doesn't pick up any additional yield for taking on additional volatility and for tying your money up for a longer period of time.

With the yield curve in Figure 16.10 it makes sense to extend out to 5 years, but you're not really paid to extend out beyond 15 years.

You can analyze where the best value is along the curve to reallocate your investments when the curve changes its shape. If the bonds you own become expensive and yields are more attractive for the amount of risk elsewhere on the curve, you may want to realign your portfolio. This idea of actively managing your fixed-income assets brings us to the next section.

stay short in bonds, to invest primarily in short maturities or to keep the average maturity of your portfolio low.

moving out the yield curve investing in bonds with longer maturities.

ACTIVE APPROACH

This section is for you investors who want to spend tons of time immersed up to your eyeballs in the financial world.

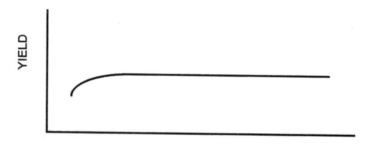

FIGURE 16.9 It doesn't pay to extend.

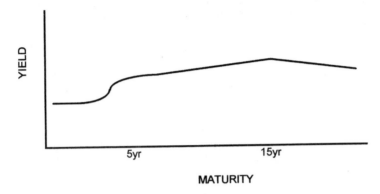

FIGURE 16.10 Extend out to 5 years, not beyond 15.

Forecasting Interest Rates

This approach involves timing. You are trying to figure out when interest rates are at their high so you can buy and when they are at their low so you can sell. You can use the information in Part Three to help you forecast where you think interest rates are going. Keep in mind this is a tough game. Wall Street pays people million-dollar salaries if they've correctly forecast interest rates a few more times than they've been wrong.

Beware of taking an interest rate guru's word as gospel. These gurus can have their own agendas. For example, their employer may want to sell a new bond offering, so the guru is encouraged to be positive on that sector or on interest rates. They're also generally interested in staying employed, so they'll rarely deviate too dramatically from recent experience. That way if they're wrong, they're not very wrong, and no one should get too upset with them.

Your own research, observation, and common sense are usually your best guides. The only drawback is there's no one to yell at if you're wrong.

Duration Management

This approach is an extension of the first. When you think interest rates are heading higher, you want to be more defensive, and shorten your portfolio's duration. You can do so by buying bonds with shorter maturities and larger coupons. Conversely, when you are bullish, you would extend the portfolio's duration so that its value will go up more when interest rates fall. To accomplish this, you would sell your shorter-duration bonds and buy bonds with longer durations. For example, you could buy bonds with longer maturities or smaller coupons, even zeros.

Asset Allocation

This involves forecasting the outlook for different types of bonds or asset classes. Here are a few examples. You could time when to move between: stocks and bonds; dollar and foreign currency–denominated securities; or different types of bonds. With this strategy you shuffle your money around between asset classes. Your objective is to sell the overvalued asset type and buy the undervalued. If you take some gains and don't see anywhere enticing to go, remember you can always go to cash. Actually it is preferable to go to a cash equivalent, such as money markets or T-bills, where you can earn interest while you wait to find something more enticing. If you're like a certain prognosticator I know who's always crowing that the financial sky is falling, then buying gold bars, painting them brick red, and building a tool shed with them might not be a bad idea.

Swaps

yield pickup
the alternative investment will provide you with more yield than the original.

This is about swapping one bond for another; you sell the bond you own and buy a bond that is substantially similar to the one you owned before but is different. What? Why? Well, there are a number of reasons why you would do this. You might do it because the new bond offers you a **yield pickup**, or perhaps the bond you are considering may offer more of an opportunity for capital gains. You might do it for tax reasons. In fact, there are a number of reasons you may choose to make a swap:

✔ Upgrade quality.

✔ Extend or shorten maturity.

✔ Increase current income.

✔ Increase yield-to-maturity.

✔ Improve call protection.

✔ Consolidate small holdings.

✔ Increase liquidity by buying securities that are more marketable.

✔ Diversify holdings.

✔ Adjust to state law changes.

✔ Realize tax benefits.

Many bond investors think they are getting a yield pickup when they actually aren't. The trap is most often sprung when interest rates rise. For example, let's say you bought a bond when its YTM was 6.25%, but now similar bonds have a 7.5% YTM, so you decide to sell the old one and buy the new one in order to make 1.25% more a year in interest, right? Well, literally yes, but actually no. The bond you already own will have gone down in value as the interest rates have risen, so you will have to sell that bond at a loss. Therefore, you will have less money to reinvest into the new bond. So, while the YTM may be higher, you would have less money earning that interest. Your actual investment return (dollars earned) would probably be about the same from either bond. (In fact, it may be a little lower with the new bond because you had to pay the broker/dealer to buy and sell the bonds.)

Here's an example: A guy I met on a town committee wore my ear off regaling me with his bond woebegone tales. He had bought zeros for his kids' educations. The YTM was 6.73%. Later on he got a cold call from a guy telling him he could buy a similar zero for 7.04%. This sounded super, but he was flabbergasted when he asked for a bid on the bonds he owned and found out they were worth less money than he'd paid for them. He had understood that over time zeros accrue toward their face value, so he had assumed they would be worth more than he'd paid for them. What he didn't understand was that while zeros' theoretical value accrues a little every day toward the face value, their value in the secondary market can whipsaw all over the place. The reason the new zero offered a higher yield than he was earning on his zero was because interest rates had moved. He had bought his zero when interest rates were lower; now interest rates had moved higher. In fact, if he decided to sell the zero he currently owned, its YTM in the current market would be about the same as the bonds he was being offered on the cold call. So let's say he decides to do the trade; his net return could end up being lower after you figure in the loss on his bonds and trading costs. Staying put may result in a higher return than executing the trade.

How can you tell if a swap is a good idea? You need to multiply each alternative's face value by its yield-to-worst (YTW). If you own $25,000 face value that you bought at a 5.45% YTW, your annual return is $1,362.50. Compare this with the new alternative that has a 6.15% yield, but after realizing the capital loss on the other bond and paying trade costs, you'd only be able to buy $22,000 face value with the proceeds from the sale. With the new bond you'd earn $1,353, which is less than the $1,362.50 you're currently earning, so you'd do better to stay put.

Investors often miss opportunities to pick up income, as well. Most investors don't realize that it's possible to swap into a bond with a lower yield and earn a higher return when you sell at a gain, because you are reinvesting more money at the new lower rates.

To figure out which bond is the better alternative, use the same procedure as before. However, before you can fairly compare the two bonds, you need to subtract the capital gains tax you'll have to pay on the sale from the proceeds.

For example, you have $20,000 invested in a bond that matures in five years and has 10% coupon. It provides $2,000 a year in income (so it will pay $10,000 in interest over the remaining life of the bond). You can sell this bond for $25,000 and reinvest the proceeds in a 5-year bond with an 8.25% coupon, so the annual income is $2,062.50 a year income ($10,312.50 over the life of the bond). So, the new bond looks better, right? However, if your tax rate is 25%, you'll have to pay Uncle Sam $1,250 in taxes on the $5,000 capital gain from selling your bond ($25,000 minus $20,000), so you'll actually only make a $9,062.50 return on the new bond versus $10,000 if you remained invested in your original bond. (Note that you're not considering swapping out of the bond because it's a bad investment but because there's an opportunity to pick up yield elsewhere.)

One of the most popular bond swaps is the tax swap. A tax swap is a method of turning paper losses into actual losses. The advantage of realized losses is that they can be used to decrease a tax bill. The prerequisite for this trade is of course for interest rates to have risen after you've bought a bond so that you have an unrealized capital loss But what if you still want to be invested in the security even though you'd like to write off the loss?

Well, actually there is a law to prevent people from selling just to write the loss off their tax bill and then buying the security right back. It is the **30-day wash sale rule**. As the name suggests, you can't buy the same security for 30 days before or after the sale's trade date when there's a loss. But in bond land, there is a way you can have your loss and stay invested—just like having your cake and eating it, too! The reason you can do this with bonds is because for a bond to be deemed a substantially different security you only have to change two of its three distinguishing criteria:

1. Issuer.
2. Coupon.
3. Maturity.

So, for example, you can sell your United Airlines bond at a loss and immediately buy a bond (if there is one) that has the same maturity, slightly different coupon, and is issued by Delta Air Lines, which upgrades your credit quality. You can see in Table 16.2 how fixed-income tax swaps allow you to buy something similar but different.

30-day wash sale rule
rule against selling a security to realize a loss for tax purposes and then turning around and buying the security right back. Any such sale is termed a wash sale, and may not be used as a loss for tax purposes. You cannot buy an equivalent security within 30 days before or after the sale's trade date.

TABLE 16.2 Swap Candidates				
	Issuer	Rating	Coupon	Maturity
You own:	United Airlines	Baa1/BBB2	8.70%	10/7/08
Swap candidates:	United Airlines	Baa1/BBB	8.31%	6/17/09
	Delta Air Lines	Aa1/AA1	8.10	1/1/09
	USAir Inc.	Aa/AA3	6.76	4/15/08

So while it's a different bond, you can buy a replacement that will keep the characteristics that are most important to you the same and still be able to take the loss. The best part is you don't have to wait 30 days and be at the mercy of the market; you can sell your bonds and buy the alternative bonds simultaneously, so there is no market risk.

Contrarian Investing

We touched on this strategy earlier in the chapter, when we talked about how when mutual fund investors are bailing out in droves it can be a signal to buy. Contrarian investing involves looking at what the masses are doing, and doing the opposite. Since the idea in the market is to do what everyone is going to be doing before they do it, the contrarian philosophy figures the best way to do this is to put the trade on while everyone is still following the old trend. That way you're sure to be there first.

However, as you may have guessed, there's more to it than just saying, "Hey, everyone's buying—I think I'll sell," because the momentum of the masses could push the price/yield a lot further in their direction. For example, after the birth of my first child in the winter of 1995, I noticed the market had been moving higher for a long time; and since I was too tired to think, I just reacted. For someone a long way from retirement, I committed the cardinal sin and converted my IRA assets into money markets. Well, two years later after I'd gotten some sleep and picked up the *Wall Street Journal* again, I reinvested in the markets at astronomically higher levels. (I'm sharing these embarrassing moments with you hoping you'll learn from my mistakes.) What this demonstrates is that like any type of indicator, contrarian indicators should simply serve as a triggers that start you thinking.

When everyone seems to love or hate something and the basis for this passion seems to be more emotion than reason, I call that a frothy market. Prices have been churned up so much there's a froth on the surface and little substance supporting its height or depth. If you were to blow on it, it scatters away. The classic example is the tulip bulb mania that so gripped Holland in the 1630s that "the ordinary industry of country was neglected, and the population, even to its lowest dregs, embarked in the tulip trade."[1] One tulip root was exchanged for "two lasts of wheat, four lasts of rye, four fat oxen, eight fat sheep, two Hogshead of wine, four tuns of beer, two tuns of butter, one thousand lbs. of cheese, a complete bed, a suit of clothes and a silver drinking-cup. . . . At first as with all gambling mania, confidence was at its height, and everybody gained." Land and housing prices collapsed as people sold their property at bargain basement prices in order to get cash to invest in bulbs. "At last, however, the more prudent began to see that this folly could not last forever. . . . It was seen that somebody must lose fearfully in the end. As this conviction spread, prices fell, and never rose again. Confidence was destroyed, and a universal panic seized upon the dealers. . . . Substantial merchants were reduced almost to beggary, and many a representative of a noble line saw the fortunes of his house ruined beyond redemption. . . . Tulips which had, at one time, been worth six thousand florins, were now to be procured for five hundred."

The question to ask yourself is, "Is there a substantive reason for the current fervor, other than extreme investor infatuation or disgust?" If there is, ride on. If there isn't, then it may be time for a contrarian play.

---

[1]*Extraordinary Popular Delusions and the Madness of Crowds*, Charles Mackay, LL.D., 1841. © by Andrew Tobias 1980. New York: Three Rivers Press, p. 94.

PORTFOLIO DESIGN

As we've mentioned before, the first thing you've got to do is identify your needs. Then you can combine any number of strategies to tailor your portfolio to your own personal requirements.

For example, my grandmother has a fixed pool of cash that must pay for her needs for the rest of her life. Keeping pace with inflation, avoiding reinvestment risk, and providing a steady income stream are her primary concerns. When designing Gram's portfolio, I combined the monthly income strategy with the laddered portfolio. This would give her monthly income with lower reinvestment risk and make principal available every April in case she needed it to pay taxes.

An example at the other end of the risk spectrum would be to combine the 90–10 strategy with asset allocation and duration management. A portfolio could be 10% zeros and the rest rotated among stocks, bonds, and cash. Adjustments to the bond mix could be determined by adjusting the duration to reflect the investor's outlook for interest rates.

Whatever your personal requirements, it is important to conceive of your financial portfolio as a whole. Building a portfolio is like building a wardrobe. If you don't think of the whole closet, you'll find that you have too many blue suits or that you don't have the black turtleneck that would match everything. If you don't consider the whole ensemble and plan, you'll end up wasting a lot of money.

You need to ask yourself, "What is the overall risk level you are targeting?" Once you arrive at the answer, you can mix investments of different risk levels to arrive at your target. For example, for a moderate level of risk, you can invest in securities that all have moderate risk; or you can split your assets between conservative and aggressive alternatives so overall the risk averages out to be moderate.

Once you decide how to allocate your money between different asset classes, then you can decide on which specific security will best fit each criterion.

Sometimes when you're looking at the financial heavens, you need to back up for perspective. Pull yourself off the telescope. Just lie down on the grass and take in the whole sky. If the sheer number of investment alternatives, like the infinite number of stars, begins to become intimidating, get back on the telescope and examine one sector of the investment sky at a time.

Conclusion

That's probably enough for now. Hopefully, you've picked up a couple of useful compass points to help direct your navigation through the wonderful, expansive world of bonds. You now know more about bonds than almost everyone you saw today. Not bad.

During the first week of April last year, I was in a no-load mutual fund office making our IRA contributions. A man came in, talking at speed in a loud voice, "Hey, a friend of mine just bought a bond at 13%; I want to buy some of those." Keep in mind, at the time long rates weren't even 6%. Since he couldn't even furnish the name of the issuer, it was very difficult for the investment advisers either to explain why this phantom bond was yielding 13% or refute his claim. Of course, one possible explanation was that his friend's money was on its way to a South Seas island in someone's briefcase, and his friend would not only never see any of this fabulous interest but probably wouldn't see his money again, either.

What we can learn from our overexcited customer in the preceding paragraph is: It's crucial not to get caught up in the market's emotion. Instead of being naive and therefore vulnerable, you now know how to compare investments and decide rationally which makes the best financial sense. You've got the tools, so stay cool.

My last word to you before you boldly set forth with your newly acquired arsenal of fixed income knowledge: Just remember the market is extremely efficient; if it sounds too good to be true, it probably is. So, go ahead, take what you've learned, adapt it to your own situation, and do what's right for you. The knowledge you've gained mixed with some common sense puts you among an elite group of investors.

Good luck, and here's to a bond bonanza!

Fixed Income Web Sites

GENERAL

American Bankers Association	American Bankers Association: consumers—calculators (www.aba.com)
Ask Dow Jones	Interactive business news and market research (http://ask.djinteractive.com)
Bankrate	Rates (www.bankrate.com)
Bloomberg	Rates, market data, news (www.bloomberg.com)
BONDTALK.com	Headlines, rates, commentary (www.bondtalk.com)
Reuters	International indexes and news (www.bridge.com)
Briefing.com	Bond market commentary (www.briefing.com)
Bureau of the Public Debt Online	Information and purchase of U.S. Treasuries and savings bonds (www.publicdebt.treas.gov)
CBS MarketWatch	Bond market update (http://cbs.marketwatch.com)
Default Risk	Papers about fixed income default risk (www.defaultrisk.com)

General Accounting Office	Statistics on tax collections (www.gas.gov)
The Bond Market Association	Education, rates, historic data, links (www.investinginbonds.com)
Investopedia	Mostly stocks, but has some bond information (www.investopedia.com)
Smart Money	Rates; investment strategies (www.smartmoney.com)

PUBLICATIONS

Barron's Online	Weekly financial newspaper (www.barrons.com)
The Bond Buyer Online	Daily municipal bond newspaper (www.bondbuyer.com)
Bond*Week*	Weekly bond newspaper (www.bondweek.com)
Investor's Business Daily	Daily financial newspaper (www.investors.com)
Standard & Poor's	Link to *CreditWeek*, the weekly bond newspaper (www.standardpoor.com)
The Wall Street Journal Online	Daily financial newspaper (http://online.wsj.com)

Glossary

accrual bond   the bond's interest is added to the principal amount and isn't paid out until maturity.

accrued interest   bond investors earn interest every day, but it is paid out only periodically; most pay semiannually, and a few pay monthly. Accrued interest has been earned by the investor but has not yet been paid out.

alternative minimum tax (AMT)   this tax applies to 1% of the population. Its intent is for the wealthy to pay taxes on private-purpose municipals. AMT adds together passive losses (such as those from tax shelters and deductions for charitable contributions) and income from private-purpose tax-exempt bonds, then subtracts a certain amount and taxes a percentage of this income that is above a minimum level.

appreciate   the investment value rises higher.

arrears   what was not paid and is owed to someone; back pay.

asset-backed security (ABS)   security consisting of a group of credit card, auto, boat, or other loans whose loan payments pay its interest.

asset class   grouping of like securities. Tax-exempt securities, floating rate notes, zero coupon bonds, and international bonds are examples of asset classes.

ask   the lowest price anyone who owns the security is willing to accept as the selling price. It is the price the bond owner is "asking" for the bonds. This is also known as the offer because it is the price the owner is offering the bonds for to potential buyers.

average life   the time it is estimated that it will take a mortgage-backed security to return half of the principal to the investor. Also known as average maturity.

axe   trader jargon (short for "axe to grind"). It means traders have something they want to get rid of.

backed   the interest payments are pledged to be paid by (e.g., the bond could be backed by a bank, equipment, escrow account, etc.).

back-end load   mutual fund sales charge that is subtracted from the price when you sell your fund shares; also known as a contingent deferred sales charge (CDSC).

basis point (bp)   the smallest measure when discussing bond yields; 1 basis point equals .01%. Traders sometimes call them "beeps."

bearer bonds   these bonds have attached coupons that are ripped off and turned in for interest. At maturity the bond itself is turned in for the principal payment. Whoever has the paper is the one who gets the money; there is no other record of ownership. Bearer bonds are now extremely rare in the United States. The Tax Reform Act of 1982 prohibited their issuance to help fight money laundering. Ownership is now transferred electronically, and there is no physical bond.

bearish   bad; negative; down; decreasing in value. In the bond market this means interest rates are headed up and bond prices are going down.

bid   the highest price anyone is willing to pay for a security in order to buy it. For example, you may say, "I want to earn 7½%," which for the bond you're interested in might mean a price of 101. Your bid for the bond is 101. That is the price you propose to the present bond owner.

bid/ask spread   difference between what someone wants to buy the bond for and what someone wants to sell it for. An example of a bid/ask spread is 100-29/101-01. The ask is always higher than the bid. When the buyer and seller agree on a price, there is a trade—the bonds are sold and ownership transferred.

bond   debt security. Investors loan the issuer money who pledges to pay back the money plus interest.

bond equivalent yield (BEY)   a cash equivalent or short-term discount instrument's simple yield will look higher than a coupon bond because the coupon bond pays interest and can be compounded every six months. To compare the two, you must translate the discount's simple yield into a bond equivalent yield.

$$\text{BEY} = \frac{365 \times \text{Discount rate}}{360 - (\text{Discount rate} \times \text{Days to maturity})}$$

To calculate the BEY for money market instruments that use a 360-day year, such as CDs, substitute 360 for 365 in the numerator.

book   record of the bond trader's positions—what bonds are owned (long) and what are short. Similar to your portfolio statement.

bp   *see* **basis point**.

broker   a third party that serves as an agent, trading securities on your behalf. With bonds, brokers will mark up the price when you're buying and mark down the price when you're selling. Therefore, their cut is included in the price, so you can't see how much they're making. There is no commission like with stocks. Don't panic. With bonds, comparing yields is more important and relevant than price in determining value. If the broker took "too much", the yield would become unattractive.

bullish   good; positive; up; increasing in value. In the bond market this means interest rates are headed down and bond prices are going up.

call   an option contract that gives the buyer the right to purchase a security from the owner at a specific price before the contract's expiration date.

callable   a callable bond can be retired by the issuer before the maturity date. It is called at a premium, above the price it was issued at, after stipulated dates. For example, a bond could become callable five years after it's issued at a price of 103. It remains callable at that price until two years later when it becomes callable at a price of 101. If it is not called, it will mature at 100.

capital appreciation bonds (CABs) municipal zero coupon bonds that are sold at a deep discount from the maturing face value.

capital gains aka cap gains. When you sell an investment for a higher price than you paid for it.

Chapter 11 when an entity is unable to pay its debts and has declared protection under the bankruptcy laws. This 1978 law keeps the company in possession of and in control of its business. It allows the creditor(s) and debtor a lot of freedom to reorganize the business and hopefully be able to pay off the debts and become a viable business again.

chart graphing data to create visual representation of trends; used in technical analysis.

close price of the last trade for the day.

coincident indicator economic measure that tends to give readings that reflect how the economy is currently doing.

collar an adjustable rate bond's maximum and minimum interest rate. The bond will not pay interest higher than the upper collar or lower than its lower collar.

collateral hard assets, things that are pledged when someone borrows money. If the borrower does not have money to pay off the loan, the items pledged must be given over. Your house is collateral for your mortgage—if you don't pay your mortgage, the bank gets your house.

collateralized mortgage obligations (CMOs) a security made up of mortgage-backed securities. It is split up into pieces called traunches that are designed to have specific volatility and maturity characteristics.

commercial paper short-term securities with maturities from 2 to 270 days; issued by banks, insurance companies, and corporations that have cash to lend out.

compounding interest is earned on both the principal and all the interest that was earned before and reinvested.

confirm short for "trade confirmation," this lists all the particulars of the trade.

consumer price index (CPI) prices of domestic and imported goods and services purchased by U.S. consumers as calculated by the Bureau of Labor Statistics.

contrarian doing the opposite of what the majority is doing. It is kind of similar to using reverse psychology on your kids. A contrarian indicator is an indicator that you'd think would mean the market is likely to move in one direction, but the market actually moves in the other direction. A contrarian investor is one who does the opposite of what the investing masses are doing. If the majority is buying, he/she is selling and vice versa.

conversion ratio   set when a convertible bond is issued, this ratio calculates how many shares of common stock each convertible bond can be exchanged for when the bond is converted (conversion ratio equals par value divided by conversion price).

(convertible) premium   how much more you have to pay for a convert over and above the price it would cost if it were a straight bond. The premium is expressed as a percentage of the convert's theoretical value. The reason for the premium includes such factors as the ability to convert the bond into common stock and the ability to buy it on margin.

convexity   Measures the rate of change in a bond's sensitivity to interest rate moves. It's the rate of change in a bond's duration (price volatility).

correlated   objects are said to be correlated when their actions tend to resemble one another; objects that are not correlated react dissimilarly to events.

coupon   stipulates how much money the lender/investor will earn. A 10% coupon means the investor will receive 10% of the amount she or he lent for as long as the contract states. For example, $1,000 lent will earn $100 a year until maturity, when the $1,000 is paid back.

coupon yield   the interest the issuer has promised to pay, an annual percentage of the face value.

credit derivative   contract between two parties that bets on the future value of another security.

credit rating   outside evaluation of a borrower's credit standing and ability to pay financial obligations. In the case of a bond rating, it evaluates the issuer's ability to pay bond investors the money owed them.

crossing bonds   the same investment firm acts as agent in a trade between two of its customers without the firm's trading desk ever owning the bonds.

currency risk   the risk that the currency your foreign bond is issued in will appreciate in value so your bond's proceeds will be converted back into fewer dollars than they would have been before.

current yield   to calculate, divide the bond's annual dollar interest by the current market price.

cushion bonds   bonds trading in the secondary market that have coupons significantly higher than current interest rates. Their larger coupon offers a cushion against price fluctuations when interest rates move, so these bonds tend to experience less price volatility. Since they are trading at substantial premiums, many investors won't buy (they erroneously think they are expensive). Therefore, the YTM is often higher than similar bonds with lower coupons, offering an attractive yield pickup.

CUSIP number   stands for Committee on Uniform Security Identification Procedures number. Pronounced "Q-sip". Every bond that is issued is assigned a

CUSIP number to identify the issue. It is analogous to the social security number that identifies you.

cyclicals bonds issued by companies whose successes tend to follow business cycles: When the economy and consumer demand are strong, the company does well; when they falter, the company also struggles.

debenture bond whose interest and principal payments are not secured by hard assets that could be sold if the company goes under. The bond is sold on the basis of the company's past performance and good name.

deflation prices of goods and services are declining.

deliverable the security is able to be transferred into an account. It is often not a physical security only an electronic notation.

depreciate decline in value.

discount price below par; price less than 100.

discount bond or **zero coupon bond** bond sold at a price way below its face value. No interest is paid until the bond matures. At maturity, the principal, interest, and interest-on-interest is paid to the investor. The interest-on-interest calculation assumes semiannual reinvestment of "phantom" interest at the bond's interest rate.

discount rate (1) An annualized rate of return based on the par value of a T-bill; (2) what the Federal Reserve charges member banks on a collateralized loan. It is the base rate that all other interest rates are pegged off.

discount window where member banks can borrow money from the Federal Reserve at below market rates if they need to increase their reserves. This borrowing is discouraged and is only used in really tough spots.

diversification spreading out your risk by splitting up your investable assets among several different types of securities. The hope is that they will react differently to stimuli, like interest rates or unemployment figures, so your investment returns won't all go down at the same time.

dollar-cost average to invest equal dollar amounts in an investment at equal time intervals. This technique has been found commonly to result in a lower average cost than trying to time the market.

double tax-free you don't have to pay state or federal taxes on the interest you earn from the bond.

due diligence period when issuer is checked out to make sure what it asserts to be true is, and to make sure all the ducks are lined up for the new offering.

durable goods goods with a life of 3 or more years.

duration the measure of bond price volatility in years. Duration equates the bond to a zero coupon bond (e.g., a bond with a 4-year duration has the volatility of a 4-year zero).

easy policy also known as being accommodative. The objective is to get more money into the domestic monetary system in an attempt to stimulate the economy.

escrowed to maturity   money has been put aside and held in a separate account to pay all of the bond's future interest and principal payments. The payments are assured and do not come from the issuer any longer.

euro (€)   common currency shared by 12 European countries that agreed to function as one economic and financial unit beginning in 1999. The monetary system is governed by one central bank. Trade and employment barriers have been dropped.

Eurobond   bond underwritten by banks and investment firms from several different European countries. Eurobonds can be denominated in any currency. They are sold to investors outside the country whose currency pays the issue's principal and interest.

Eurodollar bond   a bond whose principal and interest are paid in U.S. currency held in foreign banks, usually European banks. They are not registered with the SEC.

European Union (EU)   begun in 1950, the EU has 15 member states, with 13 others soon to be added. It includes countries that have not adopted the euro as their domestic currency.

ex-autos   short for excluding automobile sales.

exercise   to use the right you purchased in a futures or option contract.

ex-food and energy   short for excluding food and energy statistics.

face value   amount the borrower must pay the investor at maturity. This amount is used to calculate the interest payments.

fast markets   when prices in the secondary market are rising or falling with extreme speed.

the Fed   short for the Federal Reserve Bank, the United States governing bank authority.

Federal Reserve Bank   the United States' central bank, charged with maintaining the health of the country's banking system. There are 12 Federal Reserve branches owned by the member banks in their region. These branches monitor the member banks to make sure they comply with the Federal Reserve Board regulations. They also provide member banks with emergency funds when needed at below market rates through their discount window. The Federal Reserve is also charged with monitoring and maintaining the country's economic health. They do this by affecting monetary flows.

Fed funds rate   the interest rate a bank will charge another bank that needs an overnight loan.

fixed income investments   also known as bonds. Bond issuers are obligated to pay the income stipulated in the contract until the security matures. At that time the issuer pays back the principal borrowed from the investors. Most bonds have level income payments. A few pay variable income streams that change according to a set formula. Bonds with their promised income are different from stocks, which pay income only when it is earned.

flat the issuer is no longer paying interest on the bond.

floor slang referring to a physical location where traders meet face-to-face to trade the securities that are listed with them. An example is the cavernous room where the New York Stock Exchange (NYSE) conducts its trading.

front-end load mutual fund's sales charge that is added onto your purchase price.

full employment considered to be around 5.5% unemployment, a level of unemployment that is felt to be transitional (people temporarily out of work or between jobs). If unemployment falls below this level, it is felt inflation pressures will begin to heat up.

fundamental analysis researching economic indicators, financial statistics, and issuer's financial position in an attempt to predict the future direction and behavior of the economy, interest rates or a certain bond issue.

futures a contract agreeing to buy or sell a certain amount of something (e.g., bonds, gold, cattle) at a set price on a specific date.

G-8 eight developed nations that have formed a loose economic alliance (formerly the G-7). Their economies and interest rates tend to move in the same direction. The G-8 includes: Canada, France, Germany, Great Britain, Italy, Japan, Russia, and the United States.

global bond bond issued in several countries' currencies simultaneously.

govies trader slang for government securities.

guaranteed bond bond backed by some other corporation, for example the issuer's parent company.

handle trader lingo for the part of the bond's price that is a whole number. When a bond's price is 98^1/$_4$, the handle is 98.

heavy hitters big players, size traders, large investors.

hedge fund originally used to mean any mutual fund that uses futures and options defensively to limit risk. Hedge fund now usually refers to speculative funds that use these same techniques as an aggressive tool to compound their investment returns. These funds are known for their excessive volatility; they can give their investors incredibly stellar returns or they can lose most of your money for you.

hit trader slang meaning you accept the price and agree to exchange money for the bond. Short for saying, "Yes, I will buy/sell at that price. Let's trade the bonds."

illiquid the lack of interest in the bond makes it very difficult to sell, because finding buyers is so tough.

indenture formal agreement between bond holders and the issuer covering such issues as: type, size of issue, terms, what backs the issue, any provisions that further protect the investor (such as a sinking fund), call privileges, and appointment of trustee on behalf of bond holders.

index bond   a sampling of corporate bonds that is supposed to act similarly to a sector of the bond market as measured by an index.

indications of interest   syndicate members canvas their major clients about their interest in an upcoming new issue to determine if the yield they are thinking about is too high or too low and whether they have to make adjustments.

inflation   when prices of goods and services are rising without any improvement in productivity or quality.

institutional investors   large investors such as pension funds and insurance companies.

institutional trading   sector of the bond market where bonds are traded in very large size—for example, $1 million. The smaller-sized trades done by individuals are usually done on retail trading desks.

interest   money that a borrower owes the lender in addition to the amount borrowed. It is the cost of borrowing. Lenders demand this additional money for the inconvenience of being unable to use the money they have lent to the borrower.

in-the-money   the price of the underlying security has moved so that if you exercised the option you would make money. The contract has intrinsic value.

Investment Company Institute (ICI)   private company that monitors the mutual fund industry.

lagging indicator   economic measure that tends to show how the economy was doing a while ago.

leading indicator   economic measure that tends to presage what the economy is going to do in the future.

letter of credit (LOC)   a bank or large investment firm stands ready to make the issue's payments should the issuer become unable to make them itself.

liquid   there is a significant amount of interest in the issue, so buyers can be found if you want to sell. The bond can be easily traded in the secondary market.

long   owning a bond or other security.

lots   created when you bundle together a bunch of the same security, usually done to take advantage of economies of scale.

M1   currency in circulation, commercial bank demand deposits: NOW (interest-bearing checking) and ATS (automatic transfer from savings) accounts, credit union share drafts, and mutual savings bank demand deposits.

M2   includes M1 plus: overnight repurchase agreements issued by commercial banks, overnight Eurodollars savings accounts time deposits under $100,000, and money market mutual fund shares.

M3   includes M2 plus: time deposits over $100,000 and term repurchase agreements.

margin account investment account where the investor borrows money from the investment firm in order to buy securities, paying a higher interest rate on the money borrowed.

matrix pricing assigning an inactively traded bond a value by comparing it to other bonds that have a known price and adding an appropriate yield spread.

maturity the length of time until the loan ends. When the bond matures the borrower pays the investors back the borrowed principal and any remaining interest owed. This ends the contract between the investors and the borrower.

MOB spread spread of muni futures over bond futures.

money supply total amount of U.S. currency or money equivalents in the domestic economy, primarily the currency that's in circulation plus deposits in savings and checking accounts. There are four measures of money supply: M1, M2, M3, and L (the last includes longer-term liquid assets).

mortgage-backed security (MBS) security consisting of a group of real estate mortgages.

mortgage bond a bond backed by a property mortgage.

moving out the yield curve investing in bonds with longer maturities.

municipal bond debt obligation issued by a state or local governmental entity.

mutual reciprocity the agreement between the federal and state governments that they will not tax the interest from each other's bonds. It applies only to interest. If the bonds are sold before maturity any capital gains would be subject to the applicable tax rate.

negative convexity a bond possessing this characteristic finds its price becomes more reactive when bond prices are going down and less responsive when prices are rising.

net asset value (NAV) the dollar value of all the securities in a mutual fund at the close of the day divided by the number of outstanding shares.

newly industrialized country (NIC) emerging market; offers diversification and profit potential but also risk.

on special the bonds are cheap because the owner is desperate to unload them.

original issue discount (OID) the bond issue was not issued at par but instead came to market at a discount. If you sell the bond in the secondary market, you must check to see if the price is above or below the accrued amortization line to determine if you owe capital gains tax.

originator issuer of mortgage-backed bonds.

out-of-the-money the futures or option contract has no intrinsic value; if it were exercised today the contract holder would lose money.

outstanding has been issued and has not yet matured or been called.

over-the-counter (OTC) when stocks and bonds aren't traded on the floor of a formal exchange there is no physical place where the traders meet face-to-face to trade the securities; they are traded over the phone, fax, and computer line.

par   price where the bond's dollar value equals the face value it will mature at ($1,000, $25,000, etc.). The price at par is 100 (i.e., the bond at par is trading at 100% of its face value).

parity   a convertible bond's theoretical value if it were a straight bond without the conversion option.

plus   add 1/64 to the price given.

point   if the price changes from 102 to 103, it has changed a point. A one-point change in the price affects the bond's dollar value by 1% of the face value. For example, a point is worth $10 when bond has a $1,000 face value; a point is worth $50 when a bond has a $5,000 face value.

portfolio   a collection of investments made by one entity.

position   total holding of a certain security; the amount invested in something.

premium   price above par; price greater than 100. When a bond is trading at a premium the bond's dollar value is higher than its face value (the principal amount you get at maturity).

premium recovery period   how long it is estimated it would take the convertible bond owner to make back the premium through the yield advantage.

prerefunded bond (pre-re)   outstanding higher-coupon bond whose interest is no longer paid by the issuer but is paid by a Treasury security.

prepayment risk   the possibility that a bond owner will receive his/her principal back from the issuer before the maturity date.

primary market   when bonds are first sold to investors by the issuer. This is not a physical place; it is more a point in time and a transaction.

principal   amount of money the borrower must pay back to the lender/investor at maturity. It is usually the amount borrowed from the investor. Also known as the **face value**.

producer price index (PPI)   monthly measure of the change in wholesale prices as calculated by the U.S. Bureau of Labor Statistics.

prospectus   document sent to people considering investing in securities such as stocks, bonds, mutual funds or unit investment trusts. It details what the investment objectives are, what it invests in, and how it has performed in the past.

proxy   stand-in for; e.g., an in-the-money convertible bond can be exchanged for stock, so it is considered to be an alternative and equivalent form of the common stock.

put   contract that enables the option holder to sell a security to the other party at a set price until the contract expires.

put bond   investor has the option to put the bond back to the issuer at set intervals.

real interest rate   what you're left with after inflation deflated your return (real rate of return equals nominal interest rate minus inflation rate).

realized   security is sold thus locking in the profit or loss.

reciprocal   as used in calculating a municipal bonds' TEY; the reciprocal of a number is found by subtracting the number from the number one.

refunding bond   new bond issued to raise money to prerefund an outstanding higher-coupon municipal bond.

repo   short for repurchase agreement. This transaction is usually done with U.S. Treasuries. It is an agreement between Party A and Party B, that Party A will set Party B securities and then will buy back the securities on a certain date (often the next day) at a higher price. In essence, Party B is making Party A a collateralized loan. The difference between the two prices is the profit Party B makes for loaning the money.

reserve requirement   restriction set by the Federal Reserve's Board of Governors that regulates how much of a bank's money can be lent out and how much must be kept on hand in the form of cash and liquid assets. It is a percentage of demand deposits and time deposits.

resistance   price level where in the past a security has tended to stop rising and then falls to lower levels; acts as a ceiling.

retail investors   individual investors who invest smaller quantities than institutions. You and me.

retire   the issuer pays off the loan/bond in full, so the issue is no longer outstanding.

rich   expensive, pricey, costing more money, so the yield is lower relative to other bonds that have similar characteristics.

risk   chance the investment could go down more or up less. As investors, we are usually more worried about the going down part.

savings bonds   type of bond issued by U.S. government. There is no secondary market, and there is a penalty for early redemption.

scale   list of a new bond offering's maturities and the expected yield at each level. Scales can be subject to numerous revisions before the offering and during the few hours the bonds are being offered.

seasoned   securities have been outstanding and traded in the secondary market for a while.

secondary market   when bonds are traded by investors after the bonds have been issued and are outstanding (i.e., between the issue date and the maturity date). The trade involves two parties other than the issuer, who is no longer involved. This is not a physical place; it is more a point in time and a transaction.

secure   a hard asset backs the bond's interest and principal payments in case the issuer becomes unable to make the payment.

securities   financial instruments that you can invest your money in; bonds or stocks.

Securities and Exchange Commission (SEC)   federal agency that regulates the securities industry. It makes rules to discourage fraud, and then polices, arbitrates, and punishes misconduct. It was created by the Securities Exchange Act of 1934 to enforce the Securities Act of 1933.

SEC yield   standardized yield calculation established by the SEC that subtracts the premium paid for any bonds within the portfolio from their higher income stream.

semiannually   every six months (i.e., half year).

serial bond   portions of a serial bond issue mature at different times—the issue has a number of maturity dates. For instance, different bonds in the issue may come due each year for the next 10 years. The other type of issue is a term bond.

settlement date   when the money for the trade is due. If it is not received, the trade is canceled.

short   when the trader has sold the bond before owning it (i.e., without being long the bond).

simple interest   interest is paid once, so there is no compounding during the year; the interest rate used for discount securities.

sinking fund bond   that is money put aside and held in a separate account to retire portions of a bond issue at different times.

size   large quantity.

slug   U.S. Treasury bond that is created to exactly match the cash flows of a pre-refunded municipal bond (from SLGS—State & Local Government Series).

sovereign risk   the risk that the government where the bonds are issued will take actions that will hurt the bond's value.

spot   current price.

spread   the difference between the yields (yield spread) or the difference between the prices (price spread) of two securities. It is used to compare the past behavior of similar bonds with different maturities, different bond sectors, or bonds of different ratings.

stay short   in bonds, to invest primarily in short maturities or to keep the average maturity of your portfolio low.

straight-line amortization   the same increment is added to the price every day.

strike price   price stipulated in a futures or option contract that the contract can be exercised at (i.e., the price the security can be put or called at).

STRIPS   stands for separate trading of registered interest and principal of securities. They are Treasury-issued zero coupon bonds. They are issued at a deep discount from the maturing face value. The difference is the interest and interest-on-interest.

support   price level where in the past a security has tended to stop falling and rebound to higher levels; acts as a floor.

syndicate   group of investment firms formed to distribute a new offering to investors. Some members take market risk because they buy the issue and own it until they can sell it to investors. Other members only sell the issue and are not at risk. The manager or comanagers who coordinate the syndicate take on the most risk and allocate who gets how many bonds.

tanks   traders' slang for plummets precipitously with astounding momentum. Other expressions conveying the same meaning: bites the dust, falls out of bed.

taxable equivalent yield (TEY)   converting the yield of a tax-free bond into the equivalent yield it would have if it were a taxable bond in order to land the same number of after-tax dollars in your pocket.

technical analysis   studying graphic patterns of financial data (prices, yields, averages, trading volume, etc.) in an attempt to predict future patterns and trends.

term bond   bond where the entire issue's face value matures on the same day.

30-day wash sale rule   rule against selling a security to realize a loss for tax purposes and then turning around and buying the security right back. Any such sale is termed a wash sale, and may not be used as a loss for tax purposes. You cannot buy an equivalent security within 30 days before or after the sale's trade date.

tight policy   also known as being restrictive. The objective is to make it more difficult for people to get money. Since money becomes expensive it discourages borrowing. This tends to slow down the economy, so inflation doesn't get out of control.

TIPS   stands for Treasury inflation protection securities. They are inflation-indexed Treasuries.

tombstone   newspaper advertisement for a new bond issue that lists which investment firms are in the syndicate, who the issuer is, and size of the issue.

total return   a comprehensive measure of your investment's performance. It includes change in price, plus income, plus or minus any change in currency valuation if it's denominated in a currency other than U.S. dollars.

$$\Delta \text{ price} + \text{income} \pm \Delta \text{ in currency value} = \text{total return}$$

trade date   when the seller promises to sell the bond to a buyer, at an agreed price.

traded through   it refers to some line you have graphed: the bond's average price, prices at the end of the day, etc. When the bond's price or yield passes above or below this line it is said to have traded through.

trading at   the yield used to price the bond. The secondary market feels the bond should offer the investor this yield; thus, the bond's price adjusts so the investor receiving this coupon will earn this yield.

traunche   division within a CMO that has its own unique characteristics and is sold as a separate security.

Treasury bill (T-bill)   short-term (maturities up to a year) discount security issued by the U.S. government.

Treasury bond (T-bond)   long-term debt obligation (maturities greater than 10 years) issued by the U.S. government.

Treasury note (T-note)   intermediate debt obligation (maturities 2 to 10 years) issued by the U.S. government.

underwriter   investment bank that agrees to buy a new issue and distribute it to investors. It assumes the risk and makes the underwriting spread on securities sold.

underwritten   when an investment bank buys a new issue, assumes the market risk, and attempts to resell it to the public; a syndicate underwrites the new issue.

volatility   the characteristic of having up and down changes.

Yankee bonds   dollar-denominated bonds issued in the United States by foreign banks and corporations.

yield pickup   the alternative investment will provide you with more yield than the original.

yield-to-call (YTC)   estimated yield investor will receive if the bond is called before maturity by the issuer.

yield-to-maturity (YTM)   the yield you would receive if you reinvested the coupon you earn at a rate equal to the yield-to-maturity. It is a more accurate yield than current yield because it includes the positive effect a larger coupon has on your investment return.

yield-to-worst (YTW)   the lowest yield the bond you are considering could yield. When you compare the different types of yield (yield-to-call, yield-to-maturity), whichever is the lowest is the yield-to-worst and is the appropriate one to use to compare with other bond yields.

zero coupon bond   *see* **discount bond**.

Index

SPECIAL OFFER FOR READERS OF
GETTING STARTED IN BONDS
FROM TELEVISION'S MOST-WATCHED
BUSINESS NEWS PROGRAM,

NIGHTLY
BUSINESS
REPORT

**Order the award-winning home video:
"The NBR Guide To Buying Bonds"
at a special discount price.**

Winner of a Platinum award in the 2002
WorldFest/Houston and the Excellence in
Financial Journalism Award from the New York
Society of Certified Personal Accountants,
"The NBR Guide To Buying Bonds" is hosted
by NBR co-anchors **Paul Kangas** and **Susie
Gharib**. It also features extended interviews
with the author of Getting Started in Bonds,
Sharon Saltzgiver Wright and a leading bond fund manager,
Gail Seneca of Seneca Capital Management.

Subjects covered include:
- How to tell if a bond is a good buy;
- Risks associated with bond ownership;
- Pros and cons of various types of bonds/bond funds.

SPECIAL PRICE FOR READERS OF THIS BOOK:
**$19.95 (regularly $24.95), plus $4 for shipping & handling
Florida residents please include 6% sales tax.
To order: go online to <u>www.nbr.com/bondsvideo</u>
or call 1-305-949-8321 ext. 230
Allow 2-3 weeks for delivery.**

Nightly Business Report is not affiliated with John Wiley & Sons. This offer does not constitute
an endorsement of this book or its contents by Nightly Business Report, its affiliates or NBR
Enterprises/WPBT2 Miami.

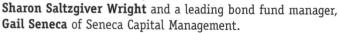

N B R   V I D E O   L I B R A R Y